# RING OF FIRE

# RING OF FIRE

## WRITERS OF THE YELLOWSTONE REGION

BILL HOAGLAND, EDITOR

THE ROCKY MOUNTAIN PRESS

P.O. BOX 2713

CODY, WYOMING 82414

# Contents

# Introduction

This is a book about landscape and environment, about weather and time, and about the people who live and work in and around the world's first national park. It brings together 36 writers from Idaho, Montana, and Wyoming in the Yellowstone caldera, that volcanic ring of fire that gives the region its hot springs, mudpots and geysers.

The writers of the Yellowstone region are a diverse group. Some are full-time writers; some work other jobs and write on the side. Some are ranchers, some are shopkeepers, some are educators, some work for state or federal agencies, and one is a librarian. Some are famous; and some are unknowns. Some were born here; others moved here because of a writing job, or other employment, or because the place was just too beautiful to leave after they first experienced it. Yet each writer here is representative in his or her own way of attitudes and interests that can be found in the communities and backwoods cabins throughout the region around Yellowstone National Park.

We are not tourists, we writers of the Yellowstone region. We live here year-round. We practice our trade in winter, when our rivers freeze over and the snow blows into deep drifts, pinning cattle to fences, threatening their lives. And we write in summer, when our little towns bulge with visitors come to camp, hike, ride horses, and fish, to sample this spectacular landscape we see every day, but never take for granted. We live with the political issues associated with wolves and grizzly bears. Sometimes we disagree about grazing fees, mining claims, "let-burn" policies, and the impacts of tourism, just as our neighbors also disagree about these issues. But conflicts do not scare us; rather, trouble seems to engage us. We are here to stay.

I was on a four-month-long sabbatical from my teaching job at Northwest

College in Powell, Wyoming, when I first began searching for writers to include in this book. I made several trips around Yellowstone, stopping at bookstores to ask proprietors what they thought of such a project. Their advice was invaluable. I read widely from all sorts of books and magazines. I made calls for submissions and poured over manuscripts of new writing. My criteria for selection were that the writing had to be passionate, personal, honest and accurate—and it had to deal with the character of the landscape and/or the people of the Yellowstone region.

Soon after I began this project I realized that this anthology had the makings of a new community. The writers in Montana had little knowledge of their counterparts in Wyoming and Idaho. The same went for the writers from Idaho and Wyoming. Yellowstone National Park has served as a big oasis separating us from one another with its size and its grand diversions.

And yet our interests turned out to be very similar. We have a respect for nature that never falls to sentimentality. We care about nature, we care a lot, but we also know that our surroundings can kill. Our landscapes are imposing. The animals that live here with us are some of the most exotic in all of North America. Our skies are huge, and our mountains are stark. Beside such magnificence, we are humbled.

I wish to thank Northwest College for that sabbatical which helped me begin this project. Thanks also to Morgan Tyree and the Big Empty Imaging Company. His graphic design skills are unparalleled, and his sense of humor is worthy of emulation. Thanks go out to all of the writers who submitted to this publication for their patience. Finally, I must thank my wife, Julia, and my children, Ted and Gigi, whose faith in me has often exceeded my own.

# Geoffrey O' Gara
## Lander, Wyoming

*Geoffrey O'Gara is a journalist, travel writer, and public television documentary producer. His most recent television work includes a documentary on Wind River Indian Reservation youth, titled "Generations," and a 60-minute piece for Wyoming Public Television called "Compass West." His latest book is* What You See In Clear Water.

# Return to Wyoming

As you drive across the unending, unbroken desert between California and Wyoming, you will pass occasionally in the dark little roadside clusters of trailers or prefabricated houses. Faint brave lights glow from behind slipping venetian blinds, even at the most exhausted hour, and you may be distracted for a moment from thoughts of your own home and family, and think instead of the sheer quantity of fragile and particularized lives that are undertaken out there, unglimpsed except by a dreamy all-night driver.

As my trip neared its end, I began imagining that as I approached each of these lonely settlements, there was someone looking out one of the windows in my direction. The someone was vaguely awake, wearing a nightshirt or underwear, absently lighting a cigarette, putting a plastic-covered kitchen chair next to the window. The light was then shaded, and the person looked out and saw first the deep bowl of stars, then the faraway suggestive shapes of the mountains, and finally the flame of headlights bound somewhere unknowable. And at that moment our souls tangled hungrily, trying to change places.

I drove back into Wyoming on Interstate 80, the belly-binding superhighway that cinches the state's southern plains. At Rock Springs I turned north, and for the first time then I saw just above the bulge of the globe the white tips of the Wind River Mountains, visible through the low current of trembling air along the horizon, with only the meditative space of the Red Desert between us. It was early dawn, and now the fantasies of strangers' lives fell back before much stronger images: my children in their beds, arms and legs akimbo, sighing as sleep lightens and lifts off them. Perhaps the youngest has snuggled in with my wife, his head by the window she opened before going to bed, being a lover of night breezes; he smells the lilac and expressions rush across his sleeping face. On the wooden slats outside, the wind fluffs the dog's tail, and he lifts his head crossly.

Right on the heels of my happy surge of anticipation followed a contrary desire to slow and savor the approach. Just north of the town of Rock Springs I dropped off what's called the Rock Springs Uplift on a rutted dirt road and drove east into the Red Desert, an encirclement of hills that interrupts the sharp peaks of the Rockies with a unique sump of sand and rock and biota with nowhere to go. The Continental Divide splits along its borders, and water—what little falls here—flows inward and disappears. The basin is about four thousand square miles altogether, and it has some fine duny sands, some ridges Mohawked with forest, and bands of wild, roaming horses. Harsh winds, sudden downpours that turn the clay soil to slippery muck, and rattlesnakes are among its resistible attractions. Two-track "roads" run crazily around in it, a maze of scars that signify both the ancient quest of westering wagons and the careless scribing of last year's uranium prospector, fading off into the sagebrush or centering so high that only a truck can pass; it's easy to get lost.

On many trips, the Red Desert has been for me the vestibule to the valley where I live, an extraordinary interlude of silence after the mechanical fury of Interstate 80 and the huge power plants of Rock Springs. Generations ago this expanse of windblown plain was the weariest of prospects to travelers on the Oregon Trail, who had endured so much of the empty plains by the time they arrived here that they plunged on blindly. Now such an uninhabited landscape is a rare thing, with an entirely new value. After so much traveling, through crowded cities and along shop-strewn roadways, the open spaces and the snug isolation of Wyoming towns seem foreign and beguiling. All over the country the builders are winning careless victories over the landscape, and there seems to be no enforcement of climate or topography to hold us at bay; here the environment still stings, and a community huddles in its own warmth.

I drove into a landscape low-slung and undulating, gray and sienna and pale green with lichened cobble and hard clay, sagebrush and wild rye; as the car worked its way down off a small plateau, the most distinguished feature on the empty plain ahead was the shadow of a cloud passing, and it was majestic.

I heard a faint whistling noise over the sound of the Mustang's engine and looked back over my shoulder toward Boars Tusk, a volcanic spire. To the southwest I saw a small yellow box puttering along a narrow track. John Mioncynski would be in the cab, traveling the track to check for vandalism or theft. U.S. Steel used to haul taconite across the desert from its mine in South Pass to the Union Pacific hopper cars in Rock Springs; the mine closed recently, so Mioncynski was hired to take these rides now and then until the salvage people could sell the track. Mioncynski, a rangy, quiet man who raises goats and plays piano, knows the flora and fauna of the Red Desert as well as anyone, and a ride on the train was a kind of lesson.

I had ridden the little railroad car with him a few months earlier, and on the way back I climbed up on the roof with Philippina Halstead, an artist and writer from the area, so we could get a better view of the passing landscape. Both she and Mioncynski lived in the vicinity of Atlantic City, another little Wyoming town not far from mine, a little higher, a little less sheltered, a lot smaller, a lot more precarious. A century ago newcomers mined gold in Atlantic City, and now fewer than fifty people lived there year-round, barely getting by. Many of them had had jobs at the taconite mine; times were hard now, and some would have to move away. Towns are often reborn in country as handsome as this, but how does it feel to be a leftover from the last community, and what depth of history can survive such turnover? In recent years even folks I assumed were better rooted than I was—those generous people who put the new roof on our cabin when we first moved to Wyoming—would suddenly up and leave. Those who stay don't talk about it much. It would only lead to questions like: What about you? Yes, indeed, you have given some thought to moving on, much to your chagrin.

But it was so beautiful up there on that little yellow box, legs spread and toes dug in, hands gripping the riveted metal edge of the roof—a gang of five horses came flying out of the desert and crossed the track ahead of us, racing for a while—and it didn't seem worth it to get all serious. Instead, we recalled a friend from back East who had lived in Wyoming for a few years, and then returned to the coast; on a recent visit she looked around a bar in Atlantic City with a frown and said, "Who are all these new people?"

The Mustang was overheating again, and I pulled over at the foot of the Oregon Buttes, a salient chunk of hard sandstone rock that sits square and tall, rising up out of the dry barrenness of the desert with limber pine furring its crest. Nineteenth-century migrants followed the Sweetwater River west into South Pass, just to the north; it was a favorite passage through the northern Rockies. They passed between the buttes and the snow-capped Wind River Mountains, and sometimes they wandered a little north and found the valley where I live. A few went no farther; they set up vegetable farms and sold their goods to the westering wagon trains. I let the car rest awhile and then tried to crank the engine so I could refill the radiator. There was not even a click. I tried the lights; I tried the radio. Nothing.

I got out of the car, but instead of opening the hood and looking for the problem, I wandered away from it. The afternoon was getting on. I hiked up the side of the butte, not a difficult climb, but the sky clouded over halfway up, and a few drops of rain fell, slicking the path. Two red-tailed hawks cried *keeeeeeeer* and dove away from a stand of dead trees near the top. The top was flat, and covered with fine gravel, crunching under the boot. The sides of the butte fell away quickly, leaving a few pinnacles standing off away from the main block of the butte's flat top. A marmot stuck its gray head out at me, and then scuttled down and around the cliff facing south.

Deer, bitterbrush, lupin, marmots, bitterroot, even elk, in the winter—the top of the butte was an island, marooned by the desert all around, a floating and, because it was so small, fragile place for those creatures that survive on its grasses and lichen and rodents. In a few hundred feet you could drop from evergreen to aspen groves to sage desert. The butte's narrow confines and the inhospitable border lands surrounding it made it a most particular place, and dear to a traveler's heart. If there had been people there, they would surely be eccentric in their isolation, and, I imagined, most attractive to me.

My mind again reached forward to the valley where I live, just over the next swell of land, just across the winding Sweetwater River, around the steep flank of Limestone Mountain, across Beaver Creek, into the trough of the Little Popo Agie River, and on to town. When the dog heard the particular sound of the Mustang, he would get up, totter the way he always did, and amble over to me as I climbed out, with his crooked old tail wagging, as if I'd left just yesterday; he would put his head down and butt my leg, and do the little half hop which has replaced the leap he used to make against my chest; and then he would yip just like a puppy, and welcome me home.

And was I quite ready to call Wyoming home? Well, not quite. I would make a finicky distinction, on the pretense that I had been able to cull some wisdom from my travels.

Wyoming was not my home, but the place I lived. My home was, and always would be, in California. California! Bountiful, silly, misleading California. When it's really your home, you can call it names. I have so much more hope for Wyoming....

Wyoming would be, happily, the home of my children. And it was the place where I lived. The place I traveled away from for the pleasure of coming back to it.

It was twilight when I started back down. Like a fluffed quilt in a darkening room, the desert hills stretched below off toward the horizon. Honeycomb badlands formed a stitch running east. I heard a faint beat, then a louder glissade of violins, and finally the voice of Rudy Lewis telling us that "on the roof" was the only place he knew.

A yellow smudge by a dry creek bed, light from the window of a rockhound's tiny trailer...north up a dry wash, a solitary pronghorn grazing, invisible until the sound startled him erect.

And down below I could see a faint radio glow from the Mustang's dashboard. The song sounded as sweet here as it might on the Upper West Side of New York; my trail was starblazed now, and I kept coming down it as though it were a fire escape. Not quite the troubleproof paradise of the song, but a place with room enough, and a car that knew the way. I was singing, and my feet were doing their awkward best to turn descent into dance. It was just a few more miles to go, to the place where I live.

# MARK SPRAGG
## CODY, WYOMING

*Mark Spragg has written screenplays for several Hollywood studios. His most recent film,* Everything That Rises, *was selected as a finalist for the 1999 PEN Center USA West Literary Award for Teleplay. Also a writer of short stories and essays, Spragg has been a recipient of Wyoming Arts Council Literary Fellowships, and the Blanchan Memorial Award for nature writing. "Greybull" is from his new book,* Where Rivers Change Direction, *winner of the 2000 Mountains and Plains Booksellers Award for non-fiction.*

# Greybull

"How long's that going to take you?"

I lever myself out of one of the fifty-five-gallon oil drums we use to store grain and stand holding two filled coffee cans of oats. I have the last rotation of horses tied in the stalls, and these two cans are the last I have to deliver. A bay in the far stall whinnies.

My father stands in the barn's doorway. He wears laundered, pressed jeans and a silver-belly gray hat. The hat is free from sweatstain and horseshit. The hat's crown catches and holds the morning light. It is the hat he wears to town. His hands are clean. His thumbs are hooked in his pockets. His shirt blouses in a slight breeze. Its pearled snaps come bright and dull as he shifts his weight.

"I'm almost done," I tell him.

I walk into the stalls and squeeze between the hot, impatient bodies of the unfed pair. Their heads are turned together at the ends of their halter ropes, their noses nearly meeting, their large dark skulls rising up like a pair of bodiless wings. My father steps into the granary. The horses' rhythmic chewing echoes off the low ceiling as would the sound of a troop of drunks staggering on gravel. Bars of sunlight leak through the weathered board and batten barnside and hatch the row of horse rumps. Grain dust and motes of powder-dry manure hang in illuminated scrims in the walkway behind the horses. A pair of slate-blue butterflies falter in and out of the blades of light. A horse snorts. Another coughs. The barn cats scrabble above us in the loft. A speckled roan spraddles onto the toes of his back hooves and pisses. The smell of hot urine spikes through the general scents of grain, animal sweat, the tang of pine needle and manure. It is the third summer I've wrangled horses for my father. I'm fifteen, and five-foot-three. I've been up since four. My body still vibrates from the twelve miles I've ridden gathering this bunch off night pasture.

"You had your breakfast?"

"Yes, sir."

"I thought I might go over to Greybull."

"What's in Greybull?"

"A horse sale."

I come back into the granary, drop the coffee cans in the half-filled barrel of grain, and slide the cover on. The horses stamp their feet against the thick board floor, and the sound echoes in the stalls, into the loft, against the tin roof, rebounding in weak resolution. They snort. They chew. They sneeze. Their tails work the air alive against an excitement of flies.

"I didn't know we needed horses."

"You didn't know you were going to grow hair under your arms either, but there you are." He lights a cigarette, snaps the wooden match in half, and flicks it back through the granary door. "I'm thinking the price might be right."

"How do you know what the price is going to be?"

"I won't unless I go. You want to come, or don't you?"

We've shipped our spring bear hunters off and don't expect the first group of summer tourists for a few days. The river is risen too muddy to fish. The banks are collapsed, the rapids choked with the commerce of timber torn away and turned downstream. The feeder streams, also too swollen with runoff to allow us very far into the mountains with a pack trip. There will be mostly day rides. I nod and look to the shifting horses in their stalls. "As soon as this is over," I say.

My father backs his pickup to a two-horse trailer. I straddle the tongue of the trailer and guide him back under the hitch. I lower the hitch onto the ball, plug in the brakewire, and drop the safety chain over the ball. I wipe my face dry of sweat with a shirttail and get in the cab. "I need anything?"

"Unless you learned how to play something musical I guess you don't. The radio's decided not to work."

"It hasn't worked in a year."

"This year?"

"Yes, sir."

"You're sure?"

"Since Ted winched the tree over the hood." We both look to the crease that folds diagonally across the truck's hood. The paint is flaked. The hood freckled with pocks of rust, the antennae snapped off into two inches of jagged stub.

"Funny what you forget to notice," my father says. "Damn shame neither one of us can carry a tune."

I hate the racket an empty trailer makes pulled over the ruts of a dirt road, like dragging some wheeled barrel ready to come apart at the staves. On the two-lane it whistles out behind us. I forget it's there, empty or full. If we return with the weight of a horse on its floor, it will produce a sound solid and thrumming and primitively musical.

My father drives into the morning glare. The bug-splattered windshield spackles the light across our chests. The side windows are down. The treaded tires whine. "We don't get a lot of chances to be together," he says.

"We work together."

"When we work together I guess I'm your boss."

# Mark Spragg: *Greybull*

"What are you now?"

"I'm your father." He turns with a half smile. "Why don't you pay attention today and see if you can notice a difference?"

My father's shirt is unsnapped at the cuffs and fallen down his forearms. The mink-brown hair at the backs of his hands and wrists catches in the wind and morning light. I look to my wrists. Rub my palms against them. There is only a slight blond fuzz. He thumbs his hat back away from his face. "It's going to be hot today," he says. "Summer's finally got here."

"It's not like we didn't expect it."

"I guess it's not," he says and turns to have a look at me. I know that our faces appear alike: same jaw, same forehead, same eyes. I've seen photographs of him as a boy, and they look as I would look dressed in unfamiliar clothes. Our similarities have always surprised and unsettled us both. He turns back to the highway. I study the profile of his face. There are streaks of lighter skin at the corners of his eyes, where he has tightened his face, squinting into the day's work. His cheeks are smooth shaven and browned. He puckers his lips, sucks just once at the air, and rests his left arm through the windowframe. In another month the air will be choked with cottonwood fluff. It will drift against the crook of my father's arm. It will swirl in the cab as flakes of desiccated snow would swirl, but now the air is only sweetened with the specks of lesser pollen.

We break out of the forest and onto the straight drive through irrigated pastures toward Cody. The valley widens. Foothills rise in the aquamarine and grays of new sage growth beyond the alfalfa-green squares of cultivated land. When we reach the reservoir it is stained with an alluvium of mountain silt where the river enters it, smooth and struck silver and green in the sun and rising to our right as we weave along the ledge of highway, through the bare rock tunnels in the canyon.

Cody is busy with out-of-state license plates. I stare out the window at plump men in short pants and women in halter tops, shorts, their midriffs bare. They seem foreign. Sunstruck. Stunned by vacation. Their children follow in their parents' shadows. They are out of their element, all of them. When we stop for a light they stare with bland indifference. They seem to be people bred solely for utility: I think of them as bands of balded cattle. I feel predacious, superior, glad for work on the land.

East of Cody we have another hour to Greybull. It is still morning, but the air comes away from the highway in shuddering, translucent tubes of mirage. The drivers of the cars and trucks we meet lift a single index finger loose from their grip on the wheel in greeting. I've never seen a man wave with his whole arm unless trying to ward off a blow. At the horizon there is the darker rim of the Bighorns, their ridgeline churned in a froth of cumulus where the sky has ground into the mountain rock. There are smudges of bastard cloud fallen loose and ridden up and fading upon the vault of blue dome. The two-lane is straight and gray. Insects burst in patches of mustard and rust against the windshield. Fist-sized birds ride the airstream over hood, glass, and cab and die against the unexpected rise of the trailer we pull, producing the lonesome sound of a softened ball thrown against the side of a metal shed, randomly, again and again.

"You happy?" my father wants to know.

"I guess I'm as happy as I need to be." He's humming a series of single notes that he means to be a tune. "Does it matter?"

He shrugs. "It's just something that comes to mind when your radio's broken."

At the sides of the road there are alkali bluffs, struggling grassland, reefs of low-growing sage, the chalk-white soil lifted here and there into sudden blurred cones of dust devil.

"You ever been to an auction?"

"No, sir."

"You'll enjoy yourself. Kind of a picnic where everybody comes sober. You can get a soda if you're thirsty, I don't mean there's any food. Auctions make me happy even if I don't buy anything."

I nod and stare along a line of fence posts diminishing to the north in the rising crowd of sage. To the west of the fence there is a collection of raw-white Charolais bulls, mostly standing, several down to rest, one mounting another in sexual rehearsal. Their asses are shit stained. Their skins flex against the flies. They appear monumental in the sun. I think of pictures of Stonehenge I have seen. The bulls do not turn to look at us as we pass, as any scatter of broken dolmen would not turn.

"You don't have to worry about moving your arms."

I focus again on the side of my father's face. I tell him that I do not understand. I tell him I was not listening.

"You always hear about some dupe who waved to his wife or girlfriend or someone at an auction and the auctioneer took it for a bid. In the story it's always more than the man can pay."

"I never heard that."

"Well, now you have."

"I wasn't worried."

"I thought you might be. I didn't know."

The highway is crowned and the borrow ditches greened in weed from the advantage of the asphalt's slight runoff. The metal highway signs so shot full of holes they appear to be stencils of a language I haven't learned.

I put the heels of my boots against the glove box and slouch in the seat. I take off my cap and hook it over the toe of my right boot. Its bill catches in the wind. My head cools. The hair above my ears, and in a band across the back of my skull, dries stiffened with perspiration. "They just sell horses at this sale?" I ask. I realize that I don't know what to expect.

"Today's sale is mostly horses. Maybe a pen of sheep or two. I imagine some cows. A pig wouldn't surprise me."

I roll my head on the back of the seat to look to him, smiling. He looks away from the highway. Sweat has beaded on his forehead and across his upper lip. "That tickle you?" he asks.

"I have a picture in my head of getting a saddle on a pig. I don't see how the stirrups wouldn't drag on the ground."

"If I see one with withers I'll buy him for you. If he bucks you loose you won't have far of a fall."

We smile at one another. I tell him I think I'd look fine on a gaited sow. To our north a coulee breaks away in crumbling angles. Its wet bottom is spotted brown and white and black, strewn with several dozen Angus and Hereford cows and their calves.

In another mile the ashen soil is cut by a sluggish stream, and then a stack of beehives at the edge of an alfalfa field streaked with the darker greens of clover. The air smells sweet. I think of a spoonful of honey and swallow. There are cottonwood and Russian olive planted in rows for windbreaks. My eyes catch on the sharp, blockish bodies of green, yellow, and red farm equipment inching through the fields. As improbable as giant insects. Year-old stacks of weather-paled hay lean into collapse. There is a single trailer house. Several houses sided in pastel aluminum.

We don't slow down in Emblem. Population: ten. No streetlights. A building with a zip code. A roadside church. A half-dozen squat, galvanized grain silos, and more miles of irrigated farmland, a strip of it, incongruous on this arid prairie.

A sign advertises Greybull twelve, and underneath, Basin nineteen.

"I didn't think Basin could beat Greybull," my father says. He smiles. It is his standard joke. I return his smile because I am his son, and he expects it.  "Probably had to go into extra innings," he says.

"I don't think I'd like to buy anything I might eat."

"You don't think you'd eat a horse? If you were hungry enough?"

"I'd have to be hungrier than I've been so far."

The Bighorns rise up out of their foothills as we come in under them. Their heights are pleated green in distant pine, broken with the paler green of meadow. I imagine the wildflowers I cannot see. The high depressions flash white with snowfield. Here and there the soil falls away as the last thrust of rock summits, rose and amber and flashing in the sunlight. Cloud-shadow dapples their western slope. I sit up straight and pull on my cap. A butte of blunted red sandstone breaks out of the poor and wind-scoured landscape in the middle distance. A jack rabbit lopes across the highway in front of us and sits hunched on the highway's shoulder, watching as my father slows the truck. The hare's ears fall back along his skull in our airstream.

The Greybull livestock building stands to the north of the highway, glowing dully. Its corrugated tin sides shimmer in the heat. The building is two stories high, perhaps fifty-by-seventy feet, its shorter side to the highway. Several acres of pens and alleyways fall away to the west, presenting a labyrinthine puzzle of banded shadow and light. The pens are constructed of roughhewn lumber painted white, spiked up higher than the shoulders of a horse. They appear stout enough to sort a herd of elephants. Beyond the pens run railroad tracks, and then a meat processing plant, and then the Greybull River hidden behind a flush of leafed trees, mostly olive and cottonwood.

The parking lot is gravel, rutted from a recent rain, grown up at the edges in tire-broken weeds. The pickups are mud splattered, most of them hitched to trailers, their grills and windshields uneven fields of smeared insect body. There is a row of stock trucks. A semi is backed to a loading chute. Half a dozen blond children play in the shade of a tree, taking turns roping an old roan and yellow dog. His eyes are glazed in cataract. His tongue lolls from his grayed muzzle. He does not duck the loop, they don't jerk out the slack. A pretty woman with red hair drawn into a ponytail sits on the tailgate of a truck. Her checked blouse falls open, and she nurses her child. She smiles. The round globe of her breast catches the sunlight. A line of men have climbed up on the pens and look out over the milling animals, pointing, smoking, laughing. There are the lows and grunts of cattle, the bleating of sheep, the sharp whinny of a horse. The ground quivers like a thick drumskin under the drubbing of hooves. The thrum of flies fills the air as would the echo of a distant siren. I climb up the side of a pen and sit on the top edge of the board. My father stands beside me, his elbows cocked shoulder-high, resting on the top board, his chin on the overlap of his hands. A man my father's age sits at my other side. His bootheels are hooked on the board under his ass, his knees splayed up level with his hips. He rests his elbows on his knees and nods into the pen. "You like him?" he asks.

"Yes, sir, I do."

In the pen is a single dun gelding. His mane and tail, muzzle, and stockings darkened as deeply brown as wet earth. So is the line that dissects his back, from his mane to the base of his tail. His ears are pricked. His face alive with intelligence. He's well muscled and put together like a cutter. His tail's been pulled short and works his hindquarters free of flies. A crow stands on his withers, turns and walks the length of his back, looking over the swell of his belly for a meal in the fresh manure. The ground and air are dotted with crows and red-winged blackbirds. They make a racket in their competition.

"Want to see him move?"

"I guess I would," I tell the man beside me.

He reaches into his shirt pocket and pinches out a small pebble, cocks his thumb behind a loop of index finger and loads the pebble like a boy would balance a marble. It catches the dun up high in the neck, and the animal spins on his hindfeet smoothly to his left, trots to the far side of the pen, and turns and faces us. He snorts. His ears vector to each of us, scanning for annoyance. The crow has lifted into the air, flapping, and settles again on the dun's back.

"Pretty, isn't he?" The man widens his knees and spits a slick stream of tobacco juice into the pen. He's unshaven, and his lower lip bulges over the wad of Copenhagen he's laid in against his lower teeth. He lifts his hat and smoothes a hand over his bald, white head.

In the background we hear the public address system remind us that no consignment is too large or too small to appreciate. I tell the man that I don't own a cat that moves as well as this horse. He nods. "You going to bid on him?"

"I don't know."

"He'd look good under you." I smile and admit that he might. The man spits again. "Course he'd look good under me, too."

In the air, above the insect buzz and static of bird argument, we hear the market report for lambs, breeding ewes, breeding bucks, slaughter ewes and bucks, goats large, goats small, weaner pigs, sows, boars. We hear yesterday's quotes for bred heifers, heiferettes, cutter cows, utility cows, steers, bulls, cutting bulls, horses, light test.

"You ready to get out of the sun?"

I look down at my father. "Yes, sir," I tell him. I have another look at the dun and climb off the pen.

The entrance is built into a corrugated add-on at the building's west side. The screendoor is clotted with flies. They rise and fall, like a damp black cloth against the mesh as we enter. My father stands at the buyer's window, and I stand before a wall of ribbons and plaques presented for nearly every variety of prize animal. Two walled ramps rise into the building, and I follow my father up the one to our right.

The ramp opens halfway up a curving stack of bleacherseats built around three sides of the interior. They rise from the building's floor into the eaves. Before us, below us, at ground level, is a blockish half-mooned arena. Its floor curls up in fresh amber woodchips. The arena does not taper at the ends as a crescent would, more a bent alley of ground, opening through a gate at either end. Livestock is run in one side, out the other. We can look down into the auctioneer's bay. There is a window squared out of the east wall at the arena's concave side. Behind it a room-sized shed is built onto the main building, bracketed by the runways that feed and empty the arena. Inside there are two men seated over microphones and a woman standing behind them fingering through a sheaf of papers. She wears a sleeveless blouse, and her arms are muscled like a wrestler's. The air feels cool, damp. There is laughter and echo upon echo of swirled conversation. The seats and walls are painted white, the trimwork and supporting poles an inkpen blue. There are perhaps one hundred and fifty people spaced throughout the place, thickly along the rail. The colors of worn denim, faded corduroy, and work-stiffened canvas dominate. Shades of blue and brown everywhere. And the bright primary colors of chain-store shirtcloth.

There is a knee-high stack of carpet samples where we have come out into the seats. "For your ass," my father says, and takes one. I leave them for the older men. I figure my ass is fine. My father sidesteps to the middle of a row and sits. We are centered between floor and ceiling. There are five-gallon buckets spaced at the ends of every other row, half-filled with sand for butts and spit. A big man wearing bib overalls and no shirt enters at the end of our row and kicks the sand-bucket ahead of his steps. It skids to a stop short of my father's boot. A black-and-white border collie bitch follows at the man's heel. The bleacherseat squeals when the big man sits. The dog curls between his feet, tucking her nose under her tail. "Morning, Jesse," he says. My father nods. There are matted curls of gray-tipped hair cushioning the man's shoulders, grown up the back of his neck and down his arms. "What's got you out of the mountains?"

My father lights the man's cigarette and then his own. "Thought I might buy a horse."

The auctioneer repeats the prices for slaughter cows, high cutter and boning utility.

"There's some good ones coming through here today. Tom Holman's brought over some colts that know their business."

"Lost three to winter pasture."

"You looking for three?"

"Not all at once."

"That your boy?"

"One of them." My father introduces me to the big man and leans back so that I can shake his hand. His name is Evan. The dog's name is Grace. She raises her head when she hears her name and then settles. The man's hand is wet. Sweat drips on my father's thighs from his forearm where he reaches across. I smile and wipe my hand on my jeans and squint up into the lights. There are three broad-shaded floodlamps and a few banks of florescent tubing. The auctioneer tells us that domestic wool is trading active at steady to five-cent-higher prices. Some bellies out untied. Mostly in poly pack bales. Some, skirted and classed in poly bales. Greasy fob.

On the wall to the sides and above the auctioneer's bay are advertisements for feed stores, banks, ag supplies, truck dealerships, meat processing. The bay is bordered with a single strand of Christmas lights.

A numbered lot of Angus bulls are brought through and sold. They're drowsy, dusty, their noses slick with snot. I think that Angus might be a good name. I whisper the sound of the word, and then my own name, and then Angus again. My father says, "What's that?"

"Nothing," I say and nod toward the bulls. He watches me. I search the crowd for someone I know. Most of the men are middle aged or older; there are a few young couples with kids younger than me. A little boy below us stretches out on the bleacher with his head in his mother's lap. The smell of men and animals, of sweat and shit and urine, of cigarette smoke and coffee, is strong as a meal brought hot from an oven. This big shed is warming. A single woman laughs like women laugh late at night coming out of bars. The general conversation rises in pockets of clatter, crests, recedes. The auctioneer barks through the PA system as though trying to rouse some retired marching band. The woman's laughter has settled to a girlish giggle. Her body jerks with an occasional hiccup.

The auctioneer tells us that compared to last Friday, slaughter cows are fully two dollars lower, the bulk of receipts for bred cows, and cow and calf pairs. Demand and buyer attendance good. Supply 15 percent slaughter cows, 5 percent feeder cows, 80 percent replacement cows. The little boy sits up and leans against his mother. She pours some coffee from a thermos and holds the cup while he takes a sip. A block of heifers sells low. The auctioneer pleads. The bald man who thumbed the stone into the dun's neck is propped against the entrance to the rampway. He nods. I nod back. He bends low to his right and spits into one of the white buckets.

"We'll have a horse sale right along with our regular sale every month from now on," says the auctioneer. He's a pale man with a black hat and a water-blue bandanna tied loosely at his throat. His face shines with sweat. He looks like the cowboys who work for us look the morning after a three-day drunk. He sips from a white mug and winces as he swallows and then leans into the microphone. Evan tells my father that he's a replacement auctioneer. "The regular guy let a bull kick him in the hip. He's staying home until he can walk without puking." There are two signs on the wall to the replacement auctioneer's right. The first reads: *All guarantees are between buyer and seller. We act as agents only.* The one below it: *Not responsible for accidents.*

A thin man rides the dun in through the gate. He bends down over the saddle horn to clear the overhang and then straightens in the saddle with his toes turned out. He keeps the palm of his right hand pressed against the horn and reins the dun in tight circles. The little horse moves as smoothly as water running down a drain. First to the left. Then to the right. The thin man does not look into the crowd. He keeps his chin tucked and his back straight and in the middle of the horse.

"Fifty dollars," says the auctioneer. "I have fifty, and five, now five, and sixty. There's sixty. Give me sixty-five."

The bald man nods. The woman with the boy and the thermos of coffee looks back, studying the crowd.

"You have money?" my father asks.

"Yes, sir."

"Let me see it."

I reach into my pocket and take out my savings. The money's rolled and snapped tight with a rubber band. My father's eyes widen in obvious appreciation. It's a big roll. "How much is there?"

"Eighty-nine dollars."

Evan leans forward. Grace is up with her chin on his knee. "Looks like a lot more," he says. Grace begins to pant.

"It's all in ones," I tell him. "Feels better in my pocket that way."

Evan nods and rests his hand on Grace's soft head. She rolls her eyes up the length of his arm.

# Mark Spragg: *Greybull*

"You want this horse?" my father asks.

"Yes, I do."

"Then I'd stick that wad back in my pocket and go to work if I were you."

"Sixty-five, sixty-five, I've got sixty-five," sings the auctioneer. "Who's going to give me seventy?"

I raise my hand, and the woman behind the auctioneer nods and taps him on the shoulder. "And five," he says. The bald man looks my way. The blue and red stripes in his shirt seem to pulse. Dust and cigarette smoke blur the ceiling. I take off my cap and wipe my forehead with the back of my sleeve. I wonder that the building has heated so quickly. The bald man puts one finger in the air.

"Seventy-five's in, and now eighty." The auctioneer is looking straight at the woman below me. The thin man is backing the dun, releasing him, backing him again. "Holman trained, Holman guaranteed. Five years old and firing on all cylinders. Where's my eighty?"

I raise my hand.

"There's eighty. Now five, five, five, where do I have eighty-five?" The woman shakes her head, "No." The bald man puts a finger in the air. "And ninety."

I bid the ninety, and the bald man takes it to ninety-five. He tongues out his wad of Copenhagen and spits it into the butt bucket and pinches in a new chew. He winks at me and lounges back against the rampway. He looks like he just got cleaned up for dinner. "One hundred, looking for a hundred, one hundred dollars," sings the auctioneer.

"Take it to the son of a bitch." My father leans in against me.

"Who?" I've forgotten he sits beside me. I look at him as though he is a stranger.

"That winking son-of-a-bitch that can't come in and sit down."

"Where's my one hundred?"

I nod.

"And five."

The bald man smiles and bids.

"I've got the five. And ten. Is this a sound horse, Tom?"

The thin man nods and spurs the dun into a lunge and stops him in a skid.

"Now," my father whispers, and I raise my hand.

"There's my ten," sings the auctioneer. "And now fifteen. Who's got fifteen? Looking for fifteen."

The bald man bids. My father swings his leg against mine. I take it to one hundred and twenty before the auctioneer can make the offer.

"Twenty. Twenty. Twenty. Got twenty. Looking for twenty-five."

My father winks at the bald man. I wink, too.

Grace has climbed into Evan's lap. He strokes the length of her back, and when he grins the flex of his face seems to flare his ears. I look back for the bald man, but he's gone. I search the backs of the heads in front of the rampway looking for his hat.

"Twenty. Twenty. I'll take twenty-two and a half." The auctioneer looks to the woman with the kid, but she's pouring another cup of coffee. "Twenty-two and a half. Going. Twenty-two and half. Going." And he snaps his gavel and sings, "There's a one-hundred-and-twenty-dollar horse." The muscled-up woman points me out and the auctioneer tells the crowd, "Sold to the boy in the blue-billed cap." The thin man looks up into the bleachers and nods.

My father stands, and when I don't he hooks me under the arm and lifts me to my feet and gives me a push. Evan sidesteps out behind us.

In the rampway I tell my father that I don't have the hundred and twenty dollars. I tell him the eighty-nine is all I have.

"I heard you the first time." He lights a cigarette. Evan drops Grace out of his arms, and she runs ahead as though she's looking for work. I take the wad of ones out of my pocket and hold it up as evidence. "I'll loan you the rest," he says, and asks Evan if he needs a ride to town.

"My rig's in the lot. I'm going home and take a nap."

At the buyer's window the woman smiles at my father as I count out my savings. The bills are damp and stained from being in my pocket for nine months. My father writes a check for thirty-one dollars and centers it crossways on the top of my stack of ones. The cashier shows me where to sign the bill of sale, and I fold the thing carefully and put it in my shirt pocket. I snap the pocket shut.

"How do you feel?" Evan asks.

"Lighter," I tell him, and he laughs.

My father backs the trailer to the south side of the pens where Tom Holman has unsaddled the dun. The horse stands slick with sweat and shines like a river rock. He's tied up short to a post. "There son, that's the man, there son," I say as I walk to his head, running my hand along his side. He feels electric. His body humming from the showring. I stand at his shoulder and move my hand down between his front legs. He lips the collar of my shirt.

"That's a good horse," says the thin man. "You treat him right and you two ought to get along fine."

"Yes, sir. Thank you."

"This boy rope?" he asks my father.

My father swings the trailer gate open, and it flashes in the sun. "He throws a good horse loop in the corral. The only times I've seen him rope ahorseback was to catch the dog or his little brother."

"If he wants to learn, this gelding can teach him."

"You listening?" My father stands holding the gate open.

"Yes, sir."

The thin man looks down to me. A bead of sweat runs the ridge of his nose, and his sideburns are feathered damp. "This horse bucks once or twice in the spring. Usually to the left. If that's not all right I can take him back now."

"I'll watch for it," I tell him.

He nods and extends his hand. "My name's Tom Holman. In case you have a complaint." I shake his hand, and he turns and shoulders his saddle and walks away. I pull the halterrope free and walk the dun into the trailer and tie him off. When I step out my father swings the door shut, and a bull snake ropes straight up out of the pigweed and falls against the crests of spurge, moving fast.

"Goddamn," my father shouts. He's holding onto the trailer and jerking like a current runs through it. His face is caught between surprise and a smile. "I thought I was snakebit."

We watch the snake move away. He's big, more than four feet, brought liquid and bold in the heat.

# Mark Spragg: *Greybull*

My father smiles, but sucks at the air. "My legs got airborne before the rest of me. I feel like I jumped my knees through my lungs." And then, "Now would be a poor time to laugh."

We drive into Greybull and park along the curb at the A and W. My father gives me two one-dollar-bills and I go inside and order a malt and a fish sandwich and an extra container of tarter sauce for my fries.

When I'm back in the truck my father asks, "You want to eat here?" The dun stamps on the floorboards of the trailer.

I tell him that I've seen enough people today. He says he has too.

We stop at a bar in the center of town, and my father leaves the truck idling, his door standing ajar. I dip a fry into the tarter sauce and hold it against the roof of my mouth. The tang spreads until the hinges of my jaw feel like they might cramp. He slides back under the steering wheel and hands me a plastic cup of bourbon and water.

"Try not to spill that in your malt," he says and smiles. His hat is pushed back on his forehead.

I nod and balance the malt on one knee, his cup on the other, and he drives to the river and parks the truck. I set my lunch on the hood and step the dun out into the grass. We settle in the block of shade the trailer throws and watch the horse graze. He's careful not to step on his leadrope. My father sips his drink. He swirls the ice cubes against the sides of the cup.

"I'm raising you to five dollars a day." I look at my father to see if it's a new joke. He's turned his hat on its crown in his lap and leaned his head back against the trailer. His eyes are closed. I've been getting a dollar a day. A full-grown man is paid four hundred and fifty a month. He levels his head and looks at the river. "You're worth it," he says.

"I'll work harder," I tell him.

He turns to me. "If I wasn't satisfied I'd have fired you back down to just being my kid."

The dun snorts and kicks up at his belly with a hindfoot. I bite into my fish sandwich. The batter has come away from the fish and sticks to the bun.

"Course this all starts tomorrow. We're on vacation today." He takes another sip from his cup, swirls the ice, and leans his head back again. "I'll take what you owe me out of the raise. Lunch is my treat."

The dun folds his legs and rolls kicking at the sun. "Fifty dollars," I say, because that's what I've heard men say when a horse rolls: that a horse is worth fifty dollars every time he rolls.

He rolls again. "One hundred," my father says. The dun huffs and rolls once more and stands and shakes. "Looks like you got a bargain."

"Did you know the bald man?"

"The one bidding against you?"

"Yes, sir."

"Not before today. Why?"

"Just wondered. It's just something you think about when your radio's broken."

My father smiles and drags his sleeve across his forehead. The trailer ticks in the heat of the unclouded sun. "What are you going to call him?" he asks. He nods toward the horse.

"I was thinking, Mud. Or, Mouse."

"Because of his color?"

"Yes, sir."

"Either one'll work when you need to cuss him. Besides lighter, you feel any different?"

"I'm feeling bigger, I think. Like I'll wake up tomorrow and my clothes will be tight on me. Like I might have to buy new ones."

"I know how that feels." He stands. He holds his hat in his right hand. He tips back the last of his drink and scatters the ice by the trailer tire. He throws the empty cup in the bed of the truck and reseats his hat. "It won't happen overnight," he says.

The dun brings his head up just level with his chest and studies us, chewing, ears flicking, his eyes as dark as his forelock. I wonder what he sees. I wonder if he can hold us clearly in his mind, looking from glare into shadow.

# SCOTT McMILLION
## LIVINGSTON, MONTANA

*A fourth generation Montanan, Scott McMillion has also lived in New York City, South Korea and Antartica. McMillion has won several awards for investigative and environmental reporting. This essay is from his book* Mark of the Grizzly: True Stories of Recent Bear Attacks and the Hard Lessons Learned.

# You've Got to Wonder

She meant it as a joke both times, though it was an odd one for somebody like Sarah Muller to tell. Out of character. Worse than that, it wasn't even funny.

She was just finishing a shift loading luggage into the belly of an airliner at Bozeman, Montana, when she told it the first time. It wasn't yet noon on a sunny Sunday, and she was looking forward to a couple of days in the backcountry.

"I'll see you guys Wednesday," she told the crew. "Unless I get mauled by a bear."

Then she hopped in her car and drove for three hours to the northeast corner of Yellowstone National Park.

Toting luggage was a new thing for Sarah. She had spent the previous nine summers in the park, most of them working on a trail crew, learning about the sweaty end of a shovel, a pulaski, and a chainsaw. The work was good: camaraderie, fresh air, and it paid pretty well. Plus, she got to hike hundreds of miles of trails in the park, a place where most visitors never leave the pavement. But she had just bought a house and thought it was time to get a "real" job, something that lasted all year, that would make the payments and let her start fixing the place up in the evenings. That's why she had spent the morning contorting her wiry six-foot frame in a cargo hold not quite tall enough to stand up in. Trail crew had been hard work, but this was no piece of cake either. She was anxious to get out and move, to stretch her long legs. And she wanted to see Pete Walsh. He worked for an outfitter and was spending the summer at a camp along Buffalo Creek, just north of the park border in the Absaroka-Beartooth Wilderness Area. She'd met him in the mountains the previous summer, they'd hooked up again on New Year's

Eve, and that's when they became a couple.

It was July 26, 1992, and it would be her first trip back into the mountains since she had taken the new job.

The eight-mile walk from the trailhead to Pete's camp was a smooth one. She knew the trail well because she'd spent long days working on it just a year earlier. Anywhere you looked you found a pretty picture, but there wasn't much new to see. A little boring, even. She was looking forward to her destination.

She got to camp that evening, and the three-day weekend was glorious: long horseback rides, being with Pete, just being there, in the middle of the mountains, instead of standing on the tarmac watching them shimmer through the heat waves. It ended too soon. Wednesday morning came and it was time to head back to town, back to the belly of a Boeing. Pete and Sarah Harvey, the camp cook, were heading out, too. Pete offered his girlfriend a horse to ride, but she turned it down. Twenty miles in the saddle had left her more than a little sore, so she was glad to walk but didn't mind letting Pete strap her backpack to a mule.

Sarah Muller left first, taking a head start so she and the riders, who could move faster than she could, would meet somewhere near the trailhead. Pete asked her if she had everything, and Sarah remembered the car key in her pack. She slipped it into the pocket of her shorts, and Pete asked if she wanted a leather thong or something so she wouldn't lose it on the trail.

"Oh, I won't lose it," she said. "Unless I get mauled by a bear."

"I don't know why that came out of my mouth," she says years later, after five surgeries, some long stints of physical therapy, a bunch of scars, and some terrible memories that left her with a head full of questions. "That was twice I said that. In all my years in Yellowstone I never joked about that. And less than an hour later I was mauled by a bear."

Sarah first saw the bears, a female grizzly with two cubs, from about forty feet away. They were grazing through a meadow filled with brilliant yellow wildflowers and lush, waist-high grasses. It was about 10:20 in the morning, late for a bear to be using a trail in the middle of the summer on a hot day. But there they were, clambering up the south side of a small hill while Sarah strode up the north side on a collision course. They met just before each party reached the peak, and Sarah realized first what was up. She froze, her heart hammered. She didn't know what to do. A pair of spindly spruce trees stood to her left and she moved toward them but they offered no refuge. They were too small to climb or to hide behind.

"She was down grubbing plants, and I didn't even see her cubs at the time. I thought, 'Oh shit' and I started backing up. I thought it was a black bear because I couldn't see a hump on its back and I couldn't see its snout. I was moving backwards, looking for a tree to climb."

Then one of the cubs yelled.

"It was this incredible shrieking sound, like it was alarmed, giving a warning cry to its mom.

"My heart was beating a million miles an hour, my adrenaline was really up. But I still didn't really feel threatened because I thought it was a black bear. I'd come close to them before, on trail crew, and never had any problems."

Then the sow lifted her head, and Sarah saw trouble: Behind the distinctive dished face, the grizzly's beady eyes locked on Sarah's for just a flash. Then she charged. Fast. Faster than you can imagine.

"I jumped off the trail and my natural reflexes were to throw my water bottle down. I was hoping she would go for the bottle and not for me, that it would distract her."

The bear never broke stride. Sarah hoped for an instant that it would be one of the bluff charges she had heard about, that the bear would stop, that it would leave her alone. But it didn't stop. Sarah had a stuff sack in her hand, with nothing in it but toilet paper, a tiny first-aid kit, some Chapstick. She raised it, tried to cram it in the bear's mouth, but the animal went right past it and sank its teeth in her pretty face, sending her eyeglasses flying. All of this, from initial charge to first contact, took a second, maybe two. Sarah thought about playing dead, curling up into a ball, but it was too late.

"Before I even had a chance to play dead she was biting me, mauling me."

Bites broke her left arm and tore open her shoulder and her legs. One crushed seven ribs that will never heal, collapsing a lung. The bear shook her like a terrier does a rat. She heard cracking sounds when the bear bit into her ribs, but the crunching of teeth in her skull, the bear's top teeth in the back of her head, the bottom ones in her eye and forehead, was even louder. She had odd moments of detachment.

"I was thinking, so this is what it's like. This is what I've been fearing so many years. This is what it's like to be mauled by a bear. That was the thought going through my mind. I'm being mauled by a bear."

She remembers flying through the air at some point. She remembers hoping she wouldn't die because there were places she wanted to go.

"I love to travel. That thought came to me, that I hadn't done enough traveling yet. It's weird, the things you think about."

She screamed and screamed, as loud as she could. She screamed for Pete. She knew he was behind her somewhere, and she wanted his help. She screamed out to God for help. Or maybe she only thought about God. She isn't sure but she knew she wanted help.

Maybe she got it. The bear stopped biting her. The attack started and finished in seconds.

"I don't know why she left. That's the million-dollar question. Did she leave because I was down on the ground and no longer a threat to her cubs? Did she leave because I screamed so loud?"

The former seems the most likely. She had surprised a sow with cubs, it neutralized the threat, and it went away.

Sarah still wasn't sure where the bear was, though. She tried to look, but she couldn't see; there was too much blood in her eyes. Her nose was crushed. One of the bear's canine teeth had sunk through her eye socket and sinus, making a small puncture in her brain cavity.

"I wasn't sure if she was gone, but the excitement was over with."

The danger wasn't.

Sarah was alone, a long way from help. She was bleeding hard from her head wounds and she couldn't breathe; her left lung was full of blood. Bones jutted from the mangled flesh on her left arm, and one thigh was flayed open. The stuff sack was still on her left wrist, so she reached inside it for the toilet paper, trying to staunch the bleeding on her head, but there was so much blood she wasn't sure where the wounds were. The tissue was saturated in seconds, but she kept it pressed against her eye. She knew Pete and Sarah Harvey were coming up behind her, and she told herself to keep breathing, to stay calm, to stay awake. Rescuers were coming, she kept telling herself, and she wanted to stay awake so she could tell them where she was hurt. She wished the bleeding would stop.

The flies, she recalls, came in swarms.

Sarah had fallen in love with Yellowstone as soon as she got there in 1982, even though her first jobs had her selling beer in the Bear Pit Lounge at Old Faithful and cleaning toilets in a campground. Prior to that she'd been a receptionist for a concert promoter in Minneapolis.

"It was a stressful, busy, low-paying receptionist job in downtown Minneapolis," she says. "I was really sick of it."

Aside from one trip to Colorado, she'd never seen real mountains before. But she took to them like a natural. She needed only two seasons to move up from toilet scrubbing to trail maintenance, a coveted, reasonably well-paying job that not everybody—man or woman—is cut out for. In the off-season, she skied, worked some odd jobs, and hung out in Bozeman, a rapidly growing college town that was being discovered by swarms of urban refugees. Sarah liked being out on the trails but didn't care much for government work. Even out in the woods she had to deal with the bureaucracy, the paperwork, all the policies. When the crew started working in the spring of 1992, her boss pointed out how obvious her frustration was becoming.

"He said to me, 'You're not happy working for the Park Service.' I said, 'I know.' I had to find something else to do."

Plus, at thirty-four, the nomadic life was getting harder. For years, when the season started in Yellowstone, she could move everything she owned there in one trip in the car. Then it started taking two or three trips, and she still needed a storage locker. Buying a one-hundred-year-old home in Belgrade, a bedroom community for Bozeman, was a logical next step, even though the house needed a lot of work. Then she took the job at the airport, and the combination of work and new house kept her in town a lot. That's why she was so glad to finally get back to the mountains.

She recalls a conversation she had with a friend in Yellowstone, a woman ranger who worked alone in the Bechler River country, some of the most remote in the park and a place filled with grizzlies.

"I asked her, being alone, a female—not that that really matters—with all the bears around here, aren't you ever worried? Don't you get scared?"

"Not really," the friend told her. "One thing you never want to do is let your defenses down. You always want to be aware that they're out there."

Sarah had been having a great day until she ran into the bear.

"I was just as happy as can be, kind of half running down the trail. I'd had a great weekend. A new house. A good job with the airline. A semi-new boyfriend that I really liked."

# Scott McMillion: *You've Got to Wonder*

Her happiness that morning illustrates her character. The good weekend left her ebullient, feeling good about the future. A lot of people would have been a little glum, disheartened at the prospect of going back to work.

Her mind on happier thoughts, Sarah let her defenses down. "I wasn't making noise, and you should never do that in bear country. I look at it as a very stupid mistake on my part. If I had been making noise coming up that little hill, the bear would have heard me and I know she would have taken off. That was my big mistake, not making noise."

For years, she had carried bear spray while she worked on the trail crew. She turned in the canister with the rest of her equipment when she quit the job. She meant to get some more but never quite got around to it.

She hadn't thought all this through as she lay bleeding in the trail that morning. She was just glad and a little surprised to still be alive. She'd taken the kind of beating that kills a lot of people.

Pete's horse found her first, rearing and snorting as it caught the smell of blood and bear and fear. Sarah lay in the trail and raised her good arm, moaning two words: Pete's name and "bear." He thought at first it was a joke. Then he saw the torn leg beneath her shorts. He rushed to her and saw the other wounds, the mangled eye socket, all the blood. Sarah told him to have Sarah Harvey ride to the Slough Creek Campground about four miles away and get help. She wanted him to stay with her, but he was the better rider, he had the better horse, and Sarah Harvey had worked at a ski hill. She knew first aid. Nobody had a weapon, and nobody had any idea where the bears had gone. Sarah Harvey would stay and Pete would ride. It made more sense that way.

"Sarah Harvey was worried sick that the bear was going to come back. I was a little worried, too, but I was just lying there happy that I was still alive and wondering if I was going to make it or not."

Pete jumped on his saddle horse and was gone, riding like he had never ridden before. He didn't know if his girlfriend would be alive when he got back, but at least she was conscious and he thought maybe she had a chance if he rode hard enough. There was no question of moving her. She couldn't sit up and could barely breathe, let alone ride or walk. By the time he got to the trailhead and found a ranger with a radio, his horse was lathered and panting. He'd run four miles in record time.

When life is normal, Pete Walsh doesn't treat an animal like that.

Forest Service ranger Larry Sears was the man with the radio. He called for help and a team assembled fast. Ranger Colette Daigle-Berg, a medic, hopped on a helicopter, and it landed forty yards from Sarah at 11:31, less than an hour after Sarah Harvey and Pete discovered her.

Sarah Harvey had done what she could with what she had. She checked for spinal injuries, making sure the mauled woman could still move her legs, then slowly rolled her off her mangled left side and onto her back. That's when she discovered the wound in her back, the one where the bear had bitten through to her lung. It was sucking air and she packed it with the bit of gauze from her small first-aid kit. She didn't think her friend would be able to keep that arm. The bear had nearly torn it off. All the flesh was jammed up around her shoulder, and the forearm was attached only by a strip of skin on the inside of the elbow: luckily that's the part of the arm that carries the artery, the life force.

Sarah Harvey really didn't want the bear to come back.

"I remember thinking that she can't take any more. I'm going to have to lie on top of her or something if it comes back."

She quickly tethered her saddle horse and the pack animals nearby, hoping to use their eyes and ears.

"I just kept watching them because I knew that if the bear came back the horses would let me know before I ever saw it."

The pack animals were loaded with dirty laundry. She used a towel and a couple of sticks to splint the mangled arm, tying it off with a pair of dirty purple socks. She talked to Sarah, trying to keep her awake, telling her to keep pressure on the worst head wound, hoping a helicopter would come soon. She spread out a big white tarp so the pilot could find them more easily.

Once the work was done, there wasn't much to do but wait and hope. At one point, a hummingbird paid a visit, a piece of beauty flitting among the hordes of flies.

When the chopper landed and Daigle-Berg took over, Sarah Harvey could let down her own defenses. Daigle-Berg sent her on a mission to find a dropped radio, kind of like telling an expecting husband to go boil water.

"That's when I could finally cry," Sarah Harvey says. "It was very shaking. But it didn't really hit me until it wasn't my responsibility anymore."

And she cried for a long time, all the way to the trailhead on horseback, a trip that wouldn't even start for a couple of hours. She had spent years in the backcountry and would spend many more there after the attack, living for weeks at a time in the kind of place where it's no surprise to find grizzly tracks in the snow outside your tent. She's never had any more trouble with a grizzly, except in her dreams.

"I had dreams of riding into camp and everybody's been slaughtered, arms and legs all around. In my dreams, the bear always came back."

Fifteen minutes after the helicopter landed, Pete and Ranger Sears arrived on horseback. Pete took Sarah's hand.

"He was holding my right hand and comforting me and I said, 'Oh, honey, that hurts.' Here I am, all mangled all over, and I'm complaining about this little baby puncture wound. We couldn't see the hurt because there was all this blood all over."

She would learn later the bear had bitten clear through her hand. With all her other injuries, she hadn't noticed that one.

While the medics worked on her, Sarah had a little time to think, to realize she'd made a mistake, moving fast and quiet and alone through grizzly country. Rangers were asking her to describe the bear, and she did that. The animal was brown, medium-sized, and had two cubs. She knew the National Park Service had killed a lot of bears in past years, some on purpose and some accidentally. She had a request: Leave the bear alone, she asked. It was only trying to protect its children, and who could blame any mother for that?

It didn't take long for Daigle-Berg to figure out that Sarah needed a lot more help than she could get in Yellowstone Park. A medevac helicopter was summoned from the trauma center in Idaho Falls, Idaho. It got there fast, and Sarah was in the air by a little after one o'clock. As she made the miserable trip, the vibrations rattling her broken bones, her internal injuries making a sip of water impossible, more rangers and investigators arrived on the scene.

One of them was Kerry Gunther, Yellowstone's bear management specialist. This was a hard one for him. He knew the victim. Sarah was a friend of his.

Rescuers had trampled the immediate area around Sarah, and the rangers would find no bear tracks there. They did find a new trail trampled through the tall grass, however. It led from the scene to nearby Buffalo Creek and then turned north.

"This was a trail of more than one animal and very recent. The duff under the grass had been pushed downslope in a manner that indicated a heavy animal running," the investigators' report says.

They gathered the bear hairs plucked from the ground and from Sarah's body (the hairs would later prove the bear was a grizzly) and they searched the area extensively. They could find no carcass the bear was trying to protect. They found no sign she had been digging the abundant yampa roots in the meadow, no day beds, no scat or tracks on the entire length of the trail.

"It was our conclusion that while this bear with cubs may use this area from time to time she was primarily passing through at the time," the report says. "It was a chance encounter and unlikely to be repeated."

Sarah would spend two and a half weeks in the hospital in Idaho Falls, then travel twice to the Mayo Clinic in her native Minnesota for plastic surgery. Her eyes are wired to her nose, which had to be rasped back into shape. A piece of bone from her skull props up one eye. A Canadian surgeon with the unlikely name of Dr. U. Bite did outstanding work. Look at her face today and you notice nothing unusual. Just an attractive woman, tall and athletic and friendly, the type of outdoors person who often chooses to make a home in the Rockies.

Her years in Montana and in Yellowstone had built a network of friends who pitched in to help after the attack. So many flowers arrived at the hospital in Idaho Falls that they overflowed the room. Sarah sent them to the bedsides of other patients. Phone calls came from all over. So did letters, including one from Yellowstone superintendent Bob Barbee, who told of how, two days before Sarah was attacked, hikers in the next drainage to the east had come upon a grizzly cub. Then the sow appeared, but she did not attack; she just hustled the cub to safety. They were lucky, Barbee guessed.

News stories focused on her request that the bear be left alone, and strangers wrote to thank her for her attitude, to praise her strength. Friends who knew her sense of humor sent bears: stuffed ones, candy ones, and one printed on a notecard with a cartoon balloon hand-drawn on top of it. "I'm sorry, Sarah," the bear is saying.

Her scrapbook of cards and letters is not a thing you can read with a dry eye.

Doctors could fix her face, but her other scars remain. A long jagged one stretches across her arm; the limb still works, though it's tender. Others mark her shoulder and her leg. The ribs will never heal, doctors say, and they bulge some because they float freely in her body. They hurt all the time, and they mean her collection of vintage dresses no longer fits. She can't shoulder a backpack, dancing is tough, and if somebody wants to give her a hug, they have to know how to do it right.

As time goes on, she thinks about the incident less. It's no longer a daily thought. But some things bring it right back: the sound of a helicopter; seeing her border collie, Pelly, take a Frisbee in its teeth and try to shake it to death. Reading about other attack victims is hard. Sometimes she telephones them, offers encouragement and the name of her plastic surgeon.

"It helps me, too," she says.

She sold the house in Belgrade and moved to Paradise Valley, just north of the park, in a place where grizzlies are roaming again after long absences. Finding bear scat on the property makes her nervous. So does hiking. She's usually got a can of bear spray with her.

On a trip to Alaska, she and Pete each carried two big cans of it. Pete had a shotgun, too. When they tried to drive into the Yukon, Canadian customs officials said she couldn't take the spray with her. It wasn't the approved variety in that country.

"I was wearing shorts and I said, 'These are bite marks from a grizzly bear. If you take that spray away, you don't know what you're going to do to me.'"

The border guard let them through.

The attack left a lot of questions, and she's not finding many answers.

Part of her physical therapy called for swimming in a hot spring near Bozeman, wearing a suit that exposed her scars, still red and angry at the time. Children stared and asked innocent questions.

"How did you get that owie?" they asked.

"I didn't know what to tell them. I didn't want to scare them. Sometimes I'd tell them I got in a little fight with a grizzly bear and she did that with her teeth. Sometimes I'd tell them it was a car wreck."

It seemed easier, somehow.

She wonders what the attack means. She'd spent nine years in the park, walked hundreds of miles of backcountry trails, and never seen a grizzly bear except from a car. But then she'd always been with a crew: never alone and always making noise. There is roughly one grizzly for every 45,000 acres in greater Yellowstone. What are the chances of her and the bear meeting in the same place at the same time in broad daylight?

She likes grizzlies and still appreciates the thrill of seeing one in the wild, from a distance. She doesn't regret asking that the bear's life be spared, although it's doubtful the Park Service would have taken any action against a bear with cubs that attacked when surprised. Still, she can't help resenting the animal a little.

"I'll probably carry that resentment the rest of my life. Why did it hit me? I wouldn't hurt it and there are a lot of people who would."

She wants people to know that bears are out there, that they are incredibly powerful and can be dangerous. She wants people to be careful, to make noise and pay attention. There are more bears in the Yellowstone ecosystem now. They've bounced back from the terrible years of the 1960s and early 1970s after the park dumps were closed and so many were killed. But the human population is growing, too. She's not optimistic about finding enough room for everybody.

"More and more people are moving into these areas. I love seeing grizzlies in the wild, but I don't think we have enough space for them and the people. There are going to be more and more encounters and more and more maulings."

## Scott McMillion: *You've Got to Wonder*

The attack means she can't do the physical labor she had done all her life and her employment options are slimmer. She sews. She cleans houses. She wonders what to do next.

She knows she should have made noise that day, probably shouldn't have hiked alone. But thousands of people do it every day without a problem.

"Sometimes I think I want to forget it ever happened and go on with my life and try to figure out what to do next. It's like being hit by lightning, any natural sort of freak deal. But I always wonder why it happened to me. Did this happen for a reason?"

So far, she doesn't have any answers.

"But I keep thinking I'm going to."

### GREG KEELER
#### BOZEMAN, MONTANA

*A Professor of English at Montana State University, Greg Keeler is a prolific and entertaining poet, songwriter, and musician. Some of his recent books of poetry include* American Falls, Epiphany at Goofy's Gas, *and* A Mirror to the Safe. *His audio tapes bear such titles as "Aliens and Canadians," "Nuclear Dioxin Queen," and "Trash Fish." He has also written plays funded by the Montana Arts Council, the Montana Committee for the Humanities, and the National Endowment for the Arts.*

# Llamas in the Landscape

And what are these
spattering calico
over this valley
of the Horse Shoe Hills
at the True West confluence
of the Missouri headwaters?
These big cuties—
some kind of cross
between an ostrich
and a pet-shop bunny—
have come of age
tiptoeing among
the mares and geldings.
So take that saddle
off ol' Buck,
and throw a pack or two
on Sweetie and Foofoo.
The range has never

**Greg Keeler:** *Poems*

been so homey as
under these dainty puffballs,
ears straight up
and noses sniffing
thin air.
And sorry ol' Paint,
but your hooves,
your flat iron clodhoppers
are too fat and careless
for what's left
of the trail.

Yes, bring on Phoebe
and Fauntleroy,
floating over their bird-toes
like mottled balloons,
leaving the path intact
for this new age
of huge moist eyes
and batting eyelashes—
a spit for a nicker,
John Wayne in drag.

# On a Bend of the Jefferson Near Three Forks, Montana: A Post-Western

Up to our necks in logs and brambles,
hog-tied by our waders,
we veer and stumble for the next hole,
the fishing as rotten as the weather
is beautiful. But there,
framed in twigs, two otters play
in waves of light, making wilderness
look as easy as falling off a log.
Our envy is a joy
till we slog on in our satire.
Far upstream, once again,
the branches frame a spirit
freed from history—
a man in a canoe,
bearded, buckskinned,
backlit so he damn near glows.
"Any luck," we yell
from our tragicomedy.
"You bet," he winks and twinkles
then bobs down riffles
out of sight.
At dusk we plod skunked
back to the otter bend
and there's our beaming friend
plopping two soggy little wads
from his traps into his bag.

# Rock Chuck Hears a Logging Truck

Rock chuck is a rusty puff
who makes fat fists when she eats
and cheeps to remind us of
our own strong will to sit
straight up and whistle when
the world comes to pull us apart.
Her kids playing King of the Mountain
there on that pile of rocks
push each other off while Mom
stands yet the higher ground,
her atoms in sync with the same wind
that carries the hawk to them
or their scent to the coyote.
Everything here zags or circles
except the straight line of her voice,
vertical through the stream's leap,
the pine's shush, an axis of sound
in perfectly crooked spokes
to warn her world of us who are
coming to everyone's senses
but our own.

## Salmon Fly Hatch on the Henry's Fork

A whistle like grass-wind
and sun off a swan's back
stings the Tetons sharper
than blue. Salmon fly

sputters the weather woven
into her wings down the
Henry's Fork and through the
webbed water. Moon says

now, lasting into her
daytime reflection on clear
water and longer as if the
thick hatch were all there

were of night. And the
amplified day: rainbows
perking then rippling the
water into circles then

breaking those circles.
Grass bends the banks down
farther then farther with
the weight of the hatch.

There's so much reflected
here. There's so much to
be shattered then smooth
then shattered into those

**Greg Keeler:** *Poems*

clear shards that only trout
can remember and even they
are a memory under the whistle
and glare. Reflections

of swans and the Tetons will
start it again and again
in the green-early years. The
rock-bottom, glass-water years.

# Stuck in the Surface Film

I'm through with rivers, water poems
that stay the same no matter how
you twist them. Give me sage
and the desert's advice, not midges
and mayflies, the meek wanderings
of lost lovers stuck in the surface film.
I'm through with the country western
adages that wear rocks smooth
with tears. Give me the sharp fractures
of office memos: FYI: "I fall to pieces"
is hereby restricted to the water.
Did a woman in some rest home
accidentally leave her dying request
on my answering machine, or was
this just another half-recalled dream
that I'll have to answer for personally
among cactus and scorpion—all forms
that are designed to protect water,
to slow it, to hold it in?

# SUSAN SWETNAM
## POCATELLO, IDAHO

*Susan Swetnam's essays and articles have appeared in a wide variety of national and regional magazines and journals, including* Gourmet, Walking, Handwoven, *and* Journal of the West. *Her first book,* Lives of the Saints in Southeast Idaho: An Introduction to Mormon Pioneer Life Story Writing, *appeared in 1990. A Professor of English at Idaho State University, Swetnam has been named that school's Distinguished Teacher, Distinguished Public Servant, and its Outstanding Researcher. She is also a Girl Scout leader and a competitive racewalker.*

# The Firebabe

I am a most unlikely firefighter. I have feared fire since I was six, thanks to a particularly gruesome "Dragnet" episode about arson. When Yellowstone burned, I could not watch the news, the images of flames crowning high in the air, the awful rush of fire through the trees. But, at 44, a teacher, writer, and girl scout leader with plenty of other things to do, I find myself a member of a volunteer fire department in the rural Intermountain West. My mother, my students, and my friends are impressed. Actually, it is a decision of cowardice.

When we move out from town to the edge of the national forest, my husband Ford asks about fire protection, and our real estate agent is a volunteer. He easily enlists Ford, a volunteer in his youth and later, before we met. "We also have many ladies in the department," the agent says, looking at me significantly. "We believe that women can do anything that men can." "Of course she'll help," Ford replies proudly. "She's like that." Not knowing what to say, I say yes.

"Everybody's afraid of fire," smiles the man giving us nomax uniforms when I confess, sotto voce, hoping to be disqualified. I know then that I am in the company of very brave people, or lunatics. The veteran firefighters are an oddly assorted lot, but they have one thing in common: they seem to welcome fires, complaining of a summer when the department hasn't had enough calls to "stay sharp." Many are retired military men. The department also has a cadre of energetic, can-do-style middle-aged men into which Ford immediately fits, including Paul, a former technical writing student of mine at the university, Bob, our trainer, and Matt, a superb mechanic and perhaps the best firefighter in the group. Most of the women are also older, ex-combat nurses and such, long veterans of the department. Only Peggy and Kim, social work students in their late thirties and relatively new firefighters, seem at all like me. Even they are clearly tougher. Kim has spent a lot of time jumping our of airplanes, and Peggy, married to a railroader, takes no guff, despite a glamourous exterior that I later discover occasionally includes coming to fires in mascara and wearing her heavies over lace nighties. The other woman our age, Lorraine, Matt's wife, is another sort of creature completely. Large, a little rough in her humor and speech, working class mother of three teenagers, Lorraine seems to regard our one modern truck, the Quick Response Unit, as her personal property. She offers her opinions with conviction at meetings and has good grounds for those opinions, I soon realize, for she is evidently first to every fire. "Does she sleep in her uniform?" Kim wonders aloud during a break in a meeting, and Peggy and I dissolve in unfirefighter-like giggles. This is the year that the "Sportsbabe" is new on the radio, another big, blunt, no-fooling competent woman, and we begin to refer to Lorraine as "The Firebabe" among ourselves.

In my last preliminary training session, I realize that I differ from everyone else in another way. I am perhaps even more afraid of our engines than of fire itself. I have never driven anything larger than a full-sized pick-up truck, and the idea of jouncing many feet above the ground in the company of thousands of pounds of shifting water is unappealing, to say the least. The department's two regular engines are aging, quirky in the gears and steering, covered with dials and pressure gauges that look ready to explode at any moment. Indeed, before I take my trial drive, it is impressed on me how easily one could set something wrong and wreck the engine. The tanker truck—a bona fide antique—is even worse, and, when Ford proves that he is among the few competent to drive it, cheers erupt. Seeking no such glory, I am allowed to test drive Engine 2, with Paul as my amused instructor. While I do complete the quarter mile drive successfully, and even turn the thing around somehow, my performance is such that no one complains later when I manage always to be second or third to the station, always a passenger.

Despite my hopes that the department will never have another fire, the very day after Ford and I are official, we are called to one of the most dramatic fires that anyone remembers. While much of our district consists of what firefighters call the "urban interface," an area where houses encroach on national forest and BLM land, it also includes a stretch of four lane interstate highway and a nasty light industrial strip just outside the city limits, a zone of junkyards and recycling plants and ancient trailer parks. My first fire is on that strip, in a dilapidated salvage yard whose levels of deposit reach nearly to the fossil record. When we come around the corner from our canyon and look across the greater valley to see the oily black column of smoke towering hundreds of feet high, flames visible five miles away, I know that I would turn the car home if I were alone, mailing my uniform back. Ford says, "Holy shit!"—and speeds up.

It is a horrible afternoon. BLM, Forest Service, and city trucks are already on the scene helping us, thanks to a cooperative agreement for large fires that I will have cause to bless repeatedly in the months ahead. And I am never personally in danger—the department realizes what it has in me, and I am relegated to warning people not to linger under live overhead power lines. But what I see convinces me that I will never be able to fight fires. The junkyard is full of paint and bullets and exploding cars; the noise and smell are debilitating. It is all that I can do not to run away. My worst moment comes when I am directed to take water to people on the line, and see Ford and Peggy in the doorway of a shed, hosing down a smoking car. "What are you doing?" I yell, and they turn to me, baffled.

The next afternoon, we fight another fire, this one started by children playing with matches in the sagebrush. The fire is just one canyon over from ours, and it is gaining on a house as we arrive. Ford immediately joins Bob, Matt, Lorraine, and the BLM crews defending the house from its green lawn, a wonderful firebreak. I play the role of hand-maiden again. At the height of the action, when I am dispensing canteens, an all-female BLM crew goes by on a little brush unit even niftier than Lorraine's QR. They are slim and muscular and 25; they are grinning through the smoke and talking as if they were on their way to the mall. The only word to describe them, I realize, is "firebabes." I feel useless.

After the fire is knocked down and the home saved, I am dispatched with our littlest hose to work with BLM crews mopping up the burned over area. While they chop at smoldering patches, turning over hot ant hills and opening the roots around sagebrush, I bleat the hose at random sparks to prevent flare-ups. I am hot and tired and absolutely drained after these two days, wondering how I will ever be able to stand this. "Let's hope that this is *it* for a while," I say.

The nearest BLM crew member, a cheerful man in his late twenties, looks up and utters one of the most shocking things I've ever heard. "Black trees make green wallets," he grins, and I glimpse another world.

Two hours later, showered and in a sundress, I'm standing behind our house watering our lawn. The tiny hose echoes the one I handled earlier, and I wiggle my bare feet in the cool wet grass. I think about the xeroscaping advice we got when we moved out here, the surprise of our ecologically correct friends when Ford started carrying in sod, 40 pound roll by 40 pound roll, to make this little patch between us and the junipers and sagebrush. A monarch butterfly stops to drink from a grass blade near me. At this moment, a green lawn is the most beautiful thing in the world.

We never again have two such intense days piled back to back. But we have plenty to do. I learn to take to heart what Margaret, our chief's wife and a long-time firefighter herself, tells me when I confess my sense of inadequacy. If you do one thing at a fire, she says, you've helped. Don't think of the whole fire. That's incident command's job. Most firefighting is solving one finite problem, then solving another. As the season progresses, indeed, my "one things" do start to add up, though they still seem tiny in comparison to everybody else's. By the end of that first season, I've learned to work the siren and the radio on Engine 2. I've started to learn radio protocol. I've directed traffic around a rolled truck on the freeway. I've freed hose tangled around sagebrush. A few times, I've used the hose myself at the edges of very small grass fires. Once or twice, I've even forgotten briefly that I wanted to run away.

I've also gained interesting new vocabulary words. By the end of that first summer, I've learned that "candle" can be used as a verb and that "in the black" is where firefighters like to be. I've become accustomed to hearing the nouns "structure" and "vehicle" used to mean huge classes of objects, though in my heart I doubt the usefulness of a term that includes sheds in the process of falling down and million-dollar houses. I can't help but remember how hard I work with my students on exact diction, and I take some comfort when it is Paul who challenges the breadth of reference. At a fire-review meeting, he complains that a property owner directed him with particular urgency to defend an outbuilding because it contained several "vehicles." "But come to find out," he says with disgust, "those weren't *vehicles*—they were just old piece-of-shit snow machines."

My view of the world changes, too. Summer holidays will never be the same. We cheer when rain begins to fall on July 2 and doesn't stop for five or six days. Every Friday afternoon, we watch the parade of campers and trucks and motorcycles into the national forest and cringe. "Go home!" we yell at them from our deck. "Where's your spark arrester? Do you have a shovel and a bucket to go with that firewood?" I begin to feel fierce proprietary interest in the three miles of national forest where I run every day. Though I know that my colleagues in biology are right and forests need fire periodically, I have now seen first hand the smoking wreck of burned over wildlands. One day while I am running I vow that, if anyone sets fire to my national forest, I will find his house and burn it down.

Somehow, I do not quit through that first year, or the next, though I'm still afraid of fire and still manage to avoid ever driving a truck. I continue to do little things. At the end of my third year, our department command changes. Our chief retires, taking the motherly Margaret with him, and Lorraine is among the nominations for his replacement. Kim, Peggy, and I have long ago revised our attitudes toward Lorraine. Kim and Lorraine have become closer ever since they narrowly escaped together from a fire driven by a sudden wind shift; Peggy and Lorraine have worked together in the QR many times. For my part, I am simply grateful for her patience. When we say "firebabe" now, it is a term of respect and affection. The three of us and Ford join the faction working to convince her to seek the job. Along the way, we learn about the side of Lorraine that doubts and worries and listens to teasing more than we ever imagined. She is elected by a large majority, and she proves to be an excellent chief.

That's important, for our numbers are down. Our real estate agent has a heart attack, and his wife discovers that she has cancer. Several other firefighters decide that they are just too old, or move away, or change jobs and cannot respond. Sometimes only six or seven of us show up at a fire, and I know that the inevitable is soon to happen—the "one thing" that I am called on to do may soon become serious.

And it is—one afternoon in my fourth summer, there is no one but me to run the pump panel on Engine 2 during a big fire. We respond to help another department; the fire is mercifully far from our house, diagonally across the big valley, on the back side of a summit just outside the city limits in rubbly, bone-dry sage and juniper country split by deep canyons. At the bottom, there are plenty of houses with barns and horses. The fire is a big one, wind-driven, started by something in the weekend parade of vehicles to somebody else's backyard. When the call comes, Ford is in town and heads directly to the scene; I follow my usual practice and arrive second at the station, climbing into the already warmed up Engine 2 beside Tim, an energetic man in his thirties who joined the department shortly after we did. When we get to the fire, the tanker plane is already flying, and Ford is off with Lorraine in the densest smoke.

We are directed, with urgency, to "pick a house and defend it," and Tim heads just where I don't want to be, directly below the fire. I cannot whine to him as I would to Ford, so I whine inwardly as we roar into a long dirt driveway behind a cluster of houses, over dubious berms and into a nasty-looking cul-de-sac under the descending hillside. I tug down the hose, assuming that I'm to be the one to handle it, while Tim gets the pump panel going. But vile white smoke is pluming in two big pinchers, the fire itself apparently just beyond the crest a hundred yards above us. Tim regards the smoke with alarm. "I'll take this up the hill," he yells. "You run the pump panel."

It's truth time. Though I am supposed to be competent to do at least this, I have never run a pump panel; in fact, I have retreated into stubborn denial that I ever *will* when the subject is discussed in meetings. But now I must. "Remind me," I say. As he does, it sounds surprisingly easy. All I have to do is watch the gauges, make sure he has enough pressure to pump (the throttle is just a knob to twist, clearly marked), make sure that the engine temperature stays around 180 (pull the tank fill lever to cool it off), and keep an eye on the engine gauges, especially making sure that we don't run out of gas. I can do that. "Oh," he tosses over his shoulder as he starts up the hill, "and don't forget that it gets really hot under this engine if we have to sit for a while. It's pretty easy to start a fire under the exhaust pipe. You probably want to pull down the little hose to defend the truck."

This is bad news. In his haste, Tim has parked the engine on a mound of loose tinder, wood chips and sawdust, where many winters of firewood have been cut. The back end of Engine 2 is buried in loose wood chips to the bumper, in fact. I'm not sure which one of the hoses is the "little one," or how to engage it, and I vaguely remember that you have to dial the pressure down to do so, and that takes some of the pressure off the main hose, so you must be careful. But Tim is already far up the hill. And I'm suddenly surrounded by anxious homeowners. "Are you going to get it out?" one man asks. "Is it under control?" another stutters. A woman in her sixties, apparently in early shock, shakes my hand solemnly. "Thank you," she says.

This is hardly the time to start a new fire myself. "Can we help?" asks a young man in a muscle shirt, accompanied by his skinny girlfriend in flip flops. I start to tell them no, then remember the pond we crossed, and ask for buckets of water to wet the ground under the truck. I explain with what I hope is authority that I don't want to waste our water or lower the pressure on Tim's hose, even temporarily. And they surprise me, returning with a wheelbarrow full, with a pink plastic sparkly sandbucket for a bailer.

After that, the day goes well. I soon learn from radio traffic that Ford and Lorraine are safe, solving one finite problem at a time in the company of many other firefighters (though Lorraine eventually gets a lecture from the big incident command for working the line rather than acting like a chief, so intense is her eagerness to fight fires). I *do* get nervous at one point when the wind shifts and trees are obviously candling beyond the benchline. I get even more nervous when Tim starts spraying the grass just beyond my line of sight, though I quickly conclude that the gesture is essentially a show for the fifty or sixty people who have wandered up there to "help." My wheelbarrow keeps getting filled, and no one laughs at me. The gauges on Engine 2 stay where they are, as well they might, for I am watching the dickens out of them. I bail with my pink bucket. I reassure the civilians. And I have a wonderful place to watch the air tanker, the size of a DC-10, sweeping so low up the draw that I worry about it catching the top of trucks. A helicopter goes by, dangling a bucket full of water that's leaking on purpose, and I laugh out loud.

The smoke dissipates. We are dismissed, and Tim comes down the hill. "Good job!" he says. I've done very little, I protest, but he's having none of that. When he sees the wheelbarrow and the puddles in the chips under the exhaust, he whistles. "Awesome idea," he says.

For some reason, this small excursion into responsibility changes everything. The next week, we have a pump panel training, and I pay attention. I learn which lever numbers go with which hoses on Engine 2. At our next fire, an owner-arson shed event, I make myself volunteer to run the panel, and I do it right. I'm amazed to find myself a little irritated when Bob and Ford periodically come around the engine to check on me. Over the next few weeks, I jump up on the engines to engage hose take-up reels, and I hook fill lines to hydrants. "Next, you'll hog the driving," says Kim, smiling.

I don't do that (indeed, I still don't drive at all), but I do find myself actually fighting fires. I handle hose on an expressway fire that spills into the sage, taking turns with Matt, who appears to have noticed me for the first time. Then I work another hose on my own when our second crew tires. A few weeks later at midnight, my worst fear comes true, as an unidentifiable someone explodes a pipe bomb in the nature area pavilion in my national forest, starting a blaze whose glow we can see from the bottom of our street. Everybody works hard, and we stop the fire quickly, fifty yards downwind. After the big flames are out, Kim and I team up at the edge of the black and the green, opening the sagebrush roots, turning over smoldering piles, knocking down juniper flare-ups. I realize that we are doing an expanded version of what the BLM firefighter and I did, so long ago, it seems. We are very careful, and very thorough. When I finally get to bed at 3:30, I sleep soundly, knowing that the fire is really dead.

One full moon night that fourth September, we do not get back to bed at all. We're paged from sleep at 1 a.m. to fight a fire high on an open mountain slope, started by a cigarette thrown down from the winding road to the lookout, or a campfire. It's very remote. Ford and I coax the tanker to the top of the paved road, then pile with our friends into the bed of someone's big four wheel diesel truck for a ride up the dirt track. At the ultimate top of the road, we find Matt and Lorraine with the QR and a BLM party with its brush unit. The part of the fire still smoldering is farther above, inaccessible to vehicles, so Ford and I grab bladder bags and pulaskis and begin to climb "Great, *water!*" says the BLM captain when we scramble out of the draw. Ford and I cooperate to use our water most efficiently, spreading the glowing wood to hiss and sputter. We douse several junipers that threaten to re-erupt. We go down for more water and do it all over again. "Good job," says a BLM crewmember, taking a break and watching us work.

By the time that the fire is really out, dawn is just starting to light the edge of the ridge behind us, and the orange moon has moved into the center of the western sky. We decline invitations to join the crew piling back into the truck and walk down together, facing that moon. The night is cool and sweet; we hold hands. Of all the times we've been in the mountains, we've never been out this late (or this early) together, never together seen quite this glow of pre-sunrise or felt quite this air. Our friends come by, waving and beeping from the pickup, then Matt and Lorraine, our other friends; the BLM truck follows. "You don't want a ride, do you?" the driver asks, more a statement than a question.

In three hours, we'll both be in class, another life. "Can I interest you in a breakfast date after we get the tanker back to the barn?" Ford asks, then pauses, smiling at my soot-blackened face. "You firebabe."

I turn and hug him, there on the mountain track, completely happy. I am, I realize, "like that" once again. I know that I'll never be a firebabe. But I can fight fires.

## LOUISE WAGENKNECHT
### LEADORE, IDAHO

*Louise Wagenknecht has worked for the U. S. Forest Service since 1973, first in the Klamath National Forest in northern California, later for the Cibola National Forest in New Mexico, and now for the Salmon-Challis National Forest in eastern Idaho. Her essays and articles have appeared in* Western Horseman *and* High Country News, *and she has become a regular contributor to* American Nature Writing *anthologies, published by Sierra Club Books.*

# Coming Off Lee Creek

"Tell me again why we're doing this!" I shouted at the rider ahead.

"Because!" Rich shouted back, turning in the saddle as his tall Missouri Fox Trotter shuffled along, churning up the ground faster than my mount, an elderly Forest Service Quarter Horse, could lope. He laughed at my feeble joke, I knew, because he was prepared to laugh at anything today, away from the office.

I dug my spurs into Winston's orange flanks as he shied at a five-point bull elk trotting across the jeep trail ahead of us. The Fox Trotter's hooves raised little puffs of dust in the September dawn.

I looked back over Winston's tail, across the valley, to the old Junction Ranger Station, ten miles away, where Rich and I had caught our horses an hour ago. Loading them into the trailer, we headed west, rattling across the Lemhi River. In the east Mars and Jupiter blazed in conjunction above Railroad Canyon. I pointed them out to Rich.

"Uh huh," he said. "Is my bridle in the saddle compartment?"

Now, as the sun chinned itself on the spine of the Continental Divide, I looked at the pink glow on the bare peaks of the western mountains. Half an hour before, we had unloaded our horses at the county road near the valley's western edge, where sage-covered foothills and alluvial fans rose toward the jagged peaks of the Lemhi Range, more than 11,000 feet high. Stringers of aspen and conifers crept down the ridges below the timberline; meadows clothed the old slumps. A fence bisected the hills, running north and south, marking the boundary between National Forest and Bureau of Land Management lands. We approached it now at a lope, dismounting at the gate precisely at seven o'clock.

"They can't say we're late this time," Rich observed, looking at his watch. I scanned the riderless horizons with a sigh of relief. The four permittees scheduled to meet us here were unhappy enough about having to remove their cattle from the Lee Creek Allotment three weeks early.

If we of all people were late, on top of all this drought and trouble, there would be hell to pay.

Rich's restless young mare pawed, demanding action. Winston tried to go back to sleep.

"You wait here and count anything that comes by, and check the brands," Rich said. "I'm going over to the north gate. Maybe they decided to go in there." We walked our horses through the gate, and Rich closed it behind us.

I dismounted and fished a bruised apple out of my cantlebag as Rich disappeared over the rise. Winston opened his eyes long enough to eat the core out of my hand. He flung his head up, drooling juice, as two cow elk burst out of the grove of firs above us, making for the timbered ridge above the meadow. Behind them three Hereford cows lumbered, the white plastic tags on their dewlaps swinging. Carl's cattle: not the ones we were really concerned about.

The whitefaces veered for the closed gate, then, seeing me, swung uphill again without breaking stride. They had just disappeared when a horse and rider came hustling down the draw. Fast Freddie, surrounded by cowdogs, astride a sweating Tobiano paint, thundered up just as I clambered back on Winston.

"Why isn't the gate open?" he demanded, without preamble.

If the gate *had* been open, Fast Freddie would have demanded to know why it wasn't closed. I had learned that much, in four years. I looked at him and shrugged.

"Rich closed it," I said.

Freddie was not amused. "This sort of thing has got to STOP!" he bellowed, wheeling the paint off at a lope in Rich's wake. I reflected, not for the first time, that my wages weren't nearly enough compensation for these encounters.

I dug my spurs in and headed up the fence line, but Winston turned his head and nickered. Two riders approached the gate: Darwin, Carl's thirtyish son, and a woman dressed entirely in black, except for her too-blonde hair. Black hat, black shotgun chaps, black boots, black shirt, black gloves. She sat in a black saddle with much too much silver trim, on a black mare with flattened ears.

Darwin muttered a greeting. Miss Rodeo Idaho examined the scenery.

"I think they're bringing them out the other gate," I said. No reply. I turned my reluctant mount once more and spurred him up the hill, glancing back at the Fun Twins, engaged in animated conversation.

Up the ridge, down a draw, and now the sun reached us, turning the autumn frost on the short brown meadow grass to shards of winking crystal. I pulled Winston up, listening. Sounds travel strangely at 7000 feet above the sea. Ten miles away, a semi downshifted on the highway, yet I stood within a quarter mile of hundreds of moving cattle, and heard nothing of them. I once asked a local ranchwoman why no one belled their mother cows here. "Why in the world would you want to put a bell on a cow?" she demanded.

"So you can find them in the mountains," I replied. She shook her head. When I added that we did it thus in northern California, she nodded at last, understanding. Californians. That explained it.

In succeeding years, I learned not to ask questions like that, the range cows remained unbelled, and every autumn most permittees were short some cows. In spring, bear hunters found their carcasses in high alpine swales, ringed by melting snowdrifts.

I suddenly heard the high, worried bawl of a bull, and kicking Winston up the next ridge, saw below us a river of cattle, streaming down Ferry Creek to the north gate. Running, butting, aiming kicks at about ten more dogs than anyone needed, they came on. In their midst, two bulls, long separated, shoved each other angrily in a haze of dust and snot.

Winston was old and stiff, but he headed for the herd at a lope, as a rider forced his mount between the lead cows and the north gate, swung it open, and jumped aside as the avalanche rumbled down the long sagebrush slope. Red and white, roan and cream, solid black and pied, these were most of the 450 permitted cows of the Lee Creek Allotment, and their eight-month-old, 500-pound calves.

Merlin, wearing his trademark pith helmet and sneakers, pulled up alongside, his saddle attached to a stout buckskin pony about twelve hands high. His two teenage sons roved the flanks of the herd, disdainful of regulation cowboy attire in baseball caps, t-shirts, and high top sneakers.

We discussed the drought and cattle prices as the herd trailed down the foothills to the edge of the valley, to a forty-acre private pasture, part of an old homestead long since incorporated into Fast Freddie's ranch. Five other riders appeared out of the dust, converged around the pasture gate, and began cutting out Freddie's cattle.

The operation was complicated by the two bulls, which jumped over the sagging barbed wire fences again and again. The cow dogs, paying no attention to shouts of "back, BACK, GOD-DAMMIT!" worried the calves until enraged cows, bawling and slinging ribbons of drool, charged back up the fenceline, eluding the riders.

I sat beside the gate on Winston, counting cattle, checking brands, and occasionally waking up my somnolent mount long enough to head off a cow. Rich's mare was quick, with good cow sense, and Rich had by now abandoned all pretense of oversight, enjoying himself and leaving the counting to me and my little yellow notebook.

When the remainder of the herd at last began drifting toward the county road, minus almost 200 cows bearing Fast Freddie's brand, I found myself riding drag beside Carl. His shoulders hunched into a brown canvas coat despite the warmth of the sun, a stained beige cowboy hat pulled well down onto his high forehead, he did not look happy.

"You will notice," he said suddenly, "that Stew ain't here."

I cleared my throat.

"All this b.s. is becauseof *his* cows, and the s.o.b. ain't even here," he continued, acronymically.

"Maybe," I said, "he's been delayed."

Pollyanna of the Lemhis, that's me.

Carl rolled his eyes and grunted, and we rode silently on.

The herd, tired from the morning's excitement, moved slowly. At the county road, I loaded Winston into the trailer, climbed into the stifling heat of the green Forest Service pickup, and drank a warm soda while chewing on a nice hot peanut butter sandwich. Merlin's boys practiced their roping on the heels of laggard calves.

I eased the truck into gear, caught up with the herd, and crawled along in their wake, tires squishing through the splashes of wet green manure. Carl was, of course, right about why two Forest Service range specialists were spending the day "helping" four permittees to remove their livestock from the public's land. The drought would have forced them home in any case, although ordinarily we wouldn't have been along for the drive. But all summer long, Fast Freddie, who rode and salted on the allotment, had insisted that Stewart had too many cattle up there. The extra cattle, he said, bore the brands of Stew's grown children. Forest Service regulations allow up to half of a permittee's cattle to belong to his children, but Fast Freddie's suspicion that Stewart made use of this custom to smuggle unpermitted cattle onto the Forest remained.

Stewart's ranch bordered the Lee Creek Allotment, and all summer I had checked the country frequently, noting ear tag numbers and brands. Stew's cows were walking brand samplers, sometimes carrying three or more, but I had never found too many of them. Freddie was unconvinced, and since he roped with the District Ranger every Tuesday evening, his opinion counted for a great deal more than mine. So today I inched down this road, watching the daily thunderstorm spilling off the slopes of Gunsight Peak, headed straight for the herd.

The county road was fenced on both sides, and punctuated by cattleguards. Beside each cattleguard was an eight-foot wire gate. This arrangement should have made counting cattle fiendishly simple, but by the time we reached the first gate, at Merlin's ranch, the riders were leaning into the wind, feeling the first raindrops. As the downstrikes crept closer, sitting on top of a steel-shod horse struck me as a remarkably bad idea, but the cowhands seemed reluctant to dismount and open the gate. Darwin at last leapt off his horse, tied it to Merlin' s mailbox by the reins, and marched toward the gate.

"Goddammit, don't leave him there!" bawled his father in disbelief, as a clap of thunder cracked over our heads. Sullenly, Darwin obeyed him, untying the horse and leading him over to the gate, the reins over one shoulder.

Damn. I'd wanted to see that first cranky cow duck under the reins and watch the mailbox come shooting out of the ground when the horse panicked and pulled back. But no such reprieve came, and I crawled out of the cab, my yellow slicker dragging in the mud, prepared to die honorably for God and the Forest Service.

Half an hour later, I had counted Merlin's 53 cows and their offspring through the gate. Amidst the downpour and the downstrikes, I glimpsed the back of Carl's neck, growing redder and redder as he scrunched ever deeper into the saddle.

Everyone was thoroughly splattered and dripping when Stewart appeared at last, just as the thunderstorm rolled away. Resplendent in town hat and a clean shirt, his freshly shaven cheeks were drenched with so much cheap aftershave that I could smell him over the manure, horse sweat, and ozone.

"Had a meeting I couldn't get out of!" he hollered jovially, trotting up on a fat bay gelding as his wife closed up the horse trailer and got the truck turned around. All right, I thought. Now maybe this'll go faster. But as we moved the diminished herd toward the next gate, half a mile away, Freddie deserted us, slipping into his own driveway without a farewell, just as Merlin and his boys had a few minutes earlier. Perhaps they knew what was coming. For Stew reached that last gate first, flung it open with a flourish, and grinned as the remaining cattle streamed past him.

"Shit," I said. Great. Stew had just ensured that we wouldn't be able to get an accurate count of his cattle without a great deal of trouble. A mile away was an intersection. Stew's ranch lay half a mile to the right, but Carl's place was a long five miles to the left, with only one gate in that direction, at the old Clark place.

Carl looked as though he'd just discovered dog manure on his boot. Rich, Darwin, and the Queen of Darkness spurred their foaming mounts hard, trying to cut Stew's cattle back one at a time to keep them from rejoining the herd. That didn't work. It never does. But while the riders attempted the impossible, little groups of cattle took advantage of the confusion to slip into the alfalfa fields on either side of the road.

"Bloat up and die, you bastards!" Carl shouted crossly, circling a little bunch, trying to haze them back to the road.

# Louise Wagenknecht: *Coming Off Lee Creek*

Rich, his mare blowing, loped up beside me as I leapt from the idling truck in a futile attempt to keep several of Stew's cows from swerving into an open field.

"Let them go," Rich said. "Stew can get them later."

"You know," I gasped, "if they can't cut them out at the old Clark place, we'll have to follow them almost to town to get a count."

"I know," Rich nodded. "This *seriously* sucks."

At the old Clark place, while Stew made ineffectual waving motions, Carl reached the gate first, where by much spurring, cursing, and shouting, he contrived to put his 107 cows and their calves through, leaving the dregs of Stew's bunch milling behind it. I put my notebook in my back pocket, dragged the gate closed, turned the rig around, and drove slowly back down the road, counting the cattle scattered in the fields and on the roadside. I wrote the number 49 in the book.

I showed it to Rich as he rode alongside the cab. He sighed. "Well, Fast Freddie's got to go back and ride cleanup anyway tomorrow. They're out a few cows and most of the bulls, at least."

He loaded his soaking, trembling mare into the stock trailer beside Winston, then levered himself stiffly into the passenger side of the cab. I looked at my watch. Six o'clock. Rich drank for a long time from a gallon canteen.

"Have fun?" I asked as he lowered the dusty container. He laughed, shortly, mirthlessly. "Just another day in paradise."

"So, let's see," I said, scribbling in my notebook. "We just spent twelve hours of your time and my time—that's about $300 for the gum'mint, not counting the overtime we won't get—and burned up about ten bucks worth of gas, and wore out your horse, to prove that Stew probably didn't have too many cows up there. Grazing fee this year is $1.97 per cow per month, so Stew could've had 152 extra cows up there for a month before we'd have broken even finding out whether he did or did not. This is a good deal?"

Rich ignored the sarcasm. "When somebody complains, you have to check it out," he recited.

"Okay," I conceded. "But why did our fearless Ranger want us both to go? I did all the counting."

Rich was silent. "What's the matter with him?" I pushed. Does he think I can't count?"

"Let's put it this way," Rich said slowly. "He wanted to be sure the count was good."

"Uh-huh. Just like he made you go back to Walters Creek and re-check my utilization measurements, even though they came out exactly the same?"

Rich lifted his hands, palms up, and let them fall back onto his grimy green pants. "It's a different culture here," he said. "Some people just aren't used to women in field positions yet."

"For Chrissake, Rich, it's the nineties! What you mean is that our Mr. Ranger isn't used to it," I exploded. "It's supposed to be the same rules on every Forest, isn't it?" I added nastily, and immediately regretted the harangue, for Rich was chewing a mouthful of Tums, his face gone gray under the dirt.

I mashed down the clutch pedal and turned the key in the ignition. We rolled away toward the Beaverhead Mountains, that divide between watersheds and worlds, brown and old and so very dry, looming over this foreign land where nothing whatever was the way you expected it to be. I blinked hard and tried to focus on the particolored clot of cattle slowly moving away from us in the silent evening. I was tired, thirsty, and a long way from home.

## KATHLEEN KING
### POCATELLO, IDAHO

*Kathleen King teaches creative writing at Idaho State University. A native midwesterner, she first fell in love with mountains on a trip to the west at the age of 15. Her novel,* Cricket Sings, *was published by Ohio University Press, and her poems and stories have appeared in many anthologies and literary magazines. She winters in Pocatello and in summer migrates to the Gros Ventre range.*

# West Mink Creek

Willows redden beside the creek.
Hard walking on the trail, too much
snow but not enough to ski. Wind
sharpens, pushes up the canyon
toward a hunter's blind, snow
yellowed here and there by coyotes.
Near a house-shaped rock, tracks
converge in the snow. Dawn or dusk.
Next to the trail someone gutted an elk.
Evidence lies plain on rocks, frozen lungs,
grassy stomach split open, dark red heart,
liver, intestines and kidneys entwined.
Clouds part, Scout Mountain all snow,
West Mink Creek just mutters along.

# Brown Winter

Midmorning we walk the dog, footprints leaving
grassy brown trails melted in last night's frost.
Beyond Portneuf Gap, Bonneville Peak rises, white mirage
promising the river a good flow of snowmelt on sunny days.
At the edge of the golf course small sagebrush plants,
two inches high, engage the enemy lawn. Tumbleweed ambles
across the fairway, hangs up on a fence, unexpected delay.
As nine Canada geese lift from the river, wings spread to catch
wind pushing clouds toward us from the west, we watch,
impatient for new weather foretold by aching bones.
Irregular columns of basalt, old lava flow, the outwash
plain from Chink's Peak, long brown ridges tell a simple story.
Head lifted to the wind, the dog leans against me. Together
we watch the small river curve back on itself, lined by burdock.
Nothing will tame us. Many small blessings answer my prayers.

# Why We Go to the Desert

Red canyon opens wider, petrified castle spires
rising in earthy colors, burnt ocher praise of sun.
We two and our dog trudge upstream along a dry wash,
feet slipping in sand powdered by flash floods.
Nothing much lives here. Cedars brush up,
olive green leaves aromatic, durable reddish wood.
A few dried grass blades and lizards. Charged,
swift with heat, the small reptiles hurry,
patterns of movement a hymn of belonging.
In a dry stream bed the dog finds a seep,
laps at the sweet water, then lies down,
cool and mossy in the green puddle. Envious
we sit in hot shade beneath a nearby rock,
drink warm water from a plastic bottle.
Brilliant jewel, a hummingbird buzzes past.
We hike down to the San Rafael River, cottonwood
oasis. Alkali water the color of milk rushes
over stones as we hunker in the current, worship
the river miracle, cool twist in the narrow gorge.
Then lowering sun lights orange canyon walls,
yellow steeples throw longer shadows, the air chills.
Darkness follows, borne on the wings of bats.

# Developing Perspective

Afternoon draws shadows toward us
across the trail from nearby pines.
At the beaver pond one blackbird trills.
Today in Alaska Basin we saw the wind
draw a plume of cloud off Grand Teton.
You wave a hand and say, "All this."
"Yes," I agree. "The West."
We have walked away from cities.
Legs tired, we step faster now
toward camp, a fire, the night.
We cross the golden meadow
one late September afternoon
wrapped about us like a dream.

## C. L. RAWLINS
### BOULDER, WYOMING

*C. L. Rawlins worked in the U. S. Forest Service from 1977-1992 as a firefighter, range rider, and field hydrologist. He was the recipient of a National Primitive Skills Award for scientific fieldwork in the Wind River Range. He is the author of two books of poetry, including* Ceremony on Bare Ground *and* In Gravity National Park. *His nonfiction books include* Sky's Witness: A Year in the Wind River Range *and* Broken Country: Mountains & Memory.

# On Spread Creek

"Why do all the meadows have stumps in them?"

I looked at the woman, her silver hair bobbing slightly with the stride of her easy old horse. At her back was an opening in the forest, hemmed by lodgepole, bare ground filling in with fireweed and blueberry elder. It was 1974. I was taking dudes on a ride in the upper forks of Spread Creek. The only reason for the road being there was to haul logs. The dudes were incidental.

"It's a timber cut. It was thick woods before. See how square the margins are? The natural openings all have grass and sedge in them, not this shrubby stuff."

"How long ago did they cut it?" Her straw hat cast a shadow over her eyes.

I looked at the stumps just starting to go silver from the weather, at the thick patches of fireweed and a few raspberries starting to come in. "Eight, ten years. We passed some newer ones coming in. You can still see the Cat tracks."

"Cat?"

"Caterpillar Tractor, what they use to pile the slash to burn it."

"Slash?"

"The leftovers, scrap. Tops, limbs, the wood that's too small to truck out. They pile it up and torch it. See that bare hump with the thick bushes around it?" I reined into the cut-block and she followed, the hooves of the horses quieter than on the hardpacked road. Burnt stubs fingered out of a low mound. Getting off my horse, I kicked at the chalky dirt, turning up charcoal. "This was a big slashpile. The ash fertilized around it, so the bushes come in thick, but the heat sterilized the dirt where the pile burned. It won't grow much for awhile."

She ran out of questions. But at least she asked. Not many people did. I never knew whether they saw the clearcuts as necessary subtractions from the landscape, or whether they noticed them at all. The line of dudes and horses went out of sight ahead, but I saw the flash of sunglasses, her husband looking back. "We'd better catch up." I mounted and reined toward the dirt road.

From the east, following the thin crescents of horsetracks, came the wagons. The Bishop's pair of white Shires led the train. Hooped canvas thumped like sails in the noon breeze. The Bishop waved and his draft team tossed their heads. It looked like something out of a movie, or a dream. The woman fumbled for her camera. Under the plank wagonboxes, I could see the fat, black rubber tires.

The people on the wagon trips wanted it easy: they could ride gentle horses or loll on the foam-padded benches in the wagons, which made down into beds. They paid a hundred or so a day, per head, to be dragged over logging roads in the north end of the Gros Ventre Range and feel like—what?—pioneers, I guess.

We pulled into camp about three. The canvas flies of the chuckwagon were spread like sooty wings and the iron fireboxes were staked in place. The trucks were hidden behind some thick spruce, but I could see the glint of a bumper. After the horses were hobbled and turned out, I got a double-bit axe and a two-handed crosscut—the Misery Whip— and started to get wood for camp. There was a dead lodgepole near camp, and the ring of the axe brought the dudes with their cameras.

When the tree came down, Uncle Marvin limped out to grab the helm of the crosscut and we bucked the tree into three-foot lengths, cameras clicking like hail around us. "Keep it old-timey," the boss said, "because that's what they pay for." We were expected to wear cowboy hats, western shirts and boots. "No ski-resort t-shirts or baseball caps or stuff like that."

I felt like I was cheating the dudes with all this Western shuck-and-jive, while something else was being overlooked. It wasn't the horse-lore or the woods-craft that nagged. It was the deception we practiced, the rubber-tired haywagons tricked up with planks and white canvas. We were actors in a thoroughly American drama. Manifest Destiny: a Passion Play. We revived the frontier illusion, one week at a shot.

If people had asked, we might have talked about the clear-cuts and the roads, which seemed to me to be linked with our wagon-train of tourists, part of the same strange fabric, whether of history or misunderstanding. I might have taught them to recognize a few plants—mule-ear sunflower, lupine, larkspur—but most of them were impatient with such things. They wanted to learn how to saddle a horse, how to swing a double-bit, how to hinge-cut a dead pine so that it would fall, just so. I would scuff two marks, shoulder-width, on the ground with my cowboy boot and take bets that the firewood tree would fall between them.

The dudes had time and money to spend. We drew a lot of doctors and lawyers and midwestern retirees. I liked most of the people I guided, but I also liked to disillusion them. Something about them scared me: their eagerness to believe. At times, when the cameras clicked at one of our tableaux, I felt like those hired characters at Disneyland, with the white gloves and the rubber heads. Around the night fire, when my guitar was supposed to ring with "Goodbye, Old Paint" and "The Old Chisholm Trail," I'd throw in a heartbreaker by Buffy Sainte-Marie, "Now That the Buffalo's Gone." History. Conscience. In the quiet that followed, it seemed the night grew eyes.

Each day there were a few uncomfortable questions. Q: Where does this road go? A: To clearcuts. Q: What's all this rusty junk—this cable? A: Junk. The loggers left it. Q: When will the trees grow back? A: Who knows?

Faced with clearcuts, the illusion wavered. For them, I guess, it was like heading for the beach and ending up in a fish cannery. But they wanted to believe, despite the graded roads and other evidence, that they were in some way first. Where they recognized damage, they wanted to believe it was an exception, that the West was still fresh and empty. I shared that regret, because I shared their hunger, for Shining Mountains, for virgin ground, for a paradise always on the edge of what was known.

My family came to the Great Basin and the Rockies in the late 1840's, and lived as farmers, ranchers, teachers, teamsters, quarriers and mining engineers. We wintered out, proved up, and got by, but there was a longing for something besides what we had, a restless desire.

My grandad set me on a horse before I could walk. The year before the wagons, 1972, I spent three months south of the Tetons, in the drainage of Grey's River, herding and wrangling, without seeing an electric light or riding in a car. I lived on horseback, slept in a tent without mosquito net, and got a sense of how-it-all-was. I saw bears almost every day, and was bugled and charged by elk. After cooking, I stared into the fire each night, trying to gaze into the heart of the world.

But I saw other things that I didn't want to see: steep roads bleeding silt, rusty snakes of cable half-buried, and little streams blown out into collapsing gulleys, taking twelve-foot drops where the snowmelt hit raw, track-chewed soil.

Clearcuts. While Teton National Park had grown and Jackson Hole had become a profitable fantasy-preserve, the Grey's River country had been mined for quick timber. Logging roads, chopped into steep slopes, were crumbling into the creeks. Half-burnt slashpiles looked like funeral pyres. Hedges of blowdown were jackstrawed at the edge of the woods. Riding down from the roadless upper canyons into the logged-out zone was like coming on the aftermath of a battle.

I wheeled my horse and rode away, but something whispered after. As much as I loved the mountains, I had begun to know that consequences lived there, too. I had begun to sense how all events, all changes, all effects communicated to every part of the land.

My guiding didn't begin with the wagon train. I started with packtrips into the southern Absaroka Range, over trails into the forks of Pacific Creek and the Buffalo River. "What's that there?" they'd say. A bear in the berries, a moose in the willows, an eagle tipping broad wings, catching light at the edge of the sky. One night I took out my guitar and sang for the the boss's daughter: a mistake. A week later, I was stuck on the wagons where she was head cook, to wrangle, run camps and yodel at each night's fire.

But I would have done anything to be in the mountains that year. Scrubbed tin plates. Dug toilet holes. Between wrangling and guiding and driving, I walked away from camp, trying to get the feel of the place. I remember the names in that country: Togwotee Pass, Grizzly Creek, Buff Creek, Grouse Creek, Kettle Creek, Grouse Mountain. "What's over that ridge," they'd ask: Bearpaw Fork, Skull Creek, Hidden Lake, Aspen Creek, Lily Lake, Mount Leidy.

After the first snow, the dude business trickled to nothing. The boss told me I was a hell-of-a hand and offered me a big raise and a hunting camp to run. I pictured a walltent full of drunks, each boasting that he, the first goddamn thing in the morning, would bag the

## C. L. Rawlins: *On Spread Creek*

biggest son-of-bitching elk ever seen in Wyoming and You Bastards Will be Kissing My Ass. "Sorry," I muttered. On the wagon train, my working hours had been from five a.m. to eleven p.m. I was worn out. And I had to get away, from the boil of the fantasy.

When I hear, as one often hears in the West, that tourists are our only future, that we are to become innkeepers and dude wranglers and waitresses, I feel grim. It's not the travelers themselves so much as the dumb pressure of their belief, the lurching burden of our Western myth.

I'd rather drink with loggers, who at least know the smell and touch of woods, who may at times feel the power of the trees they cut, who have been afraid, hanging a big one on the stump and wondering which way to run. I'd rather drink with cowboys, who have endured animal perversity and bad weather, who see the basic link between grass and flesh, between livelihood and the land. Even in our disagreement, there's a common knowledge. My notions might lean toward a different future than theirs, but we share a reference in the land. In our arguments, the land, and not desire, is the axiom.

I have a friend, Shelley, who fiddles in a swing band. She also waits tables. We met in Utah, two musicians in a Mormon town. She was a violinist, city-bred, gently-trained, but she learned to fiddle while she got a forestry degree. She wanted to live in Wyoming and work in the woods. So she became a forester, laying out timber sales in the north end of the Gros Ventre Range.

In the late seventies, we met sometimes on the Union Pass Road when I hauled water from a spring. She wasn't happy. She would shake her head and sigh. "It isn't like I hoped," she'd say. We're cutting too much, too fast. It's pretty sad."

I was a range foreman, camped out on Pinion Ridge with a Shoshoni crew, spiking log fence to keep the Fish Creek cows from dropping south into the Upper Green with the first snows. I lived there for three summers in a tent, building buck-and-pole fence, and watched clearcuts march over ridgetops and along the little creeks, notching the horizon. We learned to pull off the narrow roads, shut down the pickup and listen for logging trucks. You could hear the drivers, miles away, gunning around the long curves. Loaded, going off the hill, they were careful. Coming back empty, they were dangerous.

The next year, I didn't find Shelley in the mountains anymore. She quit her timber job and joined a band. The guitar player, now her husband, was an ex-wildlife biologist. It can be hard, to reconcile your need to be in the woods with what you'll do to stay there. Jackson Hole absorbs a lot of refugees from those quiet wars.

I recall, from a college anthropology text, that it's hard to analyze personality apart from culture. Culture, all those shared assumptions about *what is,* provides a structure to which our identities can cling. We learn, early, to fit our perceptions into this deeper sense of order.

It's strange, looking back, how I lived out the whole frontier dance, step by step, as if there was a pattern etched in my bones. How I learned to stalk deer and swing a double-bit. How I rode horseback, leading the wagons. How I built log fences and herded stock. How I was drawn to cabins at the road's far end. How I tried to know my place, my heritage, my forebears, by doing precisely what had been done, by stumbling in the ruts. How clearcuts were a part of what I was, as much as the horses, or the wagons, or the songs.

You go so far and then the way is lost. The sun, that beacon in the west, goes down and the clouds open on expressionless dark. And the stars, that night, don't seem to be scattered diamonds, or distant campfires, or witnessing eyes. You see the dark for what it is, and look straight through your dreams. And the stars blur and prism through tears. And you turn to where the sun might rise again, and in the cold, you wait.

Things don't make more sense now, but my feelings do. I work in the mountains still, collecting rain and snow, monitoring long-range air pollution in a wilderness. But I spend more time at home. In our garden, the peas grow dreaming in their pods, rounding in the late June rain, and I know them, long before I taste and see. In August, the smell of sage accompanies thunder, and the eastern clouds toss rainbows down the lanes of mountain afternoon. The garden fills out and our baskets fill up. I like to turn the egg-sized red potatoes up with just my hands, and feel the moist cling of the earth around their skins.

At first, the trees were like ore, a wealth simply to be taken. You couldn't put fly ash back into the earth and grow more coal. So we cut the trees, sowing fire and flood. Out of that disillusionment came the National Parks and Forest Reserves.

Then, wearing science like an ammunition belt, we decided we could grow pines as straightforwardly as peas, or red potatoes. That we could go into the mountains of the west and blade roads, hack out the harvest, skid it down, haul it to the mill, dozer-pile the slash, torch it off, and *zang*: new trees for old. If trees grew here before, they damn well would again, and again, and again.

And then we had to start seedling farms for conifers, and try to replant on the cuts that didn't come back green. And then we replanted the bad plantations, once, twice, and fenced out the cows, and sent minimum-wage crews in to poison the ground squirrels in their holes, so they wouldn't gnaw the planted seedlings.

And then we found out how much sheer, cellular effort was tied up in those trees, and about nutrient losses, surface temperatures, and soil compaction. We found out that burning slashpiles didn't work like natural groundfire. Phrases like "cumulative effects," and words like "biodiversity" began to show up. And those baldspots on the aerial photos began to look more and more like a fatal disease.

I can grasp the thrill of a brand-new, yellow, articulated highwheel loader that can juggle four-foot-thick logs; the thrill of a metallic-blue Peterbilt with chrome stacks as big around as your head, and of hearing the diesel rap back from the ranks of pine; the gleam of new, oiled sawchain spinning around a 48-inch bar, the spew of fragrant chips, and the condensed whump of a big fir hitting the dirt; the rush of banking big checks that seem to come straight from Almighty God.

And you can see the results, as I've seen them in the Gros Ventres, the Absarokas, the Salt Rivers, the Wyoming Range, the Hoback, the Snake River Range, the Bighorns, the Bear Rivers, the Uintas, the Wasatch, the Sawtooth, and the Medicine Bow. You can see the scraped ground, the tangled slash, the rusty chokers, the slumping banks, the gashed streams, the silted gravel, the rutted roads, and feel the sadness that hovers over every ill-used place.

In our minds, we still hold that forested archetype, cherishing the grand scale of this

# C. L. Rawlins: *On Spread Creek*

continent. *It will come back,* we say, closing our eyes both to the stumps and to the asphalt battlegrounds. *It will come back.* And there is, too, a corresponding kind of squint-eyed, tight-fisted, broad-shouldered insistence in the American mind, an anger that strains against the massive guilt we have incurred.

*Why do all the meadows have stumps in them?* It's strange, how that question repeats itself. How, after twenty years, it acts like a lens to focus so much in so few words. Yet I can't picture the woman's face. I see her white straw hat, and the way its arc of shadow hid her eyes, and her hair, a gentle silver in the sun. And the way she held her shoulders back, waiting to hear what I'd say.

I thought I was a guide. How many questions was I asked that year? *Where does this road go? Is the trail good? What's over that ridge? What's that in the willows? What did the Indians call this place?* How many questions was I asked and how many did I think I'd answered? Yet hers is the one that still holds a voice, even if the face and name are gone.

## JAMIE HARRISON
### LIVINGSTON, MONTANA

*Jamie Harrison worked as a caterer, a script reader, and at several magazines before becoming the editor of the now-defunct Clark City Press. She is the author of four mysteries, including* The Edge of the Crazies, Going Local, An Unfortunate Prairie Occurrence, *and* Blue Deer Thaw.

# from *Going Local*

Some people looked right at you, turned on the charm; others looked all around without meeting your eyes, like dogs scared of giving offense or issuing a challenge; the third group stared resolutely at the steering wheel or the dashboard. Only a squirrelly minority bothered to argue, against all wisdom.

The mayor surprised Jules Clement by being in the second group, but Jules surprised himself by letting the fat man off the hook, bowing to good nature and small-town politics without a threat or a bribe being uttered. Eighty-five miles an hour on the interstate was kid stuff, after all, a five-dollar fine, and it was a relief to pull over a local for a change. The mayor was flushed, beaded with sweat, playing hooky in his wife's car rather than toiling over the problems of Blue Deer, Montana, and once he'd stopped dribbling excuses and relaxed, Jules had been amused to hear just a touch of wonder in his voice. "Glad to see you on the job, Jules. Hope you're healed up fine."

Nothing specific, nothing impolite, just another reminder of how most people lacked imagination. A little gunfire and they assumed he'd grown up. It was June 21, the solstice, Jules's first day back at work in almost a month. The day had a double meaning, the glass half full or half empty, the first day of summer or the longest day of the year. The weather was golden and lovely; on the other hand, he was stuck in a patrol car. Summer meant people wouldn't—theoretically—skid off icy roads, or freeze to death, or shoot each other in hunting accidents, but it also meant that the loonies would be out and about, no longer confined by bad hitchhiking weather or school, no longer lured away by steaming tropical beaches or sterile cities.

Just a week earlier, Jules, seeking a last-minute escape, had flipped to the travel section of the Sunday *New York Times* to see a color photo of the Absaroka Mountalns and a head-

# Jamie Harrison: *Going Local*

line that read MONTANA: GO BEFORE IT'S GONE. A chunk of Absaroka County was identified as "Hollywood on the Yellowstone," and Jules, heart sinking, realized that his jig might be up. The vacationing nation as a whole already seemed to have descended, or ascended, to southwestern Montana in a kind of berserk westward ho, and Blue Deer, which usually had a population of about four thousand, could now count another thousand hotel guests on a slow day. Maybe more; Jules never paid attention during Chamber of Commerce meetings.

He watched the mayor scoot east toward Blue Deer and made a U-turn away from town on the high interstate, a black backbone against green foothills. He didn't like to bother with tickets, but he loved to drive, and always turned the police radio to its lowest murmur so that it became a white noise of harmless numbers, instead of the whine of potential emergencies. He passed a town namesake, a literal blue deer swelling by the side of the road, shimmering in the heat from the pavement. Jules should have moved it out of sight, but with his luck it would have blown when he touched it, and the whole point in his first day back was to try to enjoy the job again.

He shoved the seat back and stretched his legs and worked on thinking about nothing. He drove until he hit the Bozeman Pass and the western boundary of the county, then headed east again toward the Crazy Mountains and the opposite border forty miles away. This was really the county's only paved east-west road; in the ninety miles from north to south there were actually two, but this was due to the Yellowstone River, which poured out of the northern border of the park and split the lower county in half.

By lunchtime, despite an attempt to keep life pleasant by stopping as few people as possible, his equanimity was gone. After three more speeders, a 1965 school bus filled with Deadheads felled by a broken axle, and a dozen loose sheep, the damage award had been won by some ditch-diving Poughkeepsians so riveted by a common antelope that they'd headed straight for it overland. Jules was glad that the antelope had survived the experience and chalked up another defunct miinivan to the insurance companies. The people from Poughkeepsie, dappled with Band-Aids, blamed Absaroka County's pretty views and wanted a free hotel room. Jules told them every hotel room in town was booked, but cots were kept in the basement of the Lutheran church for such emergencies. Maybe they'd opt to rent a car and head for Butte, a town that hadn't been crowded since 1920, with the exception of the annual St. Patrick's Day drunk. Jules liked Butte, but then he knew what to look for. The Poughkeepsians scowled and headed east, toward Billings.

At two in the afternoon Jules marched down the bland, modern courthouse hall, slammed through the Sheriff's Department door, tossed his hat and sunglasses on his mounded desk, and slumped against the dispatcher's counter, waiting for Grace Marble to stop typing and look at him. She took a phone call without glancing up, letting Jules stare down into her curly gray hair and cool his heels in heavyweight, uncomfortable leather shoes. After high-tops and T-shirts and worn jeans, his brown uniform felt as uncomfortable as a child's church suit, hot and stiff; his shirt was looser than it had been, but the tie still constricted him and the belt of deadly gadgets jingled and weighed him down.

Grace punched hold. "Someone wants to talk to the sheriff."

Jules gave her a stony look.

"Sweeten up," said Grace. "It isn't a tourist. It's Clarence Bost, up in Martinsdale. He says there's a tent floating in the reservoir."

"It probably blew in. The wind was blowing seventy miles an hour last week. Tell him if he pulls it out he can keep it."

Grace was sixty or so but her eyes were young, still an unfaded blue and not necessarily kindly, now oozing with reproach. "Some fishermen found it, and say it's heavy."

"No," said Jules. "I'm a month behind. Maybe two."

"You won't catch up before September anyway," said Ed Winton, who'd come up behind them. He opened his paw and a half-dozen speeding receipts floated lazily down onto Grace's keyboard. She drummed her fingers on the handset and Ed smiled. "Nice day for a drive. We want him happy, right, Gracie?"

Grace punched the hold button and used her sweet voice. "One more second, Clarence. We're seeing who's available." She listened for a minute and said, "Of course." Down went the button. "He says it's our responsibility. The reservoir's in Absaroka. And if you stick around you'll have to talk to Scotti about catching up with the court schedule. I told him you'd be back by two."

"I know where the goddamn reservoir is, Grace." Jules retrieved Ed's tickets and shuffled through, signing "Sheriff Clement," over and over, on and on. Five hours back and he was already sick of it. A meeting with the county attorney might push him over the edge.

"The Meagher County guys already told him they wouldn't handle it."

Of course the deputies from Meagher County (pronounced *mar* by local nonbicoastals) would tell Clarence to buzz off; the town of Martinsdale, a mile from the reservoir, might be in their county, thirty miles from the seat in White Sulphur Springs, but the reservoir marked the northern border of Absaroka County, forty miles away from Blue Deer but definitely Jules's headache. Jules could almost hear them cackling in White Sulphur Springs, where they needed speed traps to generate excitement.

"Harvey's on in an hour," said Ed. "Let's go."

Grace was watching Jules, prepared to make Clarence Bost a satisfied man, and Jules nodded. One very small deputy, Harvey Meyers, left to deal with the rest of a five-thousand-square-mile county, if you didn't consider the Gardiner town cop near the entrance of Yellowstone Park, fifty miles south of town. As Jules followed Ed to the parking lot he tried to imagine two Harveys for all of Maryland, a quarter of a Harvey for Rhode Island, eight for Virginia. It probably worked out to something like a gram of Harvey per acre; ten thousand New York citizens an ounce. He searched for his conscience and simply felt giddy at the idea of escape.

They drove north for mile after mile, up the western front of the Crazy Mountains, which came by their name because they sprouted illogically from barren plains like a 100,000-acre stone and evergreen Mad King Ludwig palace. On the way up the mountains looked close, clean and green and white in the sun after night rains, but you'd drive due east on a dirt road for more than half an hour before you felt you'd really reached the foothills. That was the thing about mountains—you only recognized them from a distance, or from an edge or an incline. If you were actually on them, especially in a vehicle, they tended to took like hills, even if you were used to very large hills.

Ed's musical imagination had frozen in 1975 when he reached two hundred pounds and the age of thirty. Jules asked him to pick a cassette anyway, and smiled while Ed searched through the box of cassettes, rightfully leery of what he might find. Ed said he wanted to go fast and plugged in *Sticky Fingers*, then hummed along, bobbing his graying flat-topped head, the beefy old-athlete folds of his neck rolling in time to the music. Jules giggled when "Sister Morphine" came on—after his recent stint in the hospital, the song had a new ring. But he didn't bother speeding. There were too many deer in the area, and how could anyone hurry to pull a tent out of the water on a fine summer day even after the decision had been made to enjoy the freedom of the chore? Someone had mown alfalfa, sending a sweet, lush smell for miles, and they drove with their windows down.

The upper third of the county, with only a couple thousand people and two small towns, was Ed's beat, and he brought Jules up to date on the new owners of the Clyde City Tavern, on whether the Wilsall Rodeo would be the usual whacked-out mess, and on how bad the dissension had been at a recent zoning hearing. Jules asked Ed if he'd had a good Father's Day—Ed had four children, dotted around the country. Ed said no, but didn't return the question, and looked uncomfortable. Ansel Clement had been the sheriff who hired Ed, and the real reason Jules wasn't fond of citing speeders wasn't as much a reluctance to ruin their day as the echo of his father's unseen last moments with a trucker on black beauties, a man who hadn't liked the idea of being ticketed. Jules had seen the hole in his father's chest at twelve, and had recently spent quite a bit of down time thinking about it.

Ed rolled his window all the way down and lit a cigarette. "You gotta promise me we'll stop for some food."

"No problem," said Jules. "I'm living for it."

"Get the chicken-fried steak. Or the hot beef sandwich."

They passed a rendering plant and an old Swedish church and Jules made a right onto patchy blacktop. "I'll have the fried fried," said Jules. You stick to the patty melt."

Ed laughed. He had the kind of big belly that looked healthy, and he was proud of it, regarded it as a sign of a wealthy soul á la Santa Claus. Ed condescended to keep himself under the weight limit for his job.

"Has Bost gotten any easier to take?" asked Jules.

"Nope."

Jules slowed for a pothole and a battered, shotgunned cattle crossing sign, then turned down Martinsdale's main drag. Martinsdale had one grocery, where vegetables were limited to frozen peas and iceberg lettuce, and two bars, one in the Crazy Mountain Inn and one attached to Clarence Bost's hardware store. Recent touches, like the gas pump in front of the post office-liquor store-garage, predated the Korean War. The few hardy tourists who made it this far tended to think the town had been left over from a Peckinpah or Sergio Leone movie, though even the most media-minded couldn't remember something so memorable as the jail. It sat on a slight rise near a boarded-up dimestore, a six-by-six cage with two metal screens for benches and red-painted bars on the door, open to the sky on five planes and to the grass and ants below. The cell was the real thing, still in use when the occasion demanded, on average about a half-dozen times a year.

Jules pulled up in front of the tidy boardwalk on Bost's side of the street; local merchants, faced with crumbled streets and no money, had taken the mud season into their own hands and built up. "Clarence Bost, Proprietor" was stenciled politely on the bright yellow screen door of the Mint Bar. This was Clarence's way of announcing a readiness to argue before his customers even ordered a drink. Ed and Jules walked another four feet and entered Martinsdate Hardware, marked by a blaze orange door that exactly matched most of the hammer and ax handles inside. Clarence, using up old paint, had read *Reader's Digest* on the psychological implications of colors.

The owner wasn't in sight, and Jules, fascinated, peered through the door that joined the hardware and the apricot-colored bar. Clarence wasn't there either. They found him toward the back of his hardware store, behind some dusty toy tractors and warped baseball bats. He didn't acknowledge their presence.

"What's up, Clarence?" Jules followed the owner's gaze into the shelves, wondering if he'd spied a dead mouse.

Clarence Bost still didn't look in their direction. "Problem at the reservoir. Something blue in the water."

It was possible that Clarence, who was at least eighty but used a full bottle of Grecian Formula once a week, might have entered a decline. "Blue?"

"Tent, probably."

"That's what we heard."

Jules and Ed waited. Clarence finally straightened, or attempted to—his back had grown scoliotic with age—and gave them a bleak look. "Little jackoffs from Great Falls rented one of my boats. They ran over this thing and then they tried to pull it out and tipped and I had to pull the first boat out with another one."

"Are they still out there?" Jules didn't care so much about talking to the "little jackoffs," but they might need protection from Clarence.

"They went to the bar." Clarence sighed when Jules and Ed eyed the open doorway to the dark Mint. "The *other* bar. Not mine. They said the smell drove them to drink. They were on something."

Jules thought over the hint of drugs and the word "smell" and decided not to be led off on tangents. "You think they're up to helping us get the tent out of the water?"

"Drove off in the direction of Two Dot. Didn't pay for the motor, but I have their deposit."

Clarence stuck most of his finger into his ear.

Ed sighed. "Can we borrow some rope?"

"Borrow?" said Clarence, curling a thin lip. "What good would rope be to me after you cut a length?"

Ed and Jules stared at him.

"I have to mind my property," said Clarence, picking up a can of paint. "I have to work for a living. The tent's by the dam, and you can borrow my rowboat. Now, do you want some goddamn rope or not?"

The Martinsdale reservoir floated on the high, rolling prairie like a gray-blue hallucination. The Crazies, edged by badlands buttes, domed up to the south, and when clouds swept north with the prevailing wind the sky looked like speeded-up movie footage. Trees were rare on the plains east of the Continental Divide in Montana, and only one stand of battered bonsai cottonwood had survived at the water's edge to illustrate the strength of the winds.

After a flooding May, the reservoir, often reduced to a hundred-acre mud pie by July, was still almost full. Jules counted fourteen campers and tents on the way to the dam, most of them from Billings—Montana's biggest (pop. 80,000) and possibly ugliest city, which was saying a lot, given the competition. Bost had left a rowboat drying on the bank fifty yards past the last trailer, near the dam, and Jules insisted on taking the oars. He regretted this bravado immediately, but Ed, virtually crippled by a hard life and a fair amount of bad behavior, had ruined knees and a horrible back. Jules was the boss, young and theoretically strong but for an almost healed bullet hole in his shoulder. In hindsight, neither of them had been a good candidate to pull a heavy tent from the middle of a deep lake, but they'd been too busy running away from Grace to think anything through.

The promise of the afternoon had faded somewhat in the wash of Clarence Bost's bad breath. The sapphire and fuschia tent bloomed and furled just below the surface, bumping gently against the steep dam embankment. The boys who'd run it over and jarmmed the outboard motor must have been seeing how close they could come without crashing. Jules gritted his teeth, rowed, and comforted himself with the thought that there wouldn't be much gear inside if it floated so near the surface, and if it had been light enough to blow in to begin with. The tent looked like a huge, lapis-colored sea anemone or urchin, though that stretch of imagination relied on one knowing what an anemone or urchin looked like, and the ocean was a long way away. Jules lowered his arm into the water for a tentative tug, took stock, and looked at Ed.

"It's heavy. This was supposed to be fun," said Jules.

Ed looked apologetic. "It still beats ticketing. Think of dinner."

"We won't want to if this really stinks."

"Bad hamburger won't make me forget dinner."

"Remember when we flipped that rowboat, the one that was burping methane, and found all the fried chicken strapped under the seat?"

"That won't make me forget dinner either."

Jules rolled up his sleeve again and leaned over the edge of the rowboat, but the tent was a foot below the surface and he got wet anyway. He ran his fingertips and his palm along the highest point—a mounded, buoyant object—intent on finding a seam and spare fabric or the tear the motor must have caused so that he could tie on the rope. He paused and ran his fingers back over the shape again, doubting that what he felt could be so horribly familiar.

Jules sat up so abruptly that the boat rocked. He let his wet arm fall limp onto his leg and tried not to black out. His ears rang and the cold started in his neck and ran up to his hairline, and down his torso.

"What the hell," said Ed. "Did your shoulder just kick in?"

Oh God, thought Jules. He couldn't speak, and tried to shake his head while his mind reeled with the statistical implausibility of it all. A happy camper had started a jet ski at the other end of the lake, and it added to the pounding feeling in his skull.

Ed tried humor. "Acid flashback? Piranhas?"

"There's someone in there."

Ed squinted at Jules. "What?"

"There's a body in there. I felt her."

Ed blanched. "Her?"

Jules cleared his throat and wiped his arm dry on his pant leg. He tried a crooked smile. This wasn't surprising, as his face was crooked, but it wasn't usually green He didn't want to explain that he'd recognized the unmistakable contours of a female posterior, but that the texture had been all wrong.

"Her."

## GWEN PETERSEN
### BIG TIMBER, MONTANA

*Cowboy poets and their fans know Gwen Petersen's verse grows out of her intimate knowledge of her subject, ranch life—but where she gets her sense of humor is anyone's guess. Gwen is a central figure in the annual Montana Poets' Gatherings where she always puts her audience into stitches. Her books include* The Bachelor from Hell, Scratch Where It Itches..., In the Sidesaddle, Sidekick Savvy, *and* A Tall Bush.

# Going to Town for Parts

Whenever the tractor quits or balks
Or the mower refuses to start,
I'm the one my husband talks
Into going to town for parts.

No matter I'm buried clear up to my eyes
In bread dough and Pillsbury flour,
I dust off my hands, out the door I fly,
Vowing return in an hour.

While my knight of the tractor comforts his steed
In the pickup I roar into town,
A Good Woman off on an errand of need
To the store where parts can be found.

A part man's a smart man who knows all factors
Of flange and bolt and U-Joint,
For healing the wounds of old broken tractors;
He patiently waits as I point.

"That left-handed flange with a gasket and hose,"
I say with confident air;
With a withering glance down his Cyrano nose
He asks—"just one or a pair?"

Confusion wells up and I know I'm pathetic.
"Oh, both," nonchalantly I say;
Twenty miles to drive home; my life is hectic.
I've lost the best of the day.

Back at the ranch, I seek out my husband;
"Look, one of each," I declaim.
He takes the flange with an eager hand
Then utters a tasteless name.

"A flange is no good without some bolts,"
He growls with amazed disdain,
"Anyone could see, even fools and dolts!"
My ego begins to wane.

Three trips to town and one flat tire,
And what do I find in the end?
The tractor gets fixed with pliers and wire—
No wonder I'm round the bend!

# Geezers & Crones

Two old cowpokes, Jake and Jerome,
Hung up their saddles and went to the Home,
For Old Man Time had burned in his brand
On these elderly cowboys once so grand.

Now they sit in hallways leanin' on canes,
Talkin' 'bout history and old campaigns,
Talkin' 'bout horses they've rode on the range,
Talkin' 'bout old days and the way things change.

And sittin' across from the ancient old men
Are two old cowgirls a-wonderin' just when
Them decrepit old coots will quit reminiscing,
And start talkin' 'bout some old-fashioned kissing.

Now Agnes and Alice, once pretty cheeky,
Worry most now 'bout bladders bein' leaky.
"Ya know," said Agnes, "it's purty durn borin'
Just watchin' them geezers 'n hearin' em snorin'.

"What do ya say we liven things up,
Get undressed and strut our stuff."
"Good idea," Alice replied,
"Betcha them boys'll go plumb wild-eyed."

Well, the gals got nekkid, and pushin' their walkers,
Went truckin' down the hall like old crone stalkers.
It took 'em a while and quite a few pains
To pass them geezers, leanin' on their canes.

**Gwen Petersen:** *Poems*

The old girls jiggled like Goodyear rubber.
Parts of 'em wiggled like tapioca blubber.
They promenaded on with a git-a-long hitch,
Tryin' not to scratch where anything itched.

Upon this sight, the old fellers gazed,
Then looked at each other, plumb amazed.
"What the Hell's that?!" Jake asked, frowning.
Said Jerome, "I dunno, but it sure needs ironing!"

# Cowboy Class

The courtin' cowboy took his girl
To a restaurant deluxe,
Where light was dim and candles glowed,
And meals cost lots of bucks.

With polish on his Sunday boots,
And brand new Stetson hat,
Brush-poppin' shirt tucked in his jeans,
And stomach pulled in flat,

He walked with pride until he faced
The snooty maitre-de.
"You can't come in without a tie,
Which you're without, I see.

"We take no uncouth cowboy types
In denim dungarees;
They rarely know which fork to use
Or how to eat their peas."

The cowboy nearly burst a vessel;
The insult hurt his pride.
He wished he had his lasso,
He'd have the dude hog-tied.

But holding in his mad, he searched
Throughout his pickup truck
For something he could substitute—
Alas, he had no luck.

But then behind the seat he found
A brand new jumper cable;
He tied a bow, its metal tips
A-dangling to his navel.

He showed the snooty maitre-de
His elegant new tie.
"This here's the best that I can do.
I hope you're satisfied."

The waiter sniffed, his eyeballs rolled,
His face began to twitch;
This cowboy had him buffaloed
With his offbeat necktie hitch.

Reluctantly, the maitre-de
Opened up the gate.
"You may come in, but cowboy tricks
I will not tolerate."

The cowboy grinned and said, "I promise
You have no need to fear.
Unless they're dead, I won't jumpstart
Any Body here."

# TED KERASOTE
## KELLY, WYOMING

*Ted Kerasote's writing has concentrated on the evolving relationship between people and wildlife and how an increasingly urban society can maintain its participatory ties with the cycles of nature. In addition to contributing essays and articles to magazines such as* Audubon, Outside, Orion, *and* Sports Afield, *he is the author of three books,* Navigations, Bloodties, *and* Heart of Home.

# The Lewis in the Fall

In the Rockies, in the fall, at least for a short time, it's possible to suspend your disbelief. The fine mild weather, the golden mountainsides, the sense that you are young in a youthful and precious moment, let you ignore the knowledge that snow is a few weeks—or just a night—away. The still-unsullied beauty of most of the countryside lets you think that most people will feel as you do about it and leave it alone. Driving home from my tour of the proposed New World Mine, on the border of Yellowstone National Park, it remained hard for me to believe that half a billion dollars of gold and silver could really convince people to risk a deluge of toxic tailings down one of the most stunning canyons of the planet—the Clark Fork of the Yellowstone—and endless ore trucks and power lines through grizzly country.

I had put a rod and waders in the car along with my camping gear, somehow knowing that when the tour of the mine was done, I'd be unhappy and would want to stop and fish on my way home across Yellowstone. Casting in moving water, whether surf or river, has always been meditation for me—a going down to find peace and to let go.

Passing all of my old favorite places on the Yellowstone and Firehole rivers, which now had many cars at their trailheads, I drove along the Lewis River in the southern part of Yellowstone Park, not stopping at the famous meadow where everyone has to fish because it looks like a postcard of how trout fishing in the Rockies is supposed to look: golden grass, the hills in the middle distance covered with pines, the far mountains covered with snow. Instead, I parked at the rim of the canyon slightly farther on, where no one fishes because you just about have to rock-climb down to the water.

Such strategies—searching out gnarly access routes and setting off during storms—ensure privacy in country that only twenty years ago was a great cache of private and solitary mountains. In fact, as recently as the late 1970s I walked through valleys that had waist-high flow-

# Ted Kerasote: *The Lewis in the Fall*

ers and no evidence of other humans having been there within a hundred years, not even a trail. Then came environmental awareness followed by environmental appetite. The cost of having extolled the enjoyment of wild places has been that the mountains are now full of hikers, boaters, climbers, mountain bikers, skiers, paragliders, wildlife photographers, anglers, and hunters. We now have a constituency to protect wild places, but each of us has to become more enterprising to find a smidgen of quiet and meditative space.

Which is why Merle, my golden Lab, and I were creeping down the crumbling sandstone, using the lodgepole pines as belay stations and the downsloping, rotten ledges as connective avenues between barely negotiable drops. As we slid over the last cliff and to the river's side, our removal from the upper world was complete. The road could not be seen, the sound of moving water filled the air. It was mid-afternoon and the sunlight slanted into the canyon. A breeze blew downstream, the golden halos of aspen trembling. The willows, green and burgundy tinged, hemmed the turquoise water, which sprayed haze against the black rock.

I rigged the rod; Merle had a drink; we walked upstream.

It had been a year of drought, following many years of drought, and in places the river flowed as no more than a narrow, luminescent channel between the tabular rocks of the riverbed. The hydrological conditions—almost no river—made finding the fish easy.

Stripping line from the reel, I sent a cast upstream, but the line slid back down the guides and collapsed at my feet. I hadn't stripped enough of it through the guides and had been trying to cast the weightless leader—a mistake an absolute novice would make.

I stopped a moment, thinking of how long it had been since I really fished, with all my concentration, with all my soul, with the rod and line as the divining stick of my passion about rivers and trout.

Years.

So many other passions had intruded and taken over: climbing, photography, hunting, horses. And then there was the business of the fish themselves. It is hard not to notice, at some point, that fish don't like being taken out of the water, that they do their best not to be winched toward land, which indeed is why we like to catch them. They fight.

Some of us notice this with the first few fish that we catch and give up fishing entirely. Others of us, who are so enthralled by fish as the symbols of the natural world from which we have parted, symbols that we can touch and let go and touch again, never realize or manage to forget that fish have no similar feelings. I had been in this latter group of anglers for a long time—since I was a boy. But the more fish I caught and let go (and we're talking thousands of fish, all over the world, and over decades of my life), the less satisfying the activity became. Not that I had ever addressed the question of why fishing had become less satisfying. It just had become less compelling, and I left it at that. Other activities replaced angling in importance, it's true, but the real reason was that I became increasingly uncomfortable with the knowledge that addressing the question of whether fish feel pain, addressing it in a rigorous way, would lead me into country that I didn't want to know.

During the last few years, when I did occasionally still fish and actually caught something, I bopped the trout over the head and had a meal, which continued to seem forthright and somehow equal: You, trout, eat bugs and worms and other trout, and I, human, eat you. Since the trout did not rise to its prey and spit it out and catch it again and again, which is what catch-and-release sportfishing is all about, I reasoned that neither should I. At the heart of the matter this was why, in the last decade, I had fished less and hunted more. The hunting, which had to do with food gathering and not sport, sat easier in my soul.

Getting the line stripped through the guides, I tried another cast, the rod moving through the air, the line loading and unloading it, and hissing neatly. Like riding a bike, the motion came back quickly. I tapped the rod above the spot that I wanted the fly to hit, a green delta of water below a small cascade of foam, and it landed almost there. In small bites, I stripped in line and cast again.

The line landed, floated, and darted. Before I could respond to the strike, the trout flashed through the pool, bowing the rod. Bringing the small fish in easily, I slipped my hand under it. It jumped and the barbless hook flew into the air.

Perfect, I thought, looking into the pool where the brown trout had disappeared, and then at the tiny nymph hanging on the end of my leader, amazed that it had all happened again: my knowing that the fish was just behind the spume-charged water, then dropping this little bit of hair above the spot, and predicting, almost to the millisecond, when the hit would come.

I felt a calmness settle through me, which is not only the calmness of a job well done but also the calmness that comes from being able to predict and control events. I walked upriver, taking a fish from every flume and also casting to the wide and shallow places, even though I knew that there were no fish there. It was just so lovely to watch the line unwind and alight and float upon the placid water, as if the line were the graph of my soul, gone even and smooth after the disconcerting tour of the mine site.

And I began to remember the sounds as well as the biomechanical pleasures of fly-fishing: the crisp snap of line against the spool when I had stripped just enough coils for the cast; how by throwing a rollcast upstream I could unhook the nymph snagged on rocks; how, sidearm, I could throw a cast beneath a downstream gust of wind; or how, by moving the rod over my head, I could change directions in mid-cast. And nothing went awry because I kept the line short, doing just what I could handle and walking up to the pools instead of throwing at them from afar. It was all so lovely, there in the light of September, the aspens blowing and whispering, the water tugging at my legs and spraying my arms, that I felt my chest swell and break apart, like clouds before the sun.

An ouzel jumped from boulder to boulder; a kingfisher swept across the river; far upstream, a cow elk came down to the water's edge and drank. Merle, who had been standing patiently in the water, and who likes to hunt more than fish, looked at her and looked at me and seemed to say, "Why are you wasting your time standing in this river?"

Climbing up the small, ankle-deep falls, wading slowly across the shallow pools, and casting to the narrow channels, I caught a dozen fish, some of them LDRs—long-distance releases, a phenomenon in which the fish, leaping at the end of thirty feet of line, throws the nymph back at the angler, bypassing the task of actual releasing. Other trout I brought to hand, held a moment, and slipped back into the current.

There was one more pool, then the river flattened into the upper meadows. I cast several times into the pool, which lay half in shadow, half in fractured, glittering light, letting the nymph circulate into all the deep crannies. The line dove. When I raised the rod, the fish was solid, as if I had hooked a rock. Then it flashed out of the pool and I followed it downstream, guiding it through a narrow channel before bringing it in. It made two more runs before I could grab it.

It was one of those perfectly symmetrical trout: husky, full of strength and color, and long

# Ted Kerasote: *The Lewis in the Fall*

as my forearm. And I could have killed it, because in this stretch of the Lewis you can kill fish. And I thought about it, thought about declaring that I had really been hunting for a meal today and that this trout would be a fine meal. But I hadn't been hunting at all and hadn't really fished that way for years, if I had ever done so at all. I had fished as recreation, as competition with my cousin, and as an excuse to visit wild places because I didn't know that I could go someplace and just look at wildlife or climb over mountains and still come home happy without having to reach a high lake containing fish. When I did realize that I didn't have to fish to enjoy a place, I still continued to do it out of inertia and because people were willing to pay me to fish, to write about it, and to photograph it. It is difficult, until you harden your principles, to turn down trips to remote and singularly beautiful places that you'll never get to any other way.

I had also used fishing as the social oil between friends and, throughout the years, as a way to stroke my ego, looking for, finding, and landing ever bigger fish on ever lighter tackle. Today, I had used fishing as a way to mollify my depression concerning the mine—to find some peace in a beautiful place by skillfully casting line and seeing lovely fish come up through the lens of the river and into my sun-dappled world. Which, OK, is better than taking Prozac for getting over the blues but shouldn't be confused with what a trout does when it rises to a mayfly.

That moment of predation—kill to eat to be alive (not psychically or spiritually alive, but biologically alive, the kind of alive that calories sustain)—is how I liked to think that I hunted when I hunted for elk or grouse. I enjoyed the pursuit, the physical demands, and the mental discipline, solving problems of time and distance and cutoff angles, of being silent for hours the way I have seen wolves enjoy stalking and chasing elk or caribou—but I don't believe that I've used a grouse's pain or an elk's pain to fill something else beside my stomach and my sense of doing a hard job well. In my life hunting, I hadn't tried to kill animals with larger and larger antlers as, in my life fishing, I had tried to land ever larger fish; nor had I adopted the challenges of handicapping equipment—using, say, muzzleloaders or archery to introduce a new frisson into what had become a well-worn activity—in the way I had been willing to constantly recalibrate the thrills of angling by using ever-lighter tackle, so that a two-pound trout on a one-weight rod became the sensory equivalent of a six-pound trout on a five-weight rod. In the process of becoming more technically proficient in angling, I had permitted myself to forget that on the end of my line was a creature who was fighting for its life. Never had I forgotten that about birds and mammals—one doesn't "play" them as one does fish, and their pain is too apparent to discount. Certainly, I had never tried shooting them as an analgesic for the environmental equivalent of a bad-hair day.

There has always come a moment when, hiding, I can no longer hide, when my throat and chest constrict with the knowledge that I've been avoiding a hard-to-face truth. It has been this way since I was a boy.

I let the trout go, let this lovely Lewis River trout go with a sense of letting go a life—mine as well as his. I walked up the bank and sat in the grass. Looking down the river, I wished that I was still a boy, that I could still happily catch and release fish and that it would always be the beginning of September, with the mountains, my once-private mountains, still quiet and empty.

## TIM CAHILL
### LIVINGSTON, MONTANA

*Tim Cahill is the author of six books, including* Jaguars Ripped My Flesh, *and* Pass the Butterworms. *He is Editor-at-Large for* Outside Magazine *and has worked for the* New York Times Book Review, *the* Washington Post, *the* Los Angeles Times, *and* National Geographic. *He has also written screenplays, including the Academy Award nominated documentary, "The Living Sea," and the IMAX film, "Everest."*

# Trusty and Grace

Grace attends me on my jaunts into the steep mountainside wilderness above my cabin. Sometimes I believe I can actually see flashes of Grace in the slanting light that falls through the tall pines in this cathedral of forest. I am led, by Grace, up the steep hillsides, through areas of deadfall and over mossy logs that cross the constant roaring whitewater of Falls Creek. Grace leads me through the bear and moose scat, over the forest floor, through accumulations of alpine wildflower—mountain bluebells and clematis and pink twinflower—and in the evening, Grace accompanies me to bed, where she tends to fart a lot.

Everyone should have a little Grace in his or her life, and my Grace is a 4-year-old 40 pound Brittany Spaniel whose august and noble soul is made apparent in a metabolism that operates on two speeds: hysterical and off. A faultless athlete, entirely innocent of tranquility, Grace runs at speeds in excess of 25 miles an hour. The phrase "leaps and bounds" was coined to describe the breakneck rhythm of her passage through the forest. She sails over deadfall in ten foot long broad jumps, has no trouble swimming the creek that is too high and too treacherous for humans to cross, and streaks, at top speed, down a certain rocky hillside that most folks would describe as a cliff face.

Sometimes, when Grace leads me through the forest, she maketh me to fall down beside running water, if not into the running water itself. Better to find my own way through the wilderness—it is the Absaroka-Beartooth Wilderness that rises behind my cabin in Montana—and I know that Grace will follow, appearing now and again in a jingle of dog tags, or seen as a brown and white blur racing over the mossy forest floor, or chasing one of the black bears that periodically lumber past my cabin in search of the garbage I never put out. This little drama is played out in snatches of color barely perceived through the trees: a lardy cinnamon-colored butt waddling up the hill, some young garbage-obsessed

# Tim Cahill: *Trusty and Grace*

bear harassed by a yipping brown and white streak that is the miracle of Grace.

Just lately, Grace and I have been accompanied on our walks by another dog. Trusty is an older golden retriever "type," who trudges heavily up the mountain, content to stay at my heel. Her eyebrows have gone a little white, so she has the look of a wise and aging scholar, a kind of Bertrand Russell of golden retriever types. This is well and fit, because Trusty is a dog who thinks a lot. Trusty thinks about leaves. Not leaves in mass, not forests, not sun-dappled meadows full of wildflowers. Trusty thinks about individual leaves, one at a time, and she thinks about these single leaves for hours, frowning and contemplating both stalk and blade.

Dry leaves are apparently as complex and revelatory as ones fresh from a bush or tree. The dog carries the chosen leaf gently in its mouth to a shady area, out of the sun, flops down onto her belly, and drops the green or brown object between her paws. Then she stares at it, intently, sometimes for over an hour, her patrician English logician's face crumpled in concentration. William Blake wrote the memorable opening stanza of "Auguries of Innocence" for Trusty:

> *To see a World in a Grain of Sand*
> *And a Heaven in a Wild Flower*
> *Hold Infinity in the palm of your hand*
> *And Eternity in an hour*

Presently, after an Eternity, or an hour, some concept great or small will occur to Trusty, some link to the final meaning of it all. She'll snort, a brief "hurumph," which is her canine version of "Eureka!" And the breath expelled through her muzzle will lift the leaf and set it atremble, as if to modify the physics of the entire situation and perhaps alter the very meaning of life, if not physical state of the Universe, as we know it. Something to think about for another hour, anyway.

I have been watching Trusty contemplate leaves for the last several days. She's not my dog. She belongs to a family that lives in my town, the Liskas, whom Linnea and I number among our best friends on earth. The father, Jim, once told me about the dog his kids love. The family was having a yard sale, and the dog, penned up in the back yard, longed to be out front. She attempted to climb the fence. Jim heard some strange strangled sounds and ran out back to investigate. Trusty had gotten stuck between the house and the fence in such a way that she had strangled herself. The future canine philosopher was not breathing. Jim moved fast, hoisting the dog off the fence, and clamping her nose and mouth so that he could give Trusty mouth to mouth resuscitation. Thus the dog's life was saved.

"So," I said to Jim, "your lips touched dog lips."

"And I don't even like that dog," he lied.

"She started staring at leaves after that?"

"Brain damage, probably."

Personally, I think it was Trusty's near death experience turned her into a canine metaphysician. She sees the world, heaven, infinity and eternity all in the turn of a leaf.

Linnea and I are keeping Trusty for a few weeks because Jim and his family are 1000 miles away, out east, in Minneapolis, where his young daughter is will be undergoing serious and perhaps life-threatening surgery. Her name is Courtney, and she's just a little tired of being called "a brave little girl." She's not a little girl, she just turned 15 and—like many young women her age—loves horses. Unlike most, she rides like an angel, and competes against adults in the sport and art of dressage.

The doctor, at least, treated her as an adult, fully capable of making her own decisions based on the best and most honest information her could give her.

"Am I going to die?" Courtney asked.

"I don't think so," the doctor said.

"Will I be paralyzed?"

Once again, the doctor didn't think so. What Courtney knew, what the whole family knew, was this: her spine needed to be rebuilt. If she did not have the operation, she would surely be paralyzed, probably in less than a year, and that paralysis could easily lead to death.

"Will there be a lot of pain?"

The doctor was candid: yes, for several weeks after the operation Courtney would be in serious pain.

"And afterwards, will I be able to ride a horse?"

The doctor said that, if everything went well, it was a distinct and very real possibility. But there were no guarantees in a surgery as prolonged and complex as hers.

Courtney and her mother, Geri, flew to Minneapolis, while Jim and his 12-year-old son, Daniel, drove out to save money. Linnea and I took Trusty. The operation was scheduled for July 6.

Our little town's 75th annual Fourth of July parade featured classic cars, and all the town's several fire engines, as well as floats based on the theme, "75 years of Ridin', Ropin', and Wranglin'." The Rodeo Queen contestants rode fine mounts and waved imperiously. The marching bagpipe band was, as always, a big hit, as were the miniature horses and the gaited pasafinos, and the mule train, and cowboy band called the Ringling Five, playing on the back of a flatbed truck emblazoned with their brutally honest motto: "it ain't music."

Last year, some dimwit from Portland, Oregon, traveling through the west, caught our parade and wrote an angry letter to the local newspaper, criticizing the order of march. He was incensed that a float featuring a Marilyn Monroe impersonator was positioned ahead of one carrying a man dressed as Uncle Sam. I was idiotically enraged by the letter, and fired off one of my own, suggesting that next year this patriotic imbecile could march behind Mickey Mouse and ahead of the street sweeper.

The parade is one of my favorite events of the year, a chance to see most of my neighbors, and to cheer for floats my friends and their kids have spent days and sometimes weeks constructing. I like to applaud and acclaim those organizations that I support and think do good work in the community.

"Hurray for the Big Brothers and Sisters," I holler, my hands cupped to my face like a megaphone.

"Hurray for the Rural Volunteer Fire Department!"

This year, the Shriners, a fraternal group I used to find faintly ridiculous, with their secret handshakes and Grand Poo-bahs and distinctive red fez hats, were a large presence in the parade. Many of this year's Shriners were great big men in absurd clown costumes, wearing bulbous noses like neon light bulbs and huge floppy red shoes. They rode tiny motorized tricycles in looping circles and blew amplified ooogahh horns. Later, after the parade, a few of them would get drunk, and, somewhere, in one of the downtown bars, some sentimental clown with booze on his breath would tell me, once again, that the Shrine is a philanthropic organization operating a network of 22 hospitals that provide expert, no-cost orthopaedic and burn care to children under 18. At this point, the drunken clowns usually have tears in their eyes and look altogether like a bad painting on black velvet.

"Hurray for the Shriners," I shouted at the top of my lungs.

"What a bunch of bozos," a friend standing by my side said.

I could feel my fists clenching at my sides. My forearms swelled and the muscles corded in my upper arms.

"What?" the guy asked.

"You know Courtney Liska?" I asked.

"Having that operation?"

"Shriners are paying for it."

"Hurray for the Shriners," my friend hollered.

Grace, from a Christian viewpoint, is the love and mercy God visits upon sinners. The doctrine further holds that we are all sinners by simple virtue of our humanity. That is to say, Grace is unmerited, which is why it is celebrated as being amazing. Great theological battles have been fought over the concept of Grace and the idea that it is there for the taking, entirely unearned.

My own background is Catholic. I suppose my current status in that church can best be described as long lapsed. Even so, no one who has suffered a Catholic education is ever entirely free of the belief, or at least the discipline. Quaint notions, punitive and medieval, color my perception of the physical world. I tend to see the wilderness through the broken prism of my faith.

About a 20-minute walk above my cabin, there is a place where the Falls Creek forks. Over the years, I've tracked a bit of a trail to that location, but it still requires a little bushwhacking to get there. In early July, the run-off is just beginning as snow melts on the mountains above. The creek is only 10 yards wide, but the slope is so steep that whole trees, 70 feet high, are carried down the mountain, and battered into slivers against protruding rocks. There is the sound of rushing water, constant and unrelenting, and something deeper, a contrapuntal rumbling that can felt in the ground itself and which is the sound of large boulders rolled down the streambed by the sheer and savage fervor of rushing water.

At the exact point where the creek divides, there is a rocky moss-covered triangle of earth nudging out into the rushing water. It is where I sit when I visit the Fork. A constant mist, thrown up by the creek, makes the spot 10 degrees cooler than the rest of the forest. At dawn and dusk, when the sun is low in the sky, the slanting pillars of light that fall through the mist shimmer with a rainbow's color and look precisely like the light falling through stained glass windows in a cathedral.

This place, the Fork on Falls Creek, is where I would go to pray, if I could pray, or if I thought that it would do any good at all.

Instead, on the day before Courtney's surgery, I walked up the hill with Grace and Trusty. We arrived at the Fork, and Trusty contemplated a leaf, while Grace appeared now and again, first on this side of the creek, then on that. Any ordinary dog would surely die attempting to cross Falls Creek during the run off, but this was Grace, and Grace is amazing.

Courtney went into surgery on the morning of July 6th. As they were wheeling her into the operating room, lightly tranquilized, she calmly asked her mother a favor. If she died, would it be possible for Geri and Jim to put up a memorial to her in the little park down the street from their house? It didn't have to be expensive or anything, but she'd like a little horse that little kids could play on. Before they grew up and could ride a real horse.

The surgery was scheduled for nine that morning, and would to take between seven and eight hours. It would be done around five Minneapolis time, four my time.

The day was hectic, and I was on the phone, on and off, for hours, conducting my business, such as it is. About 3:30 I stopped making or taking calls. We waited for word about Courtney from Geri. Linnea had a list of folks to call, who all had lists themselves. There were dozens of people across the country, who, like us, had spent the day worrying about Courtney. Trusty lay on the kitchen floor studying a leaf I'd supplied for the purpose. Linnea and I watched our respective telephones with the same intensity.

At 4:20, Geri called. Her voice sounded exhausted, slow and unsteady, as if each of her words had an anvil's worth of weight to it. I listened carefully and didn't hear grief.

"You sound good," I told Geri, which was a lie on the face of it.

Linnea picked up the extension phone.

"Courtney's out of surgery," Geri said. "They tell me I can see her in an hour."

The brave little girl made it. Young lady. Brave woman.

"The nurses tell me she can wriggle her toes."

Not paralyzed.

It had not yet occurred to Geri that she was relieved or happy, or overcome with joy. Linnea promised to call the half dozen people on her list.

I listened from my position at my desk. Trusty lay near Linnea's feet, staring at a new green leaf. She snorted briefly, the leaf jumped slightly, and the entire universe tilted on its metaphysical axis.

Three days later, Geri called and said that the surgery had gone so well that Courtney's therapist thought she could be up on horseback in about 30 days.

I called the dogs and together we started walking up the hill. I hadn't actually prayed at the Fork, and now I was walking up there to not actually give thanks. The dogs were happy, anyway. I had Trusty at my heel and Grace abounding.

## WILLIAM STUDEBAKER
### IDAHO FALLS, IDAHO

*Native Idahoan William Studebaker is the author of five collections of poetry, including* River Religion *and* Travelers from an Antique Land. *He has co-edited two regional anthologies,* Idaho's Poetry: A Centennial Anthology *and* Where the Morning Light's Still Blue: Personal Essays About Living in Idaho. *A whitewater canoeist and Idaho river guide, Studebaker also writes essays and articles and is a regular columnist for the* Twin Falls Times-News.

# After Breakfast at Ernest Hemingway's House, I Walk to Sun Peak Near Ketchum, Idaho

The sky is gray
one cloud
not one inch less
just a little room
beneath
for a river
a jungle of cottonwoods
a band of wild mosquitoes

& a moth
drunk on yarrow
waiting for its heart
to burst into flame.

# Blue Sky

Fairfield is the size of a match box
laid out so unimaginatively
that Main Street runs
perpendicular to all traffic
& every viable business
has turned its back on the town
& the promise of subdivisions
has begun to collapse
where houses & homes might have been.

This is small town everywhere
in the West. The postman
delivers less mail, the preacher
fewer sermons, the mortician
can't afford a hearse
& the dead get carried to their graves
in a good, used pickup.
Yet no one forgets that above them
is the blue sky they're all vested in.

Conversations are spoken with the eyes
& they follow you everywhere.
Every particle of posture is a point of gossip.
All news is old news & nothing unchanges
in a dialect encrypted with caution,
& the town crier is an old dog
black & white & wise about cows.
Her bark ignites the town pack
to a frenzy of yips and yowls.

Go around this town & you're out of it.
Go out the back door & you're in the country.
Stop & silence will be so profound

you'll forget why you thought of it.
Walk & you'll feel a light weight
like a clear bubble balloon about you.
That's when you'll understand
why you've come to invest
in so many double negatives.

This is the air you've been looking for,
the best investment your lungs have ever made.

# Winter on Bitch Creek

The few who survive
come prepared for what
is in the weather
but they are tortured
all winter by metaphors.

They hear a winded
winter front
blowing up a hill
plowing a furrow
through the sunshine.

They simply see
snowy mountains to the east,
cloud-shrouded and brewing
over Targhee.
How could they not know

about us or the coldness
that's at the heart of this
or what black needs
to feel at home in bird bones
already gone south.

## LAURA BELL
### CODY, WYOMING

*Laura Bell has worked as a backcountry guide, range manager, sheepherder, cowhand, massage therapist, and gallery/bookstore manager. Her journals and essays have appeared in the antholo-gies* Life in the Saddle, Thunder of Mustangs, *and* Camas: People and Issues of the Northern Rockies, *and she was a recipient of a 1996 Wyoming Arts Council Fellowship in Creative Writing.*

# Two Ocean Pass

I am standing at the parting of the waters, the place where Two Ocean Creek falls out of its high valley, hung undecided among the folds of the Continental Divide, and comes here to this spine of earth where its waters must choose a path. I had expected high, grand views that would lead me to imagine the waters of each ocean beyond the far horizons, east and west. I had expected that the consequences of choice would be more visible, but here the water is one and whole and there it has separated, giddy in its carelessness, to fall to opposite sides of the continent. I envy its ease. If I were water, which way would I fall?

This place of parting is sweet and sheltered. It is mid-September in the Teton wilder-ness of western Wyoming, and the aspen are dropping soft gold coins of light from their branches to the ground. Scattered loosely among and over them, Engelmann spruce and Lodgepole pines cast their own darker shadows of coolness across the water's edge. At the fork of the stream I lean an ear to the surface of water and listen hard for the voic-es of longing or regret, but all I can hear is the burbling and splashing of water falling to its place.

I am here with eight other people. We have spent the last ten days together, horseback in the backcountry of Yellowstone Park, and in our journeys have traced the paths carved by water; Mink Creek, Plateau Creek, Lynx Creek, Yellowstone River. We have camped and cooked by the waters and sung like cheerful coyotes late into the night sky, and when we have fallen to our bags to sleep the night, we have listened, as if in secret, to the con-versations of elk, owls, coyotes, and sandhill cranes.

One night I woke to the warning trumpet snorts of the wrangle horse, tied to a high-line in the trees, and watched, bright-eyed, through the mesh screen of my tent for the shape of a grizzly to pass between me and the risen moon. It didn't. Instead the campfire that smolders all night flared high to cast a comforting light on the canvas, and I heard my outfitter friend walk out through the trees with the soft whir of a Coleman lantern. A moose, he said next morning.

It has been my job to pack and cook, to cut wood and haul water and tend to the needs of both people and horses, but everyone has helped, and the trip has been a joy. At the Mink Creek camp, I was left alone in camp for the afternoon and for two hours I inched my way on hands and knees through the wet grass searching out wild strawberries, ripe and sweet and half the size of raisins. I was lost in the time of lovers and artists, and when I came to my senses my fingers were stained red and the small bowl was two-thirds full. There was nothing else in the world that I wanted to be doing. No one else I thought I should be. Next morning I stirred them into the breakfast hotcakes and watched as faces around the cook fire opened up into bright blazes, as if sheer delight is an ingredient that can be tasted.

Across the water, between the forks, a wooden sign is nailed to a large spruce tree, shoulder high on a tall man. In even, routed letters it says, "Parting of the Waters. Atlantic Ocean 3,488 miles. Pacific Ocean 1,353 miles" with arrows pointing east and west. Water miles, not crow miles, I note. The waters disappear quickly into the trees to follow their given paths; one to the Snake River and the Pacific Ocean beyond, the other to the Yellowstone and across the continent into the Gulf of Mexico.

One of the women of the group wonders out loud how many men have stood here and peed into the waters that will touch both oceans. We howl and roll our eyes at the thought, but to be honest, I get it. Maybe if I were alone and didn't have to step into the water I would do it too, just to spread myself beyond where I am captive, just to have the illusion of being in many places at once. Just to be able, in some ridiculous way, to have it both ways.

I had thought that my life would be different. I had thought that it might unfold like my parents' lives in the seeming order and relevance of a life-long marriage to each other and a commitment to their religious community. I had thought that by now I might have season tickets to the symphony, but at each fork in the water's path I have chosen the blank slate of sagebrush lands bleached hard and bare by sun. This place that I have come to is someone else's history, someone else's place of order, not mine, and for twenty years I have carved it out for myself like water across uncertain ground.

I've lost my heart to men who could give me all the space I needed and, finally, more than I ever wanted. Years ago, a man showed up at my door needing a jockey for the race horse in his trailer, and I married him four months later because he could dance and because flying flat-out in those Sunday afternoon quarter mile races was the most fun I'd ever had in my life. It was a lonely and difficult marriage that didn't last the decade, but I think now that I couldn't have chosen differently. What almost broke me gave me my life. It woke me up. It taught me to speak and gave me a relationship to his two daughters who in unguarded moments claim me as their own.

Still, I had thought that it would be different. I made a commitment and planted trees, thinking that I would sit under their shade when we were all old and sprawling. Now I hang to the ridgetops, afraid of choosing a person or even a place. I migrate every six months back and forth between two states and several jobs, but gravity pulls at my heart and asks me to fall to a simpler path. Does it matter which?

## Laura Bell: *Two Ocean Pass*

I am 44 years old and do not expect to change much in my ways. I will probably never make a lot of money even though the world has said that I can do anything that I put my hand to. The choices I have made have been odd ones, leaning towards the romantic, the poetic, the spiritual. Out of college I came west to herd sheep and then cowboy on Wyoming ranches. I hired on with the Forest Service as a manager of federal grazing lands, but signed away the security of my job to study massage and begin to put my words on paper. This life that I've chosen is a precarious one, with plates spinning and wobbling in the air around me. When asked the simplest questions about what I do or where I live, I long to answer with a word instead of a paragraph, but I make the same choices over and over, and when I am not scared to my bones, I find that I love this life with all my heart.

The light is dimming, and there are miles to go. At the meadow where we left the horses tied head-to-tail, we tighten cinches and adjust packs for the trip out to Trail Creek where we will make a quick camp for the night. Tomorrow we will pack out the Buffalo Fork trail to the Turpin Meadow trailhead, fifty miles west of Dubois, and the group will scatter back to their private lives. The conversation turns to hot showers, to dinner out and whiskey with ice cubes, but everyone moves slowly as though reluctant to begin this leave-taking. I stretch one last time and climb into the saddle, pulling my string of four pack-horses into line behind the others.

The water baffles me. Do we choose or do we fall? One school of thought says there are no wrong choices, that any choice leads us to the lessons to be learned, that choosing and falling are one and the same. I'd like to believe this but am still too fearful of making a mistake that can't be undone. Perhaps we are more like water than we think, and the path is already carved before us. At each fork I imagine that we might fall according to what we love, or perhaps what we fear. If love or fear outweighs the other, wouldn't that tilt us?

Every job I've had has taught me something about elegance of movement, about doing less and accomplishing more. The first spring that I herded sheep, I began the week-long trail to the high mountain ranges by rimrocking my band of a thousand ewes and lambs. I had tried to avoid some difficult terrain by taking them a new way, but my route was impassable. Frustrated and tired, the sheep bogged down in the heat long before we reached the noon waterhole. My exasperated camptender yelled, "Jesus Christ, these sheep have been going to the mountain every damned year of their lives. All you had to do was stay behind them and stay out of the god damned way." He didn't stay mad for long. He pulled his 4-wheel drive over a dip in the dirt road so we could crawl underneath and eat our sandwiches in its shade.

Those years, I learned how to herd with a light touch, how to let the sheep spread for miles without fearing I would lose them. I learned how to raise better lambs and read more books at the same time. I learned how, at least in the practice of sheepherding, to get out of my own way.

I earn my living now giving massage. I believe that holding to the pain will release it, so I stand under this vast and uncertain sky and wait for my fears to rise up from me like steam from the earth after a summer storm. Ease and grace is what I hope for. Years at sheepcamp taught me that less is more and that to simply follow the lacy spread of sheep was often enough. Cowboying, I learned finally to move quietly like a dancer, that from a distance I could move my horse one step this way or one step that way and put my cow where I wanted without dashing or yelling at her flanks. I learned to step back and look at a herd of three hundred cattle scattered on a winter feeding ground and, with eyes blurred across the whole of them, pick out the one cow that carried a backwards calf inside her, no hooves showing yet, a certain death undetected. I've learned these lessons of elegance and economy with animals, but I don't know how to translate them into a human life of loving and being loved. I find myself plowing that ground with head bowed and jaw set, knowing that I fight too hard.

A pair of golden eagles hangs nearly motionless in the currents above us. Their wings dip, then quiver to a still point, sure of the air that holds them. We are quiet, following the trail down Pacific Creek. Our string of twenty horses moves like some dreamlike version of crack the whip, curling through the trees and rippling over a log fallen across the trail. Ten days out has drawn us all closer to the color of dust and the smell of wood smoke, more like each other now than different. I will miss it. I will miss the ease of hitting the ground running each morning, knowing what needs to be done and knowing I can do it well. So simple.

I have cultivated my life to the blankness of a page, and now I find myself afraid to return to it. What is left are the hardest things; the messy scrawl of words put to paper, the ragged edges of a life made by hand. What is left is what I love. I choose to slip from this ridge at the drop of the reins, burning hard and bright to the path where I land. I choose to be water and love the way I fall.

# BILL HOAGLAND
## CODY, WYOMING

*Bill Hoagland writes poems, essays and magazine articles. His poetry has appeared in magazines such as* Seneca Review, Petroglyph, Denver Quarterly, Poem, *and many others, and he has been a contributor to the anthologies* 90 Poets of the Nineties, The Last Best Place, *and* New Voices. *He was the recipient of the 1995 Wyoming Arts Council's Blanchan Nature-Writing Award, and in 1998 he was awarded a Wyoming Arts Council Fellowship in Creative Writing.*

# Exposure

I was a witness
when the corpse arrived,
bagged and strapped
like a log
across the saddle,
his flesh frozen,
weird, horizontal—

a tall boy thick with health
when we knew him
kidding in the classroom,
the knack a few boys have
to escape the teacher's scolding
since his jokes were never sour,
played mostly on himself
and somehow relevant
to any lesson going.

It was early on unsettling,
although the body bag

# RING OF FIRE

had seemed secure enough.
I tell you now I felt
so damn inept, and checked
the others' eyes as if to try
to touch without a hand,
before that zipper parted
inexplicably.

There he was again
staring open-mouthed
quite through the sky,
a look incredulous, comic,
showing how he thought
he might escape our tedium
to fetch himself a moment more,
because he was so confident
he would never die.

# A Garden of Rocks

I have been moving rocks
the size of basketballs, softballs, baseballs—
a summer sport of sharp edges.

I heft a rock to my shoulder and walk,
admiring the small grains of granite.
I am reminded of atoms in a physics text—
pink granite up close is white and red
in strings and swirls and little galaxies
that flow like rivers on a fractured surface
or disappear to inner rock,
perhaps to rise again like springs.

We are all in there somewhere, I think.
Do we really need to find out where?

As I bend to place the rock
a bead of sweat falls from my forehead,
a rock now momentarily varnished and glowing.

And then I find another rock to turn
and lift and carry to a corner
by the house where nothing grew.
You go here, I tell a rock, and bump it
against another for the bold note
they sing in collaboration,
two rocks now married
and holding down a spot of dust—
a long time before they sing again.

# Water Table

However things make meaning, I'm never sure.
Last autumn, for instance, after the trees
quit drinking, our first three nights of frost
shocked us from our lethargy until our skins tingled
and our voices rang like bells.

Downhill, Alkali Creek rose three feet,
slogging up its weed-strung banks,
and walking there one morning
in fog thick as thoughts of trouble close at hand,
I startled a flock of geese who pounded the clouded air
and honked in panicked choruses
that dwindled to solo notes
as they rose to the invisible sky.

That was the day our storage cellar flooded.
Here I thought I had planned ahead so well for cold
by picking the last tomatoes—some pink,
some yellow, some still green—
then lining them on the cellar's wooden shelves,
thinking my work against frost
would haul the last of summer into fall.

But when I cracked the slatted wooden door
into the cool, dark, damp under-earth that foggy day
I flushed to see tomatoes bobbing on a lake above the sump.

That night a pair of owls called from our cottonwoods.
I lay the book I had been reading on my chest,
like open wings, and closed my eyes.
The owls exchanged their singing as if to ask:
"Still there?"
"Yes, still here, and you?"
"Still here, still here. Still there?"

## JANNE GOLDBECK
### POCATELLO, IDAHO

*A native Texan, Janne Goldbeck is a Professor of English at Idaho State University, where she has taught since 1976. Her poetry has appeared widely in journals and anthologies, including* The Bellingham Review, Centennial Review, Weber Studies, Idaho's Poetry: A Centennial Anthology, Mountain Standard Time, *and elsewhere, and her essays have been published in* Plainswoman, Idaho Arts Journal, *and* Where the Morning Light's Still Blue: Personal Essays About Idaho.

# Wintering

I am still travelling. Lately a compass in my pulses has been pulling me toward some winter I have not yet experienced, but which haunts my dreams. Its unavoidable compulsion has brought me here, a half mile or so out of the Pocatello valley, where the pavement ends and the hills begin. For a moment, before beginning to walk, I stand looking at the mounded arcs of the hills and the crested clouds rushing over them. Sometimes, up here, shapes are so compelling that I head out cross country to follow the lines of ridgetops, to feel the land's contours. But today's journey demands the decorum of a road.

I start walking. As usual in this country, the road heads uphill immediately. I must start out against gravity and against the wind. The dirt under my feet is frozen in spots, the ruts in the track unyielding. My legs ache a little, unaccustomed to the hills' upward pull. My pace suits a close inspection of where I'm going. I take long breaths. The ghost colors of November spread out around me. Clouds scud overhead. I keep walking uphill against the wind. My ears are cold under my scarf; I shove my hands into my coat pockets to warm my fingers, chilled even through my gloves. Still, I know the cold is necessary to this walk. My discomfort is marginal; I'm preparing with the hills for winter. I think I am coming home to the fierce and bonestrong beauty of late fall. I remember autumn evenings of my childhood when the pull of light and warmth indoors could never overcome the attraction of the cold, wet, exhilarating outdoors. At fifty, I am still moved by the same autumn wildness. I could jump off a hillside into the wind and soar, if only my coat were a little wider or my bones more hollow.

I'm alone—no other walkers out in this raw grey afternoon, not even the sound of dirt bikes churning up their hill tracks. I meet no pickups lurching down the road, driver and passenger eyeing me warily. I'm glad of this. Like the cold, solitude or even a certain invisibility seems essential to my journey.

The tallest of the hills are snow dusted. Whenever the road curves out a bit to the left, I catch a glimpse of them. The two-track stretches on ahead, takes a bend out of sight. In front of me stand a few scattered junipers, round-topped, then a line of them along the hill crest, a row like cattle walking home. Nothing else in sight but dry grasses and the slopes and curves that shape my path and structure my vision. Silence continues. I hear only the wind. There are not even the usual shrill calls of chickadees that shelter in the cedars or deciduous thickets along the creek. I stop, listen for a moment to catch a squirrel's chatter. Nothing. On other walks, flickers have startled me with their quick, clear whistles, their sudden flash of cinnamon red darting between trees. Today there are none; only the wind moves through the branches. In these circumstances the road becomes mysterious. Although I've been along here many times before, the parts of the road hidden from me are not predictable. I remember its general shape and direction, but, strangely, not the landmarks. The change in perspective is exciting.

I want to go even further back into the hills than this road will take me. I know that if I follow it, I will finally arrive on top of Kinport, the highest point on this side of the valley. But this is not a day for ascensions. I turn off the main road onto a narrower track that winds down a small valley to my right. Another familiar trail, but today I expect a destination that I have not reached before. All the time I have spent, in other seasons, learning the landscape, has allowed me now a deeper access to the hills and to the threshold of a sharp and powerful season. The road curves further to the left around a clump of willows. Their stems lift and twine in an intricate figure of grays and pale red. They repeat the road's shape and might be mapping all the paths up and down the hills. Alongside the willows stand light gold grasses, breast high, absolutely straight and stiff. A seasonal creek runs here, its twists and quirks imitated by the road. This land's rises, its inclines, its water channels shape the direction of both human and animal passage so that any walk is a reenactment of geographic intention.

I surrender to these motions. I have grown more used to the cold pressing against me; it's become part of my body, a condition of who and where I am. My fingers tingle slightly in my pockets, warming up. I have begun to get a second wind, a slower, steadier rhythm of breath. Ahead of me on the trail, a few deer tracks are outlined. I wonder which thickly wooded ravine shelters them.

People say they have seen elk up here—these animals haunt the edges of even the plainest accounts of hiking or hunting, emblems of the unexpected and marvelous. Sometimes a larger track in the road suggests that the stories are not all hunters' tales. On this road, though, I see nothing that could be read as elk tracks, only the fragile signs of the deer, pointing downhill, none going my way. Occasionally, I see what could be a coyote track. More elusive, less obviously grand than the elk, they are hard to see. They adapt so well to their environment, adopt its seasons and its necessities so completely that they disappear from even the hunters' stories, shadows among the sagebrush.

I come upon a derelict truck body beside the road; its wheels are gone, sections of the chassis are rusted away, though the steering column still protrudes firmly from a bed of dry grass and weeds. Just beyond the truck, my road ends at an old wooden trough, grown up with grass; an inch or two of rain water lingers at the bottom, surrounded by moss. Fallen leaves clog the sides. As I stand looking at the trough, the old truck, the clouds shift lower.

# Janne Goldbeck: *Wintering*

Snow begins to fall. Here, in between the hills in this little valley, I am protected from the wind. The snow falls vertically, lazily, collecting in small hollows and bare spots of earth. The road whitens. I still stand looking at the rotting tank, the disintegrating truck; their makers' original purposes have been transformed, subverted to a new design. They are signs I want to read. I do not brush away the snowflakes settling on my coat sleeves. At times, one falls against my eye, leaving a brief wetness in my lashes. How did that truck get here, anyway? I imagine someone driving it here, bouncing it over the ruts and potholes in the narrow road, careless of damage, to abandon it. I imagine it in summer as a haven for snakes curled under the rusty springs and remnants of grey striped upholstery. Still, though, these objects remain as indecipherable to me as the spring that will well up here sometime around April and join the snowmelt to fill the old tank and start the creek flowing again.

The snow is falling harder, in quick flurries. The hilltops have disappeared into a grey mist. I can't go further up today. Too much is going on up there. My own winter is not ready for that level of intensity. I turn around to take the darkened road back. It falls off not far in front of me, leaving a gap through which the hills across the valley loom dimly. They rise a long way off, on the other side of the town. The clouds have shadowed the land; only a few pale grasses gleam here and there. My way leads down, through the moving shadows, wind at my back. The end of my scarf keeps blowing up over my head like a pointed ear. My nose is cold and damp. I start walking, pushed by the wind, stumbling a little over frozen ridges in the track.

At the top of a small rise, I look back at the covered hills. A breeze whips up the snowflakes across my face, stinging. I am momentarily blinded. I turn and go on walking down. This is all more than I can collect: the silvery grey of sagebrush, the grasses full of light as if it came from them, the molded shapes of junipers, dark and solid, the bare graceful willows, the dark hills across the valley. And always the wind, the wind that hardly seems cold because it urges on some motion in myself, that wildness at autumn's core. I begin to run. The clouds fly overhead, all of us moving through the rising, falling, shifting, rolling hills. The road sways and turns in front of me.

The sky still darkens; the colors of the land become more somber. Snow is falling hard now, swirling ahead of me, filling up pockets in the road. I slow my pace, raise my head, and watch the flakes come down. They cling to the fuzzy nap of my gloves and begin to cover my coatsleeves. From here I can see where the shortcut road branches off back to the turnaround where I parked my car. Behind me, the outlines of the hills have vanished. I linger, not wanting yet to leave.

As I come over the last rise, a grey shape emerges from the snow to my left. I stop. No, I decide, only a sagebrush shaken by the wind. The shape comes closer. I hold my breath to see what recognizable form it will take. It slows, seems to hesitate. Then I see it is a coyote, snow holding lightly to her thick, grey fur, settling in the brush of her tail. I try not to move, to breathe so lightly that I will seem to her only another rooted part of the landscape. She has stopped too. We look at one another through the shift of snowflakes. It is too dark— even this close, I can see only the gleam of her eyes, her stillness. I do not know how long we stand in the silence, the snow lifting and dropping about us, veiling and eddying about our bodies. I have forgotten about my car just down the hill, about shelter.

She turns, finally, and trots away into the darkening evening, her shape gradually losing outline until she merges with the snow, the grey light. The hills are filling with winter.

## JULIA HOSKIN
### CODY, WYOMING

*Julia Hoskin's short stories have appeared in* Northern Lights, The Owen Wister Review, *and the* Casper Star- Tribune. *A two-time winner of Wyoming Arts Council fellowships in creative writing, Hoskin teaches classes in English and social studies at Cody High School.*

# Personal Effects

Art was casting in the chill April dusk when Jane walked up from the driveway. He wore an ancient hearing aid he'd bought at a garage sale years ago. It worked okay if he tapped it every so often, but Art seldom tapped it unless he was actually engaged in a conversation, so it was easy to slip up behind him unnoticed. Jane stood behind the horse barn, watching him draw the fishing rod back over his shoulder before casting, the line whining toward the shrubs on the far side of the yard. In the gathering dark, she could see little of him except the blue denim vest bleached nearly white by sun.

When her mother died, Art wore a suit, and the vest hung stiffly on the clothesline. His face, carved and hardened like driftwood by the Wyoming wind, was always tough to read, but afterward, remembering the vest, she took to phoning him once a week. Neither she nor Art ever had much news to report, and he spoke in the brief, guarded way people have when they're waiting for the real reason for a call. Eventually, she stopped phoning, a little embarrassed at her sentimentality.

"Whoa!" Art shouted, and then, a moment later, "Aw, crumb."

"Hello, there," Jane said, stepping forward. "Catch anything?"

"Well, Janie," Art said, leaning his rod against a shrub and tapping his hearing aid. "Didn't expect you 'til tomorrow." He pressed a bristled cheek against her hair.

"I got an itch to come early, so I left this afternoon. What're you doing out here, practicing for some walleye tournament?"

"No, no, since your mother passed on, I like to come out here evenings and do a little casting. Thought I had it, just now, but it turned out to be the dang dogwood."

"Had what?"

"Oh, I generally throw out my ring of keys and try to snag 'em. Problem is, then I can't find 'em too good in the dark like this."

Jane smiled. "You wouldn't want to cast in the daylight, I suppose."

"No sport in it, then. Be like bein' able to see the fish." He put a hand on her back, guiding her toward the driveway. "Got a lot of stuff to haul in?"

"Not really. We better find your keys, first."

"They can wait. None of 'em fit anything anymore, except the truck key and the house key. I never lock the house, and I got a spare key for the pickup in the glove box."

"You'd sure be easy to rob."

"Any burglar comin' all the way out here is welcome to my belongings. Save me gettin' rid of 'em." He tapped his hearing aid and wrestled with the car door, which was locked.

"Better safe." Jane jangled her keys.

"Sure. Wouldn't want to leave all that stereo equipment unprotected, not with deer lurkin' about." He hoisted the larger of the two suitcases. "See you in the hernia ward." He limped toward the house, the suitcase banging his ankle with every other step.

Each time she visited the ranch, her old bedroom seemed different in its strangeness. When she moved away, she'd taken anything of value and left behind relics of her awkward youth: a Black Beauty bank, left from a brief but intense passion for horses the summer they'd moved to Wyoming; a scrapbook half-filled with pictures clipped from teen magazines of the Beatles and later, the Monkees; a box of soaps shaped like owls Dan Bodell had given her on her sixteenth birthday, back when a foolish gift seemed reason enough to dump a boyfriend.

When she came out to the kitchen, Art was prying chunks of corned beef hash from a can into a skillet. "You eat?" Art asked.

"I grabbed a sandwich in Wheatland." She peered over his shoulder. "Looks like dog food."

"Why would I fry up dog food?"

Jane reached over and tapped his hearing aid.

"It's workin', it's workin'. Too bad you can't cook."

"Too bad you don't eat right. What have you been living on all this time, just hash?"

"Little hash sometimes, sometimes weenies and beans. Renata's comin' tomorrow. Maybe she's learned how to cook."

"Renata's going to be here?"

"Yep. She sent me a card last Christmas, so I got her number from Information and called her up. I figured if I was invitin' my stepdaughter to pick through my stuff before auction, better invite my daughter, too. Only fair and all."

Jane ran a hand through her bangs. Renata, after all these years. Art and Evelyn had coaxed Jane and Kylie into pity for her before Renata arrived that first summer, and they had culled a few toys from their closet shelves to lay on her bed in the spare room. Renata, it seemed, had been coached differently. She jumped out of Art's pick-up wearing the hand-tooled cowboy boots he'd sent her for Christmas and stared at them with sullen disdain. The day after she first arrived, Renata told them in lurid and wildly inaccurate detail how babies were made. That was when it started. It had never really ended.

Each summer, they dreaded her arrival and savored her departure. When Jane tacked a poster from "A Hard Day's Night" over her bed, Renata rolled her eyes and told them that the Beatles were out; nobody in McClellan listened to anything but the Rolling Stones. She laughed at the rick-rack on their dresses and called them home ec. projects. And she met all scoffs and innuendo with poorly-concealed amusement. Jane had tried to enlist Kylie's aid, but Kylie, shy and gullible and two years younger, was not a very strong ally. Kylie believed Renata when she swore that she had seen Dean Martin buying jug wine at the Plenty Mart, that her best friend had an uncle who'd been born without nostrils and worked for the McClellan Department of Sanitation, that she had once seen a cow spontaneously combust. When Renata was thirteen, she had begun bragging about boyfriends. Jane was sure the boyfriends were fictitious. Still, though Renata was skinny, with virtually no upper lip and narrow grey eyes, she had ample red hair, and it had been Jane's experience, both then and later, that boys were willing to overlook a multitude of plain features for an abundance of red hair. It was a profound relief when Renata suddenly stopped coming for summer vacation.

Jane perched on the edge of a counter. "So what's Renata been doing all these years?"

"Don't know all of it." Art turned up the flame and poked at his hash with a spatula. "Got married couple times. I think the first one was one of these dopers. I don't know about the second one. They split up I think maybe six years ago. Then she decided she wanted a baby. I don't know who the father was, and don't want to know. Anyway, it was born dead. That was a couple years ago. She's been goin' to school, too, off and on. Just about has a degree now."

Jane snorted. "By now she should have five or six of 'em."

Art looked at her dolefully. "It'd be nice if you two could get along this one last time. Don't imagine you'll have to see each other again 'til my funeral." He scooped hash onto a plate and slathered it with catsup.

"Okay, okay," she said. "Where's she been living? Colorado still?"

"Nope, northern Arizona. Not too far from where I'll be, I guess. Maybe thirty miles, if that."

Jane opened the refrigerator and surveyed the contents. "Lord, wait'll Kylie hears. Want a beer?"

"No, water'll do me. You have one." He looked grey under the florescent light, and his eyes blinked blearily. Jane put down her beer and rubbed his shoulders. "It's okay, Art. You were right to ask her." She tapped his hearing aid again, but he continued eating silently, his hand shaking a little as he lifted his fork.

Awake that night and with nothing to read, Jane listened to Art shuffling down the hall to the bathroom. She called out to him for company, but felt foolish and was a little relieved when he apparently didn't hear her and went back to bed. She rolled onto her back and reviewed her adult life through Renata's cynical eyes: two failed businesses, a marriage that ended after her husband admitted sleeping with several of her female employees . Yet remembering what Art had said in the kitchen, she had to admit that Renata had suffered as many mistakes as she had, and had also earned some sympathy. It was an oddly aggravating thought.

Renata arrived the next afternoon in a battered white Volvo, a cloud of dust obscuring the scrub grass behind her. Jane stepped out on the porch and stood awkwardly next to Art, who had chattered nervously all morning and now seemed struck speechless. Renata grinned broadly at him, said, "Hiya, Pop," and shook his hand. She glanced wryly at Jane.

"Well, Janie," she said.

Renata's hair was cut short, and crowsfeet radiated from the corners of her ashy grey eyes, the eyes of a woman who had spent her life squinting into the sun. She turned to Art and said, "You need rain."

Art wandered down to the Volvo and was peering into the driver's window. "Yep. Been a dry spring. Fella who bought the horses said Catch-Weed Creek is near dry. You don't look like you got any suitcases."

Renata reached into the front seat. "Just a backpack. I don't believe in cartin' along a lot of trash."

Art slapped the hood of the Volvo. "Your mother used to take along three or four suitcases for a trip to the grocery. Or wait," he faltered, lifting his cap and smoothing his hair. "I guess that was Jane's ma." Renata raised an eyebrow and sucked in her cheeks. After a moment, she went into the house. Art rubbed his cheek, pacing the driveway.

Finally, he said, "Well, if you get Rennie, we should be able to do the cellar in no time."

Each June, Jane's mother had taken down her sewing machine and wheeled the roll-away bed into the spare room, where Renata always slept. Now, however, Renata had claimed Kylie's old room. Jane tapped at the door and stepped in. "Art wants to get started down in the cellar. You want to come and see if there's anything you want?"

Renata turned away from the window and sighed, stubbing out a cigarette. "I suppose. What's down there, canning jars?"

"I guess so. And vases, I think. Probably nothing too valuable."

"No kidding."

Jane leaned against the wall. "Kylie's room always used to smell like nail polish and Heaven Scent."

"I never noticed." Renata picked at a cuticle. "Where is good ol' Kylie, anyhow?"

"She's having another baby, due any day now. Her doctor didn't want her driving all the way from Sheridan this close to delivery."

"Jesus, I traveled all over when I was pregnant. My boyfriend was a bull rider. We just drove and drove, following the circuit. My water broke just as he was getting bucked off a Brahma."

Jane shifted her feet restlessly, leery of personal confessions.

Renata eyed her levelly. "You don't have any kids, huh?" Jane shook her head. "Well, me neither," Renata said briskly. "Let's go help Art sort through his goddam jars."

They spent the rest of the afternoon in the cellar. Art seemed anxious for them to take things. "This is a real nice meat grinder. You don't see many these days. Practically an antique. Now this flower holder is kind of pretty. You could use it for hair ribbons or what-not." Renata lounged on the stairs, smoking and shaking her head whenever Art held up a colander or chip and dip set to show her.

Jane kept thinking of the days after her mother died. She and Kylie had divided the family photos, of which there were surprisingly few, and sorted through their mother's jewelry and most of her clothes, touching each brooch and handkerchief reverently, reminiscing in hushed voices until they had sickened of their own yearning and began tossing everything in a big box, still musty from the basement.

Jane finally let Art talk her into a case of canning jars she would never use and a cow-shaped clock that her mother had received by sending in labels from cans of evaporated milk. She thought she might give the clock to Kylie, who had been fond of it.

At last Art said, "Well, I guess the rest goes to auction. Say, Rennie, can you cook?"

"If forced to, by starvation or abusive husbands." Smoke swirled around the cellar light.

"Well," Art said, "I fear starvation if you don't. Janie here was never much in the kitchen, and I suppose neither of you are keen on weenies and beans. Come upstairs and see what you can do."

Renata groaned and led them up the stairs. "What would you two have done if I hadn't shown up?"

"Ate beans and wished we could cook," Jane said.

"My, my, aren't you a pathetic pair? I guess I'd better see what I can do." She peered into the refrigerator. "Good God, you can hear your own echo in here. Don't you grocery shop in months with 'R' in 'em, or what?"

Art was leaning over the kitchen table, reading a copy of *Grit* he'd received in the mail that day. When he didn't answer, Jane reached around him and gently tapped his hearing aid. Renata gave them a hard look and turned away, shaking her head.

"Pardon?" Art looked up, startled.

"We're having an omelet," Renata said loudly. "Any objections?"

At the dinner table, Renata minced her omelet with a fork and stabbed each minute piece, chewing rapidly. Jane ate dispiritedly. Art had recently read an article about health care and kept up a running monologue during dinner. "Don't keep you in the hospital for nothin' anymore. Fella I used to run with, Bob McGinn, got a kidney stone middle of the night and was practically blubberin' with agony, and they tell him to come back if he don't pass it. Fool insurance companies don't pay, that's why. I shoulda gone in the insurance business, only I never been snake enough to do it."

When he finally ran down, Jane pushed back her chair. "Thanks, Renata."

"What for?"

"Cooking dinner. It was...nice."

"Yeah, well, you get to do the dishes. I'll skip out on Lawrence Welk reruns or whatever the evening's entertainment is. See you in the morning." Renata scooped up her cigarettes and ashtray and strode from the room. The kitchen door slammed.

Jane leaned back in her chair, her arms crossed. "What got her in such a mood?"

Art shrugged. "She's a knotty one. I never could figure her out. If you don't mind, I might just catch the end of the season opener on the portable T.V. in the bedroom."

Renata was a messy cook. Spots of hardened egg dappled the stove, shreds of cheese stuck to the linoleum floor. The kitchen finally in order, Jane sat on the porch steps, drinking beer and listening for animals. The yard light whitewashed the tree trunks and made little wells of shadow under the juniper and jack pine. Suddenly the Volvo door opened and Renata got out and strolled up to the porch.

"Sounds funny without the horses," she said, "don't it?"

"I heard a coyote a few minutes ago."

"There aren't any coyotes left around here."

"Mm-hmm. Listen." After a moment, they heard a dog barking across the basin.

"That's a dog."

"I know that, but I heard a coyote yipping a few minutes ago."

"You heard a dog yipping."

"I know what coyotes sound like."

"How many beers does that make?"

"Two," Jane said hotly. Renata went in the house and came back with two cans of beer. She sat on the porch railing and drank rapidly.

"What were you doing, sitting in the car like that?"

"Just sitting in the car like that. I like to, sometimes. It reminds me," she said. "of getting out of bed at one or two in the morning and standing out here in my nightgown, trying to catch a breeze."

"You never."

"Sometimes I'd stand under the yard light, bowing to my audience. I never sang or danced or nothin', just bowed. I was real good at bowing."

"How'd you sneak out without anyone hearing you?"

"Sneak? Hell, I could've ridden out on the vacuum sweeper, and you all would've just gone on snoring. I think your mother knew, though. I heard her tiptoeing around a few times when I came back in. Probably disappointed I didn't run off."

"My mother wasn't like that. She was nice."

"Yep, real nice," Renata said, pitching the first beer can into the weeds, "Sometimes I almost couldn't tell she hated my guts."

"We all liked you, Ren. At least, as much as you'd let us."

"Well, that wasn't much, I'll admit. Your mother, though, she resented the hell out of me before I ever got here. Know why? I made her feel guilty."

"How did you arrive at this brilliant piece of psychology?"

"Oh, her going to such pains to prove I was the extra kid. Christ, some years she didn't even bother making room in the closet for my stuff. Little revenges, stuff like that. I gave it right back, too, every subtle little way I could think of. I never did forgive her for messing around with my Dad."

"For heaven's sake, Ren, they were married."

"Not when it started, they weren't. He was married to my Mom. Didn't know that, did you? It's true. Married and messing around. Met her at a bar, I understand."

"Oh, for godsake. Seen Deano at the Plenty Mart lately?"

Renata ignored her. "My mom wasn't the long-suffering, silent type, believe me. I remember one day she called me in from outside. I'd been splashing around in the puddles in our driveway, and I was sure I was in for a lickin'. She started hollerin' as soon as she saw how muddy I was, but somewhere in the middle there, yelling about my muddy jeans turned into yelling that my Dad was a two-timing son of a bitch, that he was a fool for another woman, and was leavin' us to buy a ranch in Wyoming and live there with his new family.

"When Pop came home, Mom was in the bedroom and wouldn't come out, so he fixed us supper. I remember it was tomato soup and cheese and crackers. I asked him, was it true, that he had another family he liked better than us, and I'll never forget it, he said, 'Rennie, I couldn't never like a little girl better than I like you. Now you eat up your soup.'" She swung her feet up onto the rail and leaned against a post.

"So I thought it was all okay and Mom was just in a snit, and then one morning he was gone, and Mom locked herself in the bedroom again. I kept shovin' little notes under the door, little pictures I drew of her, but she wouldn't come out, not for a long, long time.

"Then the next summer, Mom sent me up here, even though I begged not to go. I already hated your Mom, and you and Kylie seemed like spoiled brats, from what I heard, and sure enough, you treated me like scum on a cesspool. Finally, when I was fourteen, I threatened to run off with one of my boyfriends if she made me come here."

Renata tipped her head back, polishing off the last of her beer. Then she stood up, looking at the empty can. "I suppose your Mom came home one night all flushed and happy and said, 'Surprise, children! I found you a fine new Daddy, and we're all goin' to Wyoming to live happy ever after.'" She pitched the empty can so it bounced off the roof of Art's pickup.

Jane grabbed a handful of gravel and began chucking it at the old pump in the yard. "This is stupid. It'd be just like you to make up something like this, when Mom is gone and can't defend herself. I wonder why you didn't tell Kylie and me when we were kids. It would've been your best lie yet."

"I admit to having occasionally bent the truth to put myself in a good light, but you can hardly call this a story that would flatter me. I got dumped for you folks, remember. But now I figure what the hell. If I wasn't exactly Cinderella, your mother was no Snow White, either." Renata added reasonably, "You think I'm lying about this, you just ask Art." The storm door clicked shut behind her.

Jane rested her head on her knees and rocked a little. She could see no way around a long night of trying to fit Renata's story to what little she remembered of the summer Art had married her mother.

It had seemed quick, she recalled. One night Art came over for dinner, and the next day, it seemed, her mother took Jane and Kylie shopping for new dresses to wear to the wedding. Her mother and Art were married in the courthouse, in a little office so dim the lamps were kept on in the daytime. Her mother had handed Jane her gloves to hold so Art could slip the ring on her finger. The gloves were damp. When the judge said, "You may kiss the bride," Jane closed her eyes. Kylie got hiccups. It all fit. Far across the basin, a coyote yipped.

Later, lying in the dark, she tried to reassure herself by conjuring her mother's face, but it kept sliding out of focus. She remembered instead coming in with her mother from the pasture, picking burrs out of their socks, the kitchen windows opaque with steam from the pot of barley soup her mother had left simmering. The drain basket had been half-full with a wealth of beans, pearly, pink, dusky purple. She'd drawn a heart in the condensation on the window over the sink. She and Kylie used to play with their mother's purse during dull Sunday services, trying on the white gloves, pulling the precisely folded plastic rain bonnet from its tiny pink cylinder, inhaling the waxy smell of forbidden lipsticks, coral and rose and scarlet in their metal tubes. They could never get the rain bonnet back in its case. One winter both girls and their mother had the flu and shared the big double bed to make nursing them easier for Art. In the middle of the night, all three of them aching too deeply to sleep, her mother started singing "Shenendoah," and Kylie started crying because it reminded her of a movie where a cowboy sang "Shenendoah" to his dying horse. "It was Poke Along's favorite song," she wailed. It set them all giggling so hard that Art came in and said if it was so much fun to be sick, they might as well scoot over.

All the good memories were from fall, winter, or spring. From the first hatch of mosquitos until well past the days the weeds percolated with grasshoppers, Renata was with them. Jane could see her tight little grin. It was her mother's face she couldn't quite remember.

Art was already in the kitchen when Jane got up the next morning. His chair tipped back, his feet on the window ledge, he was engrossed in a tabloid.

"Says here," he said, "'Ordinary applesauce can ease the misery of arthritis. Two or three four-ounce servings daily are sufficient to provide dramatic relief.'" His finger searched the page. "'Larene Fortesque of Joplin, Missouri, suffered from arthritis so severe she was unable to tie her shoes,' it says. 'But after just two weeks of adding applesauce to her regular diet, she could return to her knitting and even beat husband Frank in an occasional game of Canasta.' Oughta get me some of that. My legs get so stiff sometimes, I walk like the Mummy after a bad night."

"No coffee?"

"Aw, crumb." Art scraped back his chair and struggled to his feet, "Forgot coffee. Don't know what's got into me. I never forget coffee. Drink enough to keep Juan Valdez in donkeys."

Jane sat at the table and watched him fumble with the coffee maker. She had never known him to swear or drink to excess, and he was so scrupulously honest that on one occasion, he'd driven all the way back to town—seventeen miles—after he'd discovered he'd been undercharged for some paint. Now when he returned to the table, she avoided his eyes and was careful not to brush his fingers when he handed her a mug.

When Renata came to the table, she had her backpack slung over one shoulder.

"Coffee, coffee, coffee," she called. "The only part of me that functions before ten a.m. is my sense of smell. I could drink a whole potful right through my nose. Fill 'er up with regular, there, Pop. I've got eighteen hours of hard drivin' ahead of me."

Art filled her cup. "Why on earth would you be leavin' so soon? You just got here, and we got lots of stuff to go through, yet. Haven't even started on the dishes and the pots. You like to cook. Might get some real use out of those."

"Oh, for pity's sake. She does not like to cook. She didn't come for that stuff, anyway."

Renata looked at her blandly. "That's right. I came to see my Dad." She finished her coffee and stretched. "Besides, anything you got here belongs to Kylie and Jane. I suspect I'll get plenty of junk one day from my own mother."

"I got some poles and lures in the garage," Art said wistfully. "You ever get time to fish, you might like 'em."

"Nope," Renata smiled at him. "I got no room in my trailer for fishing poles. You keep 'em, and when you come down, maybe I'll drive out and we'll go wet a line." She stood up and lifted her backpack. Art followed her out the door, but Jane sat, running her empty coffee mug up and down the crack in the middle of the white linoleum table. There were a few faint orange stains where Art ate.

She could hear Renata say, "What you ought to get yourself is a cowboy hat. Make you look like a real rancher."

"Retired rancher," Art corrected.

"Well, you ought to get yourself one."

"Jane and Kylie bought me one for Christmas one time, but I never could get comfortable in it. All the people that look right in cowboy hats been dead a hundred years."

When she heard the Volvo start, Jane got up and went to the door. Art stood on the porch, shielding his eyes against the early sun, but Jane pushed past him and walked to the car.

Renata rolled down the window and smiled expectantly. "I want you to know," Jane said sharply, "that my mother was a good person. I'm not too sure yet about what you said last night, but even if it's true, my mother had her reasons and she was still a good person."

Renata sighed, searching in her backpack. "Well, you go on and believe whatever makes you happy. All I know is, I got reason to resent her. Hell, am I out of smokes?"

"There's no way to know, now. No way to know for sure. That's why you told me, isn't it?"

"Could be," Renata said mildly. "Maybe partly. I've been wrestling with bygones a long time, I guess. Everybody else moved past what happened, and there I was, cussin' by myself. Maybe I just got tired of my own company." She grinned again and began backing out of the driveway, lifting a hand in farewell, but Jane stood irresolute, and turning, saw that the salute had been intended for Art, who raised a hand at half-mast in response.

Jane started back into the house, but Art took her elbow as she passed.

"Remembered something I was gonna give her," he said. He dug his wallet out of his jeans and began searching through it with unsteady fingers. "Here," he said. "Announcement of her birth. Wanted to show her I kept it all these years."

Jane sank onto the porch step. "That's real nice, Art. A real nice thing to do." Art carefully folded the newspaper clipping and tucked it into his wallet. Jane thought she heard him sniff.

"You can give it to her yourself when she comes to take you fishing," she said, struggling for patience.

Art shook his head. "She won't come see me. Oh, if I call her up, she'll talk to me, but if I write her, she won't write back, and she won't visit me again. She'd rather stew about stuff that happened a long time ago."

There it was, the opening, and much sooner than she'd expected. "Like what?" she asked and rubbed her palms on her knees, waiting for an answer.

Art chewed his lip. He put his wallet back. "I don't know," he said slowly. "Guess she just likes to stew."

I should have known, she thought. She pressed her head into her open palms. Art's hand patted her shoulder awkwardly before it slid off down her arm.

"All right," she said crossly. "All right."

In another moment, she knew, he'd suggest going back in and sorting through some more stuff. The thought of her mother's old metal colander and striped iced tea glasses in the hands of strangers didn't bother her anymore. Strangers would not sense her mother, her mother's doubts, and beauty, and memories.

Halfway across the dusty lawn, she saw a silvery glint. "Look," she said, "your keys." But Art chewed his lip, contemplating the peeling paint on the porch step. She stood and tapped his hearing aid. He turned to her blankly, and she tried to see down the years into his gaze, but it was like looking at an old photograph. There was nothing at all beyond those cloudy grey eyes.

## DAVID McCUMBER
### LIVINGSTON, MONTANA

*A world traveller with an eye for the unique writing subject, David McCumber abandoned what he calls "corporate striving" to work as a cowboy and writer. He is the author of* The Cowboy Way: Seasons of a Montana Ranch, Playing Off the Rail: A Pool Hustler's Journey, *and* X-Rated: The Mitchell Brothers, a True Story of Sex, Money, and Death.

# Under Quick Hail

Dig your sticks in silt under black water. Wish
for a barstool and a sweating golden glass
next to a sweating golden woman,
still barely possible: Nights stay gold
past eleven in June. Hurry. Weight
the dams with all your reasons. Walk
endless ditches clogged as hallways
in nursing homes. Kill thistle. Kill
burdock. Shovel out cuts in the damp earth.
She won't wait until closing. Flood it now
and save your excuses for the second cutting.
Figure on swathing soon to green
days of early darkness: Keep
all you can for the madness below zero.
Alfalfa flowers nod like addicts under quick hail.

# Trout Know the Truth

in the spin of a spent mayfly
truth in nymph and dace
truth now in the late summer thrum
from the grasses

by the river, we know mostly lies.
in the young season pretty
little fibs will do, tied on tiny hooks:
midges, tricos, ignorance of baseballs

through windows, stolen rides
on old ford flatbeds, lust
and pabst blue ribbon spilled
in freshcut moonlit fields

of timothy. later in the low revealing
water of september we require
more elaborate deceptions,
lies with wings

and legs: joe's hopper,
flying ant, forsaking
all others, just one more,
a hurried hotel room in the heat

of the afternoon. yet this year
there is no need for artifice.
we spin and love above
the river. it is enough

to know the truth in your eyes.

**David McCumber:** *Poems*

---

# A Place to Put Things

Stalls where horses dead now fifty years
ate oats grown in forgotten fields
are stalls still, rough-notched and square-nailed.
Doors hang on hand-forged hasps and hinges,
harness yoke and bridle
with mended rein remaining.
Stalls still, filled with things left idle:
A flat-head six that knew too much
of heat and cold and country. Swather wheels
that turned on ground
that turned from range to barley. Drive shafts
welded shut to pound steel posts,
rat-chewed canvas dams,
fencing pliers rusted open, fifteen
shovel handles, busted. Hip roof stops only half
the sky, so this became a place to put things
halfway cared about. Sun and snow and birdshit
fall on floorboards ricked and gaunt
as an old cow's backbone. No love
is made in the loft. Nothing up there
unless you count dented irrigation pipe
and the rear end of an Allis-Chalmers
no person living on this outfit
ever drove. Still good but long ignored. New things
break quickly. Old things get older,
fall from favor, purpose leaked away
with someone's faded plan to turn work and land to cash,
buy a pretty dress for a redheaded daughter gone.
Ninety years in the lee of a little hill
in the Belts somehow made this old. Knapweed
pokes through knotholes in the north wall. Deer
still come in the evenings to find spilled grain.
The new tractor spends nights elsewhere. Horses
graze the hillside, and the stalls no longer hold them.

## GARY FERGUSON
### RED LODGE, MONTANA

*Gary Ferguson is the author of fourteen books on nature and science, including* Walking Down the Wild: A Journey Through the Yellowstone Rockies, The Sylvan Path: A Journey Through America's Forests, *and his most recent book,* Shouting at the Sky: Troubled Teens and the Promise of the Wild. *A winner of the Lowell Thomas Award, Ferguson has appeared widely on radio and television programs, and his nature essays can be heard on National Public Radio affiliates across the country.*

# from *The Yellowstone Wolves: The First Year*

It begins at a time of few beginnings. On one of those March days gray and sharp as steel, full of snow, winter still sprawling on its belly like some belligerent sow bear, chasing the early bluebirds back down to the lowlands, showing no sign of ever giving Yellowstone back to spring. A time of illusions. Back and forward and back again, pulling and pushing, creatures of all kinds running after the season like beachcombers hurrying down the sand behind the surf hustling for treasures, only to be chased up the shore seconds later by the rush of waves. On the warm afternoons elk paw through to the ground for mouthfuls of fescue and wheatgrass, then lose their pickings the next day under a fresh layer of snow. Yesterday a mule deer carcass was starting to thaw under the drifts near Buffalo Creek, ripe enough with scent for any coyote within two hundred yards. By this afternoon it will be frozen fast again, barely detectable to even the best of noses. Tiny midges work their way up through layers of snow, food enough today for a couple of brave robins, by this evening out of reach.

Waiting. All of us, just waiting. For the glide of sandhill cranes. For the honk of Canada geese on the nest. And this year—the first time in almost seven decades—for the wander of wolves.

We're in that part of the park scientists have long considered a kind of wolf wonderland, lupis paradise—swales topped with dark coniferous forests; long, grassy meadows; and hushed, sheltered hollows rich with aspen. And best of all the Lamar Valley itself, winter home to great waves of wildlife—seven hundred bison and thousands of elk—and in late spring enough winter kill to fill the bellies of every kind of predator imaginable: coyote, raven, and mountain lion; grizzly and fox; eagle and badger and beetle. Three separate groups of wolves have been penned in this area since January—five animals near Soda

Butte, six at Crystal Bench, and three at Rose Creek. And while at this point no one can guess where any of them will end up, after nine weeks of capture and confinement—surely about as close to nonexistence as a wild wolf could endure—life is about to start up again right here, an easy lope from the ice-laden waters of the Lamar.

The date is March 23rd. Two days since the gate was locked open on the Crystal Bench pen. After literally decades of preparatory research and logistical planning, after more public comments than have been received for any wildlife or environmental program in American history, after lawsuits and death threats and hate mail, the last barrier to wolves running free in Yellowstone has fallen. "We expected the wolves to dash out as soon as we stepped away from that gate," says wolf project biologist Doug Smith, a tall, lanky thirty-four year old fresh in from Minnesota. "In fact our biggest concern, what we planned for, was how best to get out of the way." Not that this concern was based on any sort of fear, mind you. More of a caution to give the animals the kind of space they'd need to leave feeling safe, calm, not prone to hit the great wide open at full tilt. An attempt to "soften" the release. And yet true to their reputation for unpredictability, to that uncanny habit wolves have of doing things that humans clearly don't expect and can't understand, getting out of the way is the last thing the recovery team needs to worry about. As it turns out there's plenty of time for the men to flip that gate open on the Crystal pen and hustle back to the trailhead without a single wolf leaving. Time enough down along the highway to grin and shake each other's hands, smoke a round of good cigars, sit at a pullout until two o'clock in the morning listening to the blip of the radio telemetry receiver, waiting to hear a change in direction. Getting nothing.

Six hours later the team is crammed back into mission control—the wolf office south of Mammoth, a tiny brown building fifteen by forty feet—scratching their heads. Maybe they're just afraid to leave, offers Doug Smith, pointing out the strong connections wolves might make between that open door and the humans who've been using it for the past ten weeks. Indeed, while there were few times when the men and women coming through that steel gate weren't laden with goodies, dragging frozen dinners of deer and elk and moose, in truth the wolves reacted to their presence with about as much enthusiasm as the rest of us might muster for a pot luck with serial killers. Pacing in the back of the pen in what would become known as their "comfort zone"—agitated, timorous, as if wanting to spit out the taste of the encounter.

Of course there's a huge silver lining to the Crystal Bench wolves' reluctance to leave the pen, a nugget of good news the team members can fondle whenever they start getting a little bummed over the fact that nothing's happening. It's simply this: At least they're not bolting for Canada.

Outside the scientific community theories about the wolves' hesitation are flowing like junk mail. Commentator Paul Harvey tells his listeners the wolves have become welfare wards, good-for-nothings, too fond of government handouts to ever want to go back and make an honest living in the wild. Never mind that early on many wore their teeth down and bloodied their faces from hours spent chewing on the chain link, trying to get out. Forget that to make any sort of bond with a wolf you have to be on it like a shadow almost from birth, feeding it from your own hand, sleeping with it every night, hugging it like a child with a stuffed bear. But then little of what is said concerning the Yellowstone wolves has much of anything to do with what's real. In the coming months these fourteen animals will rarely be cast as anything but gods or devils, the cure sure to save us or the plague that will bring us down—always either a team of saviors or a herd of Trojan Horses. Never just a bunch of predators, coming home.

The next day the team decides to leave the Crystal group alone and heads out instead to open the gate at Rose Creek. Afterward the men return to the Buffalo Ranch, sit in the bunkhouse well into the evening, pouring down hot chocolate, playing spades and games of chess, waiting all over again. Once more the monitoring equipment is silent. The only bright spot of the day occurs later, up the valley, when the Soda Butte group (still in their pen) lets loose with five minutes of the most exquisite howling imaginable—great licks of soul music, candy for the ears spilling across the frozen landscape.

The next day Mike Phillips makes a call to noted wolf expert Dave Mech back in Minnesota, who goes so far as to suggest these wolves may well starve to death rather than walk into an area of the pen that has such strong links to humans. If that's the case, reason the team members, then what about providing them with a passage way in some other part of the pen, create an exit in a place to which they have less aversion? The team is well aware of those so-called comfort zones, the places along the pens with the long sidewalks of packed ice from the constant pacing, the bowl-shaped depressions nearby where the animals routinely bed down to rest. Perhaps all it will take is to cut a hole in the fence right at the edge of that zone. And so that afternoon a team heads to the Crystal Bench site and cuts an opening ten feet wide and four feet high near the back of the pen, then drops off a little incentive—two deer carcasses, placed just outside the new exit. Bingo. Seventeen hours later, at 9:14 this morning, a Crystal Bench wolf trips the monitoring equipment. Then more signals. At 10:24, 10:27, 10:29, 10:30. Off and on for the rest of the day. Wolves are out in Yellowstone.

Which takes us to the here and now—some three hours after the Crystal wolves start walking out. Encouraged by that success, a small team has arrived at the Buffalo Ranch, and is busy stuffing fence cutters, a deer carcass, and an amazing array of camera equipment into backpacks, readying themselves to hike in and make a similar opening in the Rose Creek pen. Everyone knows the mission: cut a hole in the back of the fence near the comfort zone to urge the male, female, and her yearling pup to leave; drop off a frozen deer carcass just outside the chain link; set up a camera with a fixed focus in hopes of getting a shot or two of the wolves taking their big walk to freedom. And get out. The snow is falling harder—wet, heavy curtains snapped back and forth like sheets on a clothesline in heavy winds. To the south, dark lumps of bison amble along the river, appearing and disappearing, hulking animals looking strangely graceful, even sprightly, tucked as they are into the folds of the storm.

The team members stop to catch their breath near a draw just east of the pen—the place where those faithful Park Service mules, Tack and Billy, usually stop when workers travel to this site by sleigh. From this location it's possible to see the southern-most portion of the half-acre pen, and today the men peer through the falling snow and see what looks to be the adult female, number Nine, trotting nervously back and forth, which is a little odd, because most times at the approach of humans Nine is hidden somewhere in her comfort zone at the back of the pen and it's Ten that's doing the pacing. The approach path drops into a small ravine hidden from the animals, then tops out again at the level of the pen. As a final precaution Mike Phillips will climb up and out of this ravine alone, peer over the lip of ground toward the pen to make certain the wolves are in fact still all there, at which point he'll wave the others on. As usual the talk is in whispers—not as part of some attempt to sneak up on the wolves; their noses alone, some hundred times more sensitive than ours, would make that all but impossible. The idea is simply for the team to throttle back the weight of its presence, to take some of the edge off the encounter.

And then it happens. "For a second or two I can't figure out what's going on," photographer Jim Peaco says about the long, soulful howl that erupts not ahead of him in the pen, where it should be, but from behind, on the open hillside to the east. One of the team members hurriedly retraces his steps back the way he came up the ravine and finds Ten standing on the ridge some ninety yards away, half-clouded in a curtain of snow, staring right at him. That confident stare. "His light gray color, the snow—he looked like a ghost," Jim Peaco says about first catching sight of him. "Just like a ghost." The howling goes on, spiced with a couple of curt barks, a hopping on his back legs and a switching of the tail, classic signs of agitation. The first few seconds are filled with something close to panic. Sinking, heart-in-the-throat distress. My God, Doug Smith is thinking, eyes wide with alarm. What happens if our intrusion ends up pushing Ten out, sends him running across the wrinkles of Yellowstone without bothering to look back, prods him to head far afield when he otherwise wouldn't have, back north toward Canada, searching for signs of his old home? Has whatever social glue that's formed inside the pen gelled enough to hold a mother and yearling daughter together with a male who just nine weeks ago was a complete stranger? or will this be the straw that breaks the family's back?

But Ten doesn't run. Apparently doesn't even consider it. The truth is that in some sixteen feedings from January through March this wolf was never inclined to recoil from humans in quite the same way the other animals did. Instead of pacing the far fence, hugging it like a prisoner on seeing the arrival of the hangman, Ten preferred to cruise at oblique angles to the workers, traveling along the less-beaten paths through the interior of the pen. Not showing aggression; none of the Yellowstone wolves offered the slightest hint of that. But not exactly cowering, either. Kind of like now. Phillips tells Mark Johnson and Doug Smith to drop the deer carcass, while Jim Peaco and Barry O'Neill fuss with setting up automatic camera gear in the midst of the chaos, fiddle for ten minutes with chilled, clumsy fingers, finally decide that it will take too long, give up on it, and begin to move out with the rest of the team. All the while Ten stands on that hillside and continues to howl. In an effort to keep from making any movements toward Ten, the men hurry off by a different route, down the steep side of the ravine; at one point Barry O'Neill, carrying a camera lens the size of a small bazooka, slips off the icy slope and slides down the hill, wedging himself beneath a fallen tree. And still Ten howls. He begins trotting the ridge line to the east well behind them, following. The snow continues, big flakes now, here out of the wind failing plumb, as full of calm as that howl seems full of anguish.

For all the apprehension over the encounter, this is a brilliant, searing experience, a kind of time out of time. It leaves everyone buzzed and breathless, including one researcher who by his own admission has been studying wolves for so long that on some days the animals seem little more than bundles of potential behavior, creatures whose primary magic is their ability to throw wrinkles into the statistical norm.

While team members are reluctant to guess the meaning of this or any other behavior, most find it hard not to think of such a display as entirely a reaction to their presence. A cry of intent. A bright, muscled howling of relationship and territory and propriety, from an animal who is clearly back in charge.

Well clear of the pen site, the men talk it out, over and over again. There's no doubt about it, Doug Smith keeps pointing out: Ten was upset. But while Phillips agrees, he says leaving was the last thing on that wolf's mind. In the final chilling, blustery minutes before walking out at the Buffalo Ranch, some are reconsidering the old adages about the astonishing sociability of wolves, the desire to stick together that has staggered, confused, even horrified humans for centuries. "Man, think about it!" Mark Johnson says. "It'd be like escaping from prison and instead of high-tailing it out of there, which would be the sensible thing, you come back, wait and watch, try to break out your friends."

What no one can guess at this point—what no one would have dared even hope—is that this adult pair has moved well past the point of companionship. Despite being locked away in chain link, Nine and Ten have mated, and Nine is already swelling with pups. In just four more weeks she'll give birth to eight offspring in a makeshift scrape of dirt under a spruce tree high on a hill outside Red Lodge, Montana. Unlike most such births, though, she'll be alone when it happens—watching, waiting for her mate: big, bold number Ten. The animal who, for all his heart and bravado—a few might wonder if not because of it— will be the first of the Yellowstone wolves to die.

The Suburbans and Winnebagos, the Jeeps and the Fords and the Subarus crawl along the Lamar Valley in the dull light of dawn, finally pulling off the side of the road west of the old Buffalo Ranch, so named for having once been used as headquarters to cowboy a dwindling bison population back into healthy herds. Where a month ago a fresh layer of grass grew, now in June tires and feet have worn away the vegetation and packed the ground into hard-pan. Those who have been here before, the veterans, pull in close beside the car next to them, knowing that in another thirty minutes the place will be packed with some forty or more vehicles. Lights are doused and doors creak open and owners stumble into the chilly air clutching tripods and spotting scopes and thermoses of coffee, smiling, offering quiet but excited greetings to those they recognize from having been here yesterday, and the day before, and the day before that. A few of the newcomers look apprehensive. They hold their arms across their chests and hunker against the thirty-degree temperatures, staring at the smears of snow still lingering in the high pockets under Specimen Ridge, maybe trying to figure out how freezing their butts off in the middle of nowhere before the sun is even up could possibly qualify as a vacation. The regulars, on the other hand—those for whom this has become something of a ritual—well, they look to be at the top of their game.

"Looks like clear sailing," Ed from Sacramento calls out in his loudest whisper. As usual he's armed with an enormous, two thousand-dollar star scope which he'll use to scan the hillsides, finding all manner of grizzly and elk—and yes, on most days wolves—only to yield it to a waiting line of excited neighbors, some who have spotting scopes of their own but absolutely none who has one quite like his. You can tell Ed is awfully pleased about his role, more than happy to help, perhaps thrilled that this is one of those very few toys middle-aged men like himself buy that actually turns out to be worthwhile. He says in truth he brought the thing all the way from Sacramento to watch the stars. No light pollution here, he explains. But as late night temperatures dropped into the twenty-something range his wife and friends bailed on him, leaving him to shiver out under the firmament all by his lonesome. Then with the wolves being so visible, well, it couldn't have worked out any better if he'd planned it. "At first we were just coming for a week," he tells me after spotting the day's first pair of grizzlies. "We've got a family cabin up in Silver Gate. But we talked it over and decided we're going to stay most of the summer. I mean what could be better than this?"

Club Wolf is in bloom. As it has been every day for the past several weeks, two hours or so at dawn, two at dusk, rain or shine, blue sky or fog. And while some of those living in the park regret the loss of peace and quiet in the Lamar Valley, it would be hard to fathom a more perfect setup for visitors. Unfold the camp chair or lean against the warm hood of your car, grab the spotting scopes and binoculars, and settle in for one of the greatest shows in the temperate world. Not only regular, almost daily sightings of wolves, but bison and elk and antelope beyond the counting, as well as frequent views of both black and grizzly bears with spring cubs.

This morning a yearling grizzly is offering up fine entertainment, engaged in a loping, hopscotch chase after a sandhill crane, the bird rising and settling back down again just in front of the bear several times over hundreds of yards, the bear finally stopping and looking around, bewildered, as if wondering how in the world he ended up there. Framing the stage on either end of the valley are isolated patches of fog, drifting slightly, swallowing up whole herds of bison and then releasing them, like a sigh.

Several of the wolf watchers are still talking about the special treat they had last night, something not seen before. One of the black yearlings from the Crystal wolf pack was wandering around not far from a pair of grazing pronghorn and, not being too familiar with such a creature, somehow got it into his head to try to catch one. With an explosive kick of his hind legs he broke into one of those fast, ears-back-in-the-breeze runs. Impressive, really. One of the pronghorns lifted his head casually, watched the yearling's approach, and when the wolf was about forty feet away the two of them simply looked at one another, then fired off like bottle rockets across the meadows and over the distant ridge south of the river, leaving wolf panting in the grass.

No wonder these people are thrilled. Mary Anne Bellingham from Billings—M. A., as she likes to be called—has been here with her ten-year-old daughter, Brynn, nearly every day for a month now, for the most part living and camping out of their Suburban. Up every morning at 5:30 to watch for wolves, then out hiking and geyser watching, then back in late evening for still more wolves. Most days Brynn is still very much asleep when the Suburban starts rolling down the Lamar Valley, though she has an uncanny ability to wake bolt upright at the sound of her mother's voice calling out animals: "Coyote ahead. Moose in the meadow on the right. Bison on the road." And of course the comment that gets the quickest rise: "Wolves are out." M. A. is the one Club Wolf member who always keeps the tripod under her spotting scope set at kid level, not just for Brynn, but for any other little person who happens to be around. "The adults get so carried away when they see a wolf," she explains. "Sometimes they forget all about giving their kids or even their spouses a look."

A few minutes later I overhear M. A. telling stories to a young couple from Utah—their first day at Club Wolf. "A month ago we saw them take an elk calf," she's saying, talking fast, nervous with excitement. "You could see the alpha female stand on the carcass, uri-nate on it. Then later the younger ones got in there and fed, were like playing tug-of-war with one of the bones. When the wolves left, one of the yearlings had the bone in his mouth. Just took it with him." The Utah couple acts as if she must be the luckiest wildlife watcher on the face of Yellowstone. They nudge closer. Maybe they're thinking that wolf watching is something like fishing, where you try to hang close to somebody who has just the right *ju-ju* to render fish helpless to resist whatever they throw off the side of the boat. "No, no," she reassures them when they tell her they've never had much luck watching things in the past. "You wait and see. Keep watching and you'll see them. We've watched them, what, about thirteen out of fifteen days now."

Still, the couple seems unsure, like it's going to take an act of God to shake them out of their curse of showing up the day after the best of everything. I'm almost glad M. A. doesn't tell them about last week, the time when three of the Crystal yearlings exploded out of the aspen trees, the black one in the lead carrying a half-eaten elk calf carcass in its teeth, only—a few seconds later—to have an incensed two-year-old grizzly run out of the woods after them. About how the yearling carried his stolen prize into a patch of conifers while one of his brothers, the gray, turned on the bruin and went nearly snout to snout with him, just a few feet separating the two animals—the wolf, satisfied he'd made his point, finally walking off into the woods to get his share of the goodies. And then how bear approached those same woods and yet another yearling wolf rushed out to engage him, this one trying to distract him, to lead him away. But bear kept his eyes on the prize, head-ed into that forest to get his breakfast, walked out ten minutes later empty handed.

All this with sixty or so people gathered at the overlook, swelling fast to nearly a hun-dred, until there was an honest-to-goodness wolf jam the likes of which this park has never seen. Meanwhile Park Service interpreter Rick McIntyre and his assistant, a sixth-grade teacher from California named David Gray, were sweeping their spotting scopes along with the action, calling out the play-by-plays like sportscasters in overtime, trying to cycle through the dozens of frenzied bystanders who didn't have equipment for a fast fifteen- or twenty-second look. And the bystanders themselves—people of all ages, from Florida and Michigan and Japan and Holland—looking at one another with open mouths and wide eyes, laughing and grabbing arms and slapping the backs of strangers standing next to them, some clearly feeling chosen, others not believing their eyes. After watching the bear encounter, one guy in his twenties from New Jersey just shakes his head, apparently won-dering if he'd been had by some Disney-style trick of the Park Service. "Animals don't do that," he says. "Do they?"

The undisputed leader of Club Wolf is Park Service Interpreter Rick McIntyre, a seri-ous, forty-something man with a sense of humor dry as the high desert. Rick has seven-teen years of wolf-watching experience under his belt, having made some five hundred sightings in Alaska's Denali National Park, and another fifty or so in Glacier, in northwest Montana. So driven was he to interpret these Yellowstone wolves for the public that in an unheard-of move he actually went out and raised the funding for his position from private donations. "This is an incredible time for Yellowstone and for wolves," he says. "I really wanted to be here."

McIntyre admits that before coming to the park he would've counted himself lucky to see one wolf in the wild all summer long. But of course things worked out a little better

## Gary Ferguson: *The Yellowstone Wolves: The First Year*

than that. "Here it is not even July, and I've already had 119 sightings. And all of those were right from the park road."

When asked about his favorite sighting experiences, Rick offers pretty much the same answer as a lot of other Club Wolf members, not to mention filmmakers and scientists. "The play," he says. "Those Crystal yearlings have spent so much time at it. Playing tag, ambushing one another, that kind of thing. One of the yearlings has this wonderful habit—when he's feeding, just for the fun of it he'll rip off a piece of the carcass and toss it in the air, wait a second, and then leap completely off the ground and catch it. It's just like a dog leaping up to catch a Frisbee.

"And then the visitors," McIntyre continues, suddenly flashing an uncomfortable, embarrassed look. "Most of these people are seeing a wild wolf for the first time in their lives. And when that happens, well, some of them seem to feel the need to hug the nearest government official, which happens to be me. I mean let's face it, in today's climate there aren't too many times where government workers get hugs from citizens." Indeed, in the coming week a couple in their sixties from the Midwest will be struggling for five days straight to catch sight of a wolf, without success. They'll keep canceling their departure, adding one day to their vacation and then squeezing out yet another, until they just can't stay any longer. When, in the last light of their final night in Yellowstone, Rick spots a yearling wolf and points it out to them, the woman will break down in tears, go up and give Rick the kind of kiss usually reserved for returning war heroes or firemen who pull little kids out of wells.

"There are times," Rick confesses, "when it feels like it's the early Sixties and I'm press secretary to the Beatles. Everything is just so overwhelmingly positive." In truth, sometimes all this enthusiasm for wolves can be a little much. By the middle of June it seems every wolf watcher in Yellowstone knows McIntyre's mini-van from a mile away. Many are the times he pulls off the road to take a leak—and remember, the poor guy's been drinking coffee since 4:30 in the morning—only to have six or seven cars full of excited people pull in right beside him, certain he must have spotted another wolf.

## FORD SWETNAM
### POCATELLO, IDAHO

*Ford Swetnam teaches in the English department at Idaho State University. He also writes poetry and essays, fights range fires, and plays pool. His books of poetry include* Another Tough Hop, 301, *and* Ghostholders Know.

# Thanksgiving Moose

You'd be amazed how many moose
Come and go in the Mink Creek drainage,
Not much permanent water there,
Nor much escape from inroad;

I scared one up last Thanksgiving
As I cut an early trail through snow
That year as generous and unexpected
As the moose who farted to his feet

And moved uphill all tanglefoot
And tangent, his gait reminding me
Of the awkward walk of ready aircrews
With whom I had taken Thanksgiving dinner

In '61 or '62, the laces
In their pressure suits
Loosened in the hope
That none would scare them up.

# Ford Swetnam: *Poems*

After brandy, my host said
"I'll show you where
We keep the bombs,"
And we drove beside a taxiway

To where some big fans
Spun above the ventilating shafts,
The bombs down there like scat
Just off an unreadable trail.

This year in the fresh clean snow
The moose went up the hill and I went down,
He and I by the grace of God alive,
Both leaving traces of our awkward startle

And of the stop from where
We both looked back to see
If what we'd seen was real,
Unlikely guests of one another.

# A Little Too Much Understory in the Yellowstone

I was talking to the night clerk
In the Yellowstone Hotel in Pocatello.
The bar had been closed an hour
And the bus was late. I was in shock
From busted love but my story
Was already old, game nobody
Would stop a car to look at, anyway.

The fight started
On the fourth floor,
A Hebgen Lake rockfall
Down those tight stairs
And narrow landings;
The deskman never turned his head
Until the man and woman,
Gin, garters, and galluses,
Hit the waxed floor
Like a pack of cigarettes
Dropped from a machine.
Then he looked at his watch.

"Meet Sunshine," he said,
"And we call the geezer Old Faithful."

# Large Americano To Go

Companionable barista, young man
With nicely gradated earrings,
Has it vaporizing before I'm in the door,
Trades coffee for money without a word,
Both smiling, we both know
I'm a large Americano
Headed for an onramp
Mondays and Wednesdays.

Twenty-five miles north, halfway there,
Coffee just cooling, ice
In the Snake River shallows,
I raise the cup
To the field of companionable goats
Whose breath is steam this stormlit morning,

And one sip north roll down the window
So the draft horses
Wearing saddles of frost
Can smell the beans,
Heads together in coffeehouse palaver.

# Last Weekend at Old Faithful

Tomorrow the roads close
And the clink and torque
Of tools putting up signs
That animals can't read
Will be loud in the silence.
Tonight there's roaring
In the upstairs bar.

We carry ice cubes onto the porch.
They clink among the crystals
Eddying in the air.
Concentric circles of animals
Shift a social distance back
Even from quiet talk.
Tomorrow the parking lot
Will be one more inedible meadow.

Text swirls in our heads.
My mother wanted
A winter week here
She'll not spend now.
Conversation freezes to the windows.
The geyser coughs
A caption without words.

## SUSAN MARSH
### JACKSON, WYOMING

*Susan Marsh's essays and articles have appeared in* American Nature Writing, Sierra, Northern Lights, Orion, Edging West, North Dakota Quarterly, Petroglyph, *and elsewhere. She oversees wilderness and recreation programs for the Bridger-Teton National Forest.*

# Beyond Thunder Mountain

At dawn, a cloak of mist wrapped Yellowstone Meadows. Wandering through a willow flat, I watched dew-beaded spider webs flicker with the first rays of sunlight. Over my shoulder and two thousand feet above, Hawk's Rest pointed its fingers of stone toward the sky, while at my feet, gentians strung a violet ribbon along the sweet, damp earth. Beyond flowed the Yellowstone River.

The Yellowstone: haunt of wolves and grizzly bears, legendary trout water, carver of canyons in the world's first national park. From this far corner of the Teton Wilderness rose seven hundred miles of free-flowing river.

I had spent a week in the upper reaches of the Yellowstone, my task to evaluate its merit as a Wild River. The job felt like stating the obvious. At first I was eager to conduct a Wild and Scenic Rivers study—a chance for some real conservation work while spending time in the mountains. But I did not anticipate the discomfort I would feel in the position of judge.

The last time I stayed at Hawk's Rest, the ranger had shown me trail projects and outfitter camps. My only time in the company of the Yellowstone River came when I slipped away one evening to watch its glassy current slide under the pack bridge. As I stood on its banks again, I recalled that evening at the river.

From the bridge, the Yellowstone had meandered in elaborate loops, dawdling over its shallow bed. Upstream, sunset's ruddy alpenglow hovered on the west face of Thunder Mountain. How I longed to follow the river around the mountain and beyond, to where it split into twin forks cascading from the crest of the Absarokas. The Yellowstone flowed from the most remote wilderness in the Lower Forty-eight, as far as one could get from a road. Thunder Mountain blocked my view of those mysterious headwaters while an imagined scene burned itself into my dreams.

# RING OF FIRE

The sky paled into dusk as I watched the river glide beyond the bridge. Thirty feet wide between walls of willow, the current was deep enough to float a kayak. In my dreams, after visiting the headwaters, I would take my little boat and drift away, arriving days later at Yellowstone Park's Lake Hotel.

The clang of a horse's bell snapped me back into the morning at hand. Breakfast to eat, camp to break. Today, at last, I would see what lay beyond the citadel of Thunder Mountain. I left the river to its silent flow.

The fog had dissipated by the time Ray and the mules filed onto the trail ahead of us. I rode between Jamie, an archeologist with a knack for finding stone tools at every rest stop, and Rebecca, who oversaw field management of the Teton Wilderness. Ray, a veteran ranger, worked for Rebecca.

Dust boiled in a powdery storm behind the mules. Ray twisted in his saddle, watching for loose ropes and shifting loads. Jamie eyed the ground, watching for glints of obsidian. Rebecca and I alternated between conversation and reverie. As we followed the river upstream, I stood on a stirrup for photographs, vainly trying to keep my horse's ears out of each picture.

I scribbled in a spiral notebook, recording what I saw. Aspens sprouted from under a forest fire's blackened snags. Riverside willows flashed the signatures of their species. One spread upright branches, its leaves thick and glossy. Another waved long, slender wands. A compact, silver-leafed species hugged a dry channel. Together they wove a tapestry, threading the meanders with a cloak of dense foliage. I jotted their names—Booth's, whiplash, coyote.

Hours passed as the horses carried us along a trail they knew by heart. Hawk's Rest receded into the distance, then disappeared behind enclosing curtains of cliff. Ahead lay a great wall of carved volcanic ash: Thunder Mountain. Like an accordion, it unfolded across the sky.

We stopped for lunch at Castle Creek. In the miles from Hawk's Rest, the river had dwindled from a maze of oxbows to a shallow, quick cascade. I wandered along an emergent bar where Castle Creek met the Yellowstone.

Triangular imprints of Canada geese crisscrossed the shoal. A necklace of branched impressions, like fossil dinosaur tracks, marked the path of a sandhill crane. Knob-toed bear prints were inscribed by the tiny glyphs of water beetles. Cloven tracks dented the fresh mud—a pair of elk, a skittering of deer. Traces of a moose overlay them, the deep, wide saucers of its hoof prints filled with river water.

As I studied the archive of wildlife crossings, I thought about the stack of river inventory forms waiting in my saddlebag. I should be writing this down. But the August sun combed and teased the riffles, and iridescent dragonflies darted at the river's edge. I closed my eyes to absorb the heat reflected off the face of Thunder Mountain, struck by an urge to undress and jump into the water.

I took a few photographs and scanned the shorthand in my notebook. What equipped me to evaluate this river, to answer with certainty the questions on the inventory form? They attempted to quantify the unmeasurable—beauty, wildness, the river's capacity to inspire. The importance of my task weighed on me; could I do justice to this river?

# Susan Marsh: *Beyond Thunder Mountain*

I was supposed to restrict my attention to the river itself, a problem I had not resolved in two summers of Wild and Scenic River surveys. How could I ignore the canyon around me, or the trail that brought people to this gravel bar at the foot of Thunder Mountain? Taken out of context, each stream varied from the others only in minor detail—the rocks and vegetation, the water's clarity, the shade of blue or green that settled into pools. But a river was more than flowing water. I would never see the same water curling over a boulder twice, yet every time I went to that boulder I would call it the same river. A river included the landscape it carved, each part evolving at its own pace: water, floodplain, cliff bands, rim.

And, as surely as it carried water, the river carried dreams and imagination, history and legend. I could not enter the portal of Thunder Mountain and the upper Yellowstone without falling under the spell of its particular beauty and my overlay of dreams. The earliest trappers and mountain men passed this way, the famous and the notorious: Buffalo Bill and Beaver Tooth Neal. This river bore the name of the world's first national park. I could not separate this knowledge from the water that passed before me.

Pay attention, the river seemed to say. Pay attention in bear country, especially. I focused on a set of tracks at my feet and imagined the grizzly that had left them in the slick mud. It probably dozed in a cool retreat under the willows, not far from where I walked.

A sudden shriek spun me around. I turned to see Rebecca grinning as she emerged from an ice-cold pool.

Beyond Thunder Mountain we entered a narrow gorge. The enclosing forest brought welcome shade after the hot brilliance at Castle Creek. A scent of conifers followed as we rode beneath the brow of the Continental Divide. High above, platinum blonde grass rippled between dark cliffs on a breeze that did not reach the canyon floor.

The sun was still high as we trotted across a meadow into camp. Released from cinches and woolen saddle blankets, the horses rolled in the grass and shook like wet dogs. As I unfurled my tent where I could listen to the river all night, a sequence of chords floated on the warm air. Rebecca strummed the guitar she had top-packed for sixty miles across panniers full of grain.

The trail continued upstream, inviting me to follow, so I did. The air around me lay still, while a strong wind ripped with a sound like falcon's wings among the spires of overhanging rims. Strands of cirrus streamed across the spires, making them appear to sway, making me dizzy to watch.

A half-hour from camp, I walked out of the forest into a meadow with a view straight up the river. A wedge of mountain cleaved the valley and split the current in two. North Fork, South Fork—the birthplace of the Yellowstone. Between the branches Younts Peak shone like brass in the evening sun. I imagined sitting up there in the wind, watching the sun set. No matter how far I traveled up the Yellowstone, it would always beckon farther.

I stepped onto a slab of polished stone in the river, where the waters of its forks had not completely mixed. Like eager twins, the branches of the Yellowstone tumbled from the arms of the Absarokas.

Shadows climbed Younts Peak as blue dusk filled the canyon. I bent toward the river and dipped my fingers in. On its way to North Dakota, the young river rippled down the mountainside with purpose, rushing toward important errands: to wash spawning gravel for cutthroat trout, to float rafts and dories, to water corn and sugar beets. I cupped my hands and drank.

Back in camp, I pulled out an inventory form and laid it on my clipboard. The first question droned at me like a jaded postal clerk: "Scenic quality outstanding for most of the river segment?" I paused at boxes labeled Yes and No.

Hell, no, I wanted to write. Scenery described a backdrop to observe from the window of a speeding automobile, a distraction for bored tourists, a faded postcard with a bleached-out sky. There was nothing like that here. The river I had followed all day, from the gentian-splashed willow flats under Hawk's Rest to the canyon at its source, had enveloped me with wind and sounds and smells. It absorbed our little party into its timeless flow. Here I stepped into the sublime and drank from the cup of history.

There wasn't room to put all that on the form; instead I checked the box, Yes.

Next question. "Evidence of human influence on natural processes minimal?" Yes, yes, of course, I muttered. I would answer Yes to all nine questions on the form—was there ever a doubt? I imagined calling Rebecca over to announce, "Hey, look here. I just filled out the form, and guess what—this river is a Nine." She would nod, gaze past me toward the blonde-grass cliffs, and go back to playing her guitar.

I sighed, put the clipboard away, and unfolded a topographic map.

As I pressed the sheet against the ground, everyone in camp gathered like moths to a flame. Eager fingers traced the trails. We pointed to the stretch of dark mud where we had followed bear tracks for a quarter-mile, an oxbow on Thorofare Creek where two bull moose had stood in the shadows as we passed, and a spring where we had found wild chives to enliven the evening's spaghetti. Under our fingertips, the map came alive with memories, recording our journey in the language of the land.

We crowded around the map until we could no longer see it. I wondered at its ability to deliver the bite of wild chives, the thrill of bear tracks. This map, like my river inventory forms, contained only factual information—elevations, geographic features. Why did it hold us until dark?

In simple cartographic letters, the map announced names. Yellowstone. Thorofare. Hawk's Rest, Thunder Mountain. Names of legend, recalling the river's place in history, the passing of adventurers, the magnificence of mountain and sky. I was glad to have these names to echo in my mind.

Months after the pack trip, I labored over my Wild and Scenic River report for the Yellowstone. I described the scenery, the vegetation, all those willows. Attributes that might meet the Wild and Scenic Rivers Act requirement that a stream be "outstandingly remarkable."

The handbook I referred to stated it was up to my professional judgement to determine a river's eligibility. Outstanding had not been in question when I perched on a rock watching the sunset burnish Younts Peak. At the same time, the Yellowstone at that far reach was just a little creek, murmuring over its cobbles as did hundreds of other streams in northwestern Wyoming. I would have trouble arguing with anyone who claimed it was merely typical.

I scanned my draft report—a litany of bears, trout, and willows. It read as though I were outlining the physical properties of gold, things like softness, malleability, and specific gravity. Information that described the metal but did not hint at the reasons it was so highly prized. Likewise the river: sterile descriptions told nothing of the way I had experienced it. Bear tracks, wild chives, and the sound of wind in the rimrock were more to the point. The topographic map had invoked these; my report did not.

For inspiration, I glanced through my field notes. A creased and stained map slid from the leaves of inventory forms. As I unfolded it, a particle of sand from the Yellowstone River fell into my hand. It was translucent, pale amber, and roughly round. It gathered and held the November light like a tiny sun. I sat for many minutes rolling the fragment in my open palm.

Returning to the map, I fingered an egg-blue line that curved toward the far corner of the page. I traced the Yellowstone as it swept upstream, beyond Hawk's Rest, beyond Thunder Mountain, to headwaters spilling from the apron of Younts Peak. The line began to blur, replaced in my imagination by the chatter of snowmelt over cobbles and the wind moaning among basalt spires far above.

The harsh fluorescent light over my desk faded to a moonless night in August. Frost gathered on the meadow grass as Rebecca played her guitar, laughing between forgotten, invented, and finally remembered lyrics. We lingered late, singing to a sky full of stars. Music blended with the tingkling of horses' bells and the gentle slap of the rising Yellowstone, and drifted into the night.

I began to allow words like spectacular and wild to slip into my sentences, writing with more enthusiasm.

## THOMAS MCGUANE
### MCLEOD, MONTANA

*Thomas McGuane is the author of several highly acclaimed novels, including* The Bushwhacked Piano, Ninety-two in the Shade, Panama, Nobody's Angel, Nothing But Blue Skies, *a collection of stories,* To Skin a Cat, *and a collection of essays on sports,* An Outside Chance. *A Wallace Stegner Fellow at Stanford University, he has won the Richard and Hilda Rosenthal Award of the American Academy, and was a nominee for a National Book Award. McGuane is also a rancher and serves as a director of American Rivers and the Craighead Wildlife-Wildlands Institute.*

# Fishing the Big Hole

I fish all the time when I'm at home; so when I get a chance to go on a vacation, I make sure I get in plenty of fishing. I live in south central Montana, and because of the drought and fires of 1988, it resembled one of the man-made hells like the Los Angeles basin or America in general east of St. Louis that year. I make a trip every summer to fish the Big Hole River, and that year, because I knew that is somewhat out of the range of smoke and ash and heat, I particularly looked forward to it. My friends Craig and Peggy Fellin have a small fishing lodge, with a capacity of eight, and I am perhaps their most regular annual guest.

Montana is so large and contains such a diversity of distinct regions that a trip from where I live to the southwesternmost corner, the Big Hole, provides a tremendous transition of environment, change of weather, change of terrain, change of culture. The Big Hole ranchers are different from the other ranchers in the state and many of their farming and stock management practices are also different. The age of that district is seen in the old ranch headquarters, the hoary barns, the places founded by Frenchmen and fur traders, the stables that once held famous racehorses, and, one valley over in the Bitterroot, the old mission churches.

But to head across Montana in '88 was alarming. With limited annual rainfall, much of Montana's appearance is desertic to begin with. But that year the yellow desiccation of midsummer crawled closer to the green shapes of mountains, until finally the wooded high country stood in a sort of ghastly attendance over what looked to be a dying landscape. Then all the fires began—first in Yellowstone, then in the Scapegoat and Bob Marshall areas. Inspired by this festivity, Missoula arsonists began to have at it until the feeling began to be that, generally speaking, the state of Montana was on fire.

# Thomas McGuane: *Fishing the Big Hole*

Water had become fascinating. It was fascinating to water the lawn. It was fascinating to direct a fine mist at a flowerpot. It was fascinating to take a bucket and measure the flow of water that filled the tank that watered my cows. It was fascinating to watch the saddle horses dip their muzzles in a spring. Suddenly other things in the landscape were not interesting. Wind generators were not interesting. Electricity was not interesting. Power lines were not interesting. Telephones were not interesting, and all the wires and relays over the prairie that laced this largely empty region to the fervid nation were not so very interesting anymore. Water had become the only interesting thing. It had rained one-quarter of an inch in three months. I had watched water-laden clouds go overhead at terrific speed without losing a drop. Montana was getting less rain than the Mojave Desert. The little clouds that look like the clouds on a baby's crib were the sort of thing you wanted to shout at. Wind beat the ground on the rumor of water. Cowmen hauled water to battered unusable pastures to feed cows and calves. Forest springs remembered by generations suddenly went away.

I drove west on the interstate along the Yellowstone River. A big Burlington Northern train came around a curve in the river in the dry air. It approached in silence, then was alongside me at once in a whirring rush of metal and movement. Astonishingly, the air was filled with a train smell, a sort of industrial smell that stood out sharply in the drought-stricken air. But the ash in the air was from the fires, and the smoke that poured out from the valley of the upper Yellowstone had the inappropriately sentimental tang of autumn leaf-burning. Still the train rolled on, and the first thing one wondered was whether it was a machine for starting fires or not.

As I climbed toward the Continental Divide, it did seem that things were a little greener. Some of the hay meadows actually looked like they might be producing hay instead of emergency pasture. Passing through the round red rocks of Homestake Pass, wadded together like enormous pencil erasers, I descended toward Butte and stopped to refill my tank. While the attendant cleaned the windshield, I stood inside the cool gas station and looked at pictures of Our Lady of the Rockies, being constructed. Great cranes brought workers and their equipment to her vast robes. A helicopter arrived with her head. No other town in Montana felt so strongly about the Virgin Mary, and it brought to her memory a mighty effort.

As I headed south toward Idaho and the Missouri headwaters that I love to fish, I had some nervous thoughts. I knew that sections of the Jefferson, the Red Rock, and the Big Hole itself had dried up because of irrigation. Montana has no provision for decreed instream use of water; in a bad year, agriculture can take it all without regard to fish or the fishermen who spend more than $100 million annually. Montana farmers and ranchers make thousands of new enemies each year over this issue, and those enemies are becoming a political force that would like to review not only the efficiency of their water use but other subjects as well, such as the constitutionality of their grazing-lease arrangements on public land. Vestigial rivers flowing out of the smoke only make the plight more emphatic.

I took the turnoff toward Divide and saw the Big Hole for the first time since last year. The extremely low water just kind of percolated through rubble rock. Nevertheless, the beauty of the river's narrow valley, the sage-covered walls, and the slit of railroad bed on the far bank seemed quite intact.

I turned up the Wise River from the town of that name. The river headed into the

Pioneer Mountains, and as I started up its valley I eyed its floor with the same thing in mind: Any water? A short time later I unpacked in my wonderfully comfortable small cabin on the side of the river. Water raced by! Irrigation water went overhead on a trestle-like affair. Standing underneath it on my way to dinner, I could smell the cold runoff dripping down the timbers that held it up. I was starting to feel encouraged, starting to feel that my fly rod might not have been a purely comic utensil. There wasn't even any smoke in the air.

I had a beautifully prepared meal with the Fellins and their guests. This small lodge seems to attract fairly serious fishermen. So the gloomy enthusiasms, the burst of ill-directed sexuality, the unwelcome appearance of the alter ego, the showdowns between couples, and the displays of minor violence that one associates with high-powered sporting lodges are absent here. One dines well and sleeps comfortably, storing maximum energy for the rivers.

I headed for my cabin early. The Fellins' big Labrador male accompanied me partway. He didn't stray far, because in the nearby bush there were moose, which chased him back to the house. It is a great pleasure for a family man to sleep in some building by himself once in a while; I slept the night away in a kind of mock-bachelor bliss, the windows wide open and the chilly mountain air pouring over my lofty comforter. My first home was made of logs, and the smell and solidity of those structures restored my highly eroded sense of well-being. I began to think of sallying forth with fly rod in hand to tune and sample the universe in the name of trout. This has been an issue of consequence since my bow-legged early childhood, and the feeling has grown stronger.

It was early in the morning of a beautiful summer day in Montana. What more could be asked? Hawks threw their cries against tall red cliffs along the Big Hole, then soared into transparency against the brilliant blue sky. The peculiar sluicing movement of the dewatered but still-beautiful Big Hole at the base of the cliffs and railroad bed, the powerful sage smell, the bright yellow clusters of drought-resistant resinweed, and here and there the slowly opening rings of feeding trout brought me on point. I suddenly longed to see the loop of my line stretch over moving water. The float, the gulp: This way, please.

We went to a portion of the river that split into two channels, one of which slowed down considerably and presented an ideal place to ambush fish feeding on tricorythodes, better known as tricos. These are minute, clear winged mayflies as beautiful as all the mayflies whose poetic forms have found their way into the imagination of sportsmen, certain of whom have taken pen to paper.

By the time we reached the stream the duns were hatching and the forms of rising trout, variously called "sipping," "slurping," and "gulping," opened upon the water. The duns are the immature forms of mayflies, recently transmuted from the nymphal stage, and they are reasonably easy targets for trout. The tricos are unlike other mayflies in that they complete their cycle in a matter of hours instead of days. To the angler this means that good fishing is to be had while the duns are on the water. A few hours later an even better stage, the spinner fall, commences: Duns that flew up above the riffles moult and achieve sexual maturity in a whirlwind of sparkling mayfly turbulence, and then return to the surface of the streams to lay their eggs. At this stage they are duck soup for feeding trout, and the alert angler may now slip up and catch a few.

During the emergence of the duns, I managed to catch a few small but handsome and always mythologically perfect and wonderful brown trout. Trico fishing is never easy, because the flies are so small, size 22, and they're hard to see, especially if one uses a truly imitative pattern. I ended up using a small Adams, which says "bug" to the trout in a general but friendly and duplicitous way. I was swept by the perfection of things, by the glorious shape of each trout, by the angelic miniature perfection of mayflies, and by the pure wild silk of the Big Hole River. It is for such things that we were placed on this careening mudball.

Overhead, the duns had accumulated in a glittering, transparent mass. We awaited the spinner fall. The duns gradually stopped emerging. The trout that had been feeding in the riffles tailed back into the slick water. We watched and waited for the thousands of sparkling creatures to fall to the hungry trout. Then the wind came up and blew them all away. End of episode.

We were able to float one section of the Big Hole, though the long riffles were shallow and noisy under the boat. Floating is a fine way to fish western rivers, where the slow and careful dissection of pools is less appropriate than it is in the trout streams of the East. It is also a terrific way to see the country while maintaining an air of purpose. As you float, the all-important bank unrolls before you through the course of the day like a variegated ribbon of earth and water.

It is also the fast way to get the feel of a new river. On the Big Hole there are elbows and back eddies and turning pools of white foam. There are dropping chutes of long bubble trails that hold trout. I've always thought the Big Hole had more midstream trout lies than other rivers I know. Pockets behind boulders are favorite spots, as are places where bottom structures cause angular turns of current where trout can shelter yet watch a steady procession of foods.

The wind followed us to the Beaverhead River that evening. This river is unlike any other in the state. With its brushy banks and downed trees sweeping the undercut banks, it looks almost like a Michigan or Wisconsin trout river. It has the largest trout in the state, and when conditions are difficult, as they were that evening, it's easy to see how they got to be so big. Almost as soon as the fly is presented in one of the holes and notches along the bank, it's time to pick it up and look for another place to cast. It's equally easy to lose your fly in the brush in front of you on the Beaverhead or in the obstructions behind you. The wind really defeated us that evening. Craig rowed heroically, trying to keep the johnboat in position. Just at dusk we stopped to fish a small run. There was an intense hatch of caddis, and in the cloud of insects myriad bats seethed. It seemed impossible to cast through the swarm without catching a bat. I managed that evening to catch a few of what Craig called the smallest fish ever to be caught out of the Beaverhead. But it had been a sixteen-hour fishing day, and my thoughts lay entirely with the down pillow on my bed in the cabin on the gurgling bank of the Wise River.

The next day, another banquet breakfast: baked eggs with asparagus spears, oatmeal pancakes, sausages, honeydew melon, homemade cinnamon rolls, coffee, and the kind of sleepy, merry conversation I associate with the beginning of a day astream. Then we were off on a different sort of junket. This time we drove awhile and then parked the truck and took off on a cross-country hike. I noticed that many of the wildflowers that had disappeared in my drought-ridden part of the state still bloomed here. We had a leisurely walk along an abandoned railroad bed and along the pine-covered slopes of foothills. An old Confederate whose plantation had been burned during the War Between the States had first run cattle here. Then gold-mining ventures, real ones and swindles, found an agreeable setting in the little valley. Now it was ghost towns and trackless railroad bed, sagebrush reclaiming it all into marginal pasture. I picked up an ancient rail spike and slipped it in my vest to take home for a paperweight.

We traversed a high slope above a river too small and fragile to be named, and descended to begin fishing. The river looked plain and shoaly, inconsequential and dimensionless from above, but like so many things in the West that seem flattened by distance and separation, this little river was a detailed paradise at close range. Rufous and calliope hummingbirds were feeding in the Indian paintbrush along the bank, and the thin-water stretches were separated by nice pools. One pool in particular lay at the bottom of a low cliff and held enough water to imply good-size fish. I approached it cautiously and found fish feeding on a hatch of midges. Beneath them were several good trout nymphing and flashing silver messages up through the clear water as they turned on their sides to feed. But the fish were difficult, feeding with extreme selectivity on the midges. I caught a couple of small ones before deciding the pool was spooked, then moved on. I vaguely acknowledged that I had not quite met the challenge of the midges, and challenge I've failed to meet more than once. When flies get much smaller than size 20 and the leader lies on the water's surface like the footprints of water spiders, my confidence begins to dwindle.

Then, at the bottom of a small chute, I caught a nice brook trout. This is not the most common trout in Montana, and, while its introduction was long ago, its accustomed venue is elsewhere. It is a wonderful thing to be reminded of the variety of beauties displayed in the quarry of trout fishermen. You want to cry, as a local auctioneer does at the sight of a matched set of fattened yearlings, "My, oh my!" The brook trout has a silky sleekness in the hand that is different from the feel of any other trout. Browns always feel like you expect fish to feel; rainbows often feel blocky and muscular; but the brook trout exists within an envelope of perfect northerly sleekness. He is a great original, to be appreciated poetically, for he is not a demanding game fish. Some of the most appalling arias in angling literature are directed at this lovely creature, who was with us before the Ice Age.

I moved along the stream toward the end of my trip, thinking about my own part of the state. There the tawny hills had an almost glassy hardness from lack of water, so that the handfuls of cattle grazing on them cast hard and distinct shadows, as though they stood on table-tops and flooring. I intensely valued the stream-bred rainbows I caught, small-headed relative to their breadth and wonderfully marked with bands of stardust pink. This unpurposeful note of festivity is matched by their vital show when hooked, by their abandoned vaults for freedom. The great privilege is the moment one is released, when the small, strong fish moves from your hand to renew its hold upstream. Then it's time to go.

## BURTON BRADLEY
### POWELL, WYOMING

*Burton Bradley is an Associate Professor of English at Northwest College in Powell, Wyoming, where he teaches literature, creative writing, and composition.* His magazine publications include Michigan Quarterly Review, Quarterly West, Northern Lights, Tulane Review, Wisconsin Review, *and many others. He was the recipient of the Loft Literary Center National Award for Fiction in 1996.*

# North Tongue River

Here the river, squat and flat,
meanders a bit,
sometimes into pool consciousness,
and the smallest pond thoughts.
Here's where the mountain lays itself out,
lounging green from its incessant slopes
and tree frenzy in pure flower meditation:
purple lupines and Indian paintbrush,
larkspur and wild geraniums,
with a white-capped kind of Queen Anne's lace
among mountains of mountain bluebells,
all color for color's sake:
lavender and quince and carmine and puce
and grass, god, a litany of liquid green,
chartreuse and emerald, the river alive
in light as silent as the shadows.

# Wyoming From the Tap

Nothing more than this
coldest cold water
in a turquoise mug
deep well taste
with hints
of alkali, iron traces,
a little copper,
and deeper, under the tongue
prehistoric silt,
splintered
shell, a charcoaled drop
of dinosaur blood,
and on the bottom,
just before the end of rock,
a pocket of primordial light
unopened still
in unlit air.

# The Tao of the Red-Tail Hawk

When I am right, really
right, I feel I can fly
beyond my wing span,
where there's no difference
between flying and seeing,
and seeing is nothing
but opening an eye,
and not merely to sight
a field mouse a mile away,
but to feel its small fear
twitching beneath a taloned scalp.

It is not a cruel matter,
but a requirement for balance,
like reflection in winter
atop the coldest tree,
huddled chin to chest out on a limb
leafless as a chicken leg,
with the snow forever falling
like feathers from a heaven of swans.

Summer, my eyes close
in a circle of heat sweetened air
and open above my loftiest desire,
where the last of my red life
blues into a plumage of soaring sky;
gilded by a fierce sun,
I laugh in the eagle's face.

# Trout Mind

I lie beyond mirrors
deep within my liquid center,
far from the loud water,
furiously white above,
forever passing, passing,
so much froth and bubbles—
the stuff of surfaces,
of sun weary worlds,
of life too much like death:
all that green chaos,
utterly selfish, mean growth;
nothing like this pooling,
silver minded and rippleless,
in my own sense of depths.

## GLEN CHAMBERLAIN BARRETT
### BOZEMAN, MONTANA

*A fiction writer, essayist, and teacher of writing at Montana State University, Glen Barrett has lived in Michigan, Wyoming, Washington, and Indiana. Today she lives in Bozeman with her husband, her two children, and several dogs, cats and horses. Barrett's essays often appear in* Northern Lights.

# Off the Road, or The Perfect Curve Unfound

It was the geese that took me to that world without words. And that is how I came, for a summer, to be off the road.

It was May, and I was just leaving Three Forks, Montana, heading east on the interstate, wondering if it was those words the man had said that wrecked us. "I love you," he'd told me, and I sensed when he said them a devotion to language rather than to me, which meant an approaching break up, a faithlessness. He was a writer, you see, and he spoke of how language should be like engineer's curves—perfect tools by which to measure accurately. I liked his metaphor, and the fact that he ignored his goal of exactness when it came to loving me, that he used such a generic phrase to establish his affection, suggested that he was lying.

And so I left him, and I left Seattle, the world of our watery love, to go home to another watery world—my home in Michigan. There I would live on a perfect curve of beach, placing my footprints in the sand next to no other footprints in the sand, a solitary figure needing nobody—no body.

In the late afternoon on the day I left for Michigan, I pulled into Three Forks to buy gas. When I paid, I picked up a pamphlet to read about the history of this confluence of rivers. It said that the Indians considered it one of the centers of the world, and as I drove off, I wondered if this was one of the centers, then where were the others? And how wise was it to have more than one middle to something? I knew enough about Einstein's theory of relativity to suppose it was possible, but then with his theory everything was possible. I also wondered if the Indians knew about the theory of relativity without ever having to talk about it, name it, get words into it, unlike my poet lover.

Given relativity, given springtime in the Rockies, and given that Three Forks is the place where the beating currents of three rivers come together to make the headwaters of the Missouri, I was willing to consider the proposition. And so I pulled off the road to a state park to see what it felt like to be in one of the centers of the world.

That's when the geese came. Out of the deteriorating sky, luminescent as candles in a vee, lit by the dying glow of day and the spark of inheritance which drove them north, they were flying homeward. I, too, was going home. But they were flying; I was fleeing. And they were going together, while I was alone. Once again alone, once again making the decision to leave before being left.

Because of them, I didn't go back to that perfect curve of Michigan beach. I drove for an hour or more thinking about those birds, and then, past Livingston, with an easy turn of the wheel, I exited the interstate at a green sign that simply said, "Crazy Mountains." With that turn, I forsook the one constant companion I'd always had—water—and headed north, north toward the mountains and the geese. I drove along a two-lane tar road for quite a while, crossed its center line onto a dirt lane, and finally travelled onto two tracks. By then it was pitch black, so I crawled into the back of my car to sleep that kind of darkness away.

In the morning, I awoke to snow. The world was as cold as my soul, I figured, and it made me feel good about where I'd gotten off, for I'd never spent time in a landscape that fit my personal geography; I'd always lived in lush, verdant places. Getting out of the car, I stretched while I looked around, and, seeing no one, squatted and watched my own warm waters, gathered during the night, dissolve the snowy crystals on the ground. And there in the dissolution, mixed amidst the pebbles between my shoes, were snails—lake or sea snails—empty and dry. I stood up and scuffed at the snow and dirt around me, where I discovered more and more of them, and then I went to look at a rock outcropping. Embedded in it were the same tiny shells, and imprinted in it were the fans of clams. I spun slowly around looking at this white breast of a dim sea. It was a dead ocean, and it promised a silence I felt I wanted. Why, I didn't know, other than that it had something to do with love and its absence.

I got back in my car and drove on down the two tracks toward the emptiness, until I came to a faded two-story frame ranch house that sat beneath a cliff. When I knocked on the door, an old man answered. He was pulling a canister of oxygen and had a mask over his face. He didn't talk—he couldn't because it would take too much of his air, I figured—so he just motioned me in with his long, skinny, blue, index finger. Then he dragged his oxygen can like a golfer would his bag back to the LazyBoy in the corner; he sat down and watched me with eyes that because of the mask looked unnaturally big.

I watched back.

A long time passed before a woman came in. She was strong and handsome, a palomino-colored woman with big, strong, square teeth and a ponytail. Her name was Eleanor, Eleanor Tate, and she was the owner of this operation, she told me, and the man in the chair with the oxygen tank was Franklin, Franklin Coil, her father.

What did she mean by operation, I asked.

Horsebreeding.

Did she need help, I asked, even though I didn't know anything about horses.

Yup, she said.

## Glen Chamberlain Barrett: *Off the Road*

That summer, I came to know horses—more particularly, Arabian horses. The distinguishing feature of this pedigree is not the spooned out head: those are typical of the Egyptian—the third-world branch—of the family, which leaves the other side—the Anglos—looking normal rather than dinko-cephalic. Nor should Arabs be thought of as black, as kids' storytellers would have us believe. While many start out as jet as shoe polish, just as many within two years have turned a scuffed gray. No, the distinguishing features of full-blooded Arabian horses are their unpronounceable names (they sound like the characters from *A Thousand and One Nights*) and their short backs. Most horses have six lumbar vertebrae; Arabs have just five. That short-coupled back is what gives them their smooth gait.

The other owner of this operation was Bill. Bill Tate. I didn't know he existed until he opened the door one night—about a week after I'd arrived—and walked in, stomping the slush and mud off his shoes, for it had continued to snow. Bill was Eleanor's second husband, and over the course of the summer I pieced their story together. She was from New York state and had always loved horses. At some point early on, she had mixed up her passion for horses with her love of men and married one, a chemist who taught at the university in Bozeman. She said he cheated on her first, but I came to believe otherwise. Oh, she didn't have affairs; she just had a heart filled with 35 Arabs. I suspected that whenever her chemist tried to come close, he got trampled. Finally he had enough and found a young co-ed with an empty heart.

After that, Eleanor took up with Bill, who had once been a dairy farmer in Maine, until his wife fell off a horse and died. Bereft, he sold the farm and came west in search of a new life. He found Eleanor who really didn't want a lover but needed a hired man. If she married him, she calculated, he would work for free. He was a victim, if ever there was one. That first night I met him I could tell because his eyes were set far apart, almost on the outsides of his high cheekbones, like the eyes of deer and elk and antelope—the eyes of those destined to be prey. He was silent like prey animals, too, aware that if he made too much noise, Eleanor would find him and put him to some chore.

Of the three of them, I liked Franklin the best. Most often, he was in the LazyBoy, except when he dragged himself over to the moss rock fireplace, which Bill had built two years before; it was made from his very own harvest of rocks from one of his own fields, and as I came to know Bill it became clear that this was one of his more successful attempts at agriculture. Once the rock hearth was in place, Franklin had taken it upon himself to keep the moss alive by watering it. He would stand there with his oxygen hissing and a little spray can in one upraised arm, pissing out at the moss that never grew. I greatly admired his desire to have a purpose.

I liked him for another reason, too. He liked my piano playing. The piano was in the basement room Eleanor let me use. It had gotten stuck down there when the house was built. Its first owners, who had come west right after World War I on the last and least homestead act, were so enthusiastic about free land that they decided to work from below the ground up, making the basement of a house to which they would add stories as they prospered. They put everything they owned, including the piano, in the hole in the ground and then built above it. When it came time to move their belongings up in the world, they discovered that they'd made the doors too skinny. And so the old piano sat forlornly below ground, ultimately as forgotten as the new dreams it once made melody for.

I liked to play it. I had never been very good, but I'd become used to my lack of talent and enjoyed picking at the keys. I don't think I ever enjoyed playing a piano more than that one in the Crazy Mountains because it was so out of tune it made Mozart sound Oriental. In the concussion of East meeting West, I couldn't hear my mistakes, and it sounded so good. When I finished, I would come around the corner and up out of the tunnel of stairs, and at the top would be Franklin and his oxygen tank, hissing and listening. He reminded me of a fish out of water, standing on its tail, gills panting in and out, desperate for water, and there isn't any, and it is dying. Sometimes I thought a sweet clunk to Franklin's head with a stick would be good, except that he derived pleasure from moss rocks and Chinese music, and pleasure, I have come to know, in whatever paltry form, is what makes life valuable.

It was not long before my thoughts of mercy killing were ended. One June Sunday, a misty moisty morning, I came back to the ranch from my day off. When I walked in the door and looked towards the LazyBoy to wave to Franklin (for I was becoming as mute as he), it was empty. Only the grease smudge where his head had rested and his air can with the mask hanging forlornly over its silver top valve verified that he had ever been there.

Bill was sitting in his chair reading one of his favorite Zane Grey books. "Where's Franklin?" I asked, hanging up my dripping coat.

"Dead." He did not look up. He offered no explanation.

"That's it?" I asked. "Dead?"

"Yup."

"Where's Eleanor?"

He turned a page. "Ridin' Sad."

"Sad" was Sahid, Eleanor's honest-to-God black stallion, the one that didn't turn gray, 22-years-old, her true love and her main livelihood. It was his color that brought mares from all over the country for a costly game of genetic roulette. If heritage spun out right, a new foal would be born black and stay black, and his name would be something like Sahid-al-Jasmine-al-Fed, and he would be worth $25,000 for his color alone. Eleanor hardly ever rode Sahid except in a couple of parades each year. She worried about him getting hurt. I had never seen her ride him, or seen her ride, so busy was she managing the herd. Curious, I put my coat back on and went out.

In the drizzle I walked around the house to the back, where the cliff was. It was a fault, really. The Crazies are full of them. A fault is a crack in the earth where two landforms are exposed when the world crashes against itself, crumpling, bending, pushing, and ultimately cracking. A cliff can be one of the results of this crazy self-destruction. The land leading up to this particular crack I was living under was shale, made of the old ocean bed, and the cliff was made of rich, soft, volcanic soil. It was up there, too, where Eleanor had her arena, the location selected because the ground was softer on the horses' feet. It didn't matter that it was windier and ripped the noses and ears off anyone riding her horses. The riders, after all, were just people.

At first I didn't see anything but an ink blot moving in the gray fog, kind of an animated Rorschach test. I moved closer and squatted along the fault line, watching Eleanor materialize straight-backed, riding that horse around in a prance, his front legs coming up in a high bend before snapping down elegantly. She rode by me, and I could see her back. In all that precision of movement there were big blotches of mud upon her coat from Sahid's hooves. The horse was now crossing the arena diagonally, his front outside leg stepping over his inside one while his strong hind end muscled him forward. He was beautiful. When he got to one corner, Eleanor rode him to the other corner and then crossed him back over the other direction, making a big X in the earth. After that, she posted a trot and made voltés, little circles all curlicued around the perimeter, and then she disappeared out of the arena and into the fog. I could see the precise script of the horse's feet, a perfect, geometric language signifying nothing. I had an inkling then of what it was like to live without words. I think I had come out to say I was sorry about Franklin. But Eleanor didn't need to hear that from me, any more than she needed any words from Bill or her first husband.

When I got back to the house, Bill asked, "Sad okay?"

"Yup," I said, and went to the basement to make imprecise noise on the piano.

The weather worsened that day, and by night there was a terrible wind coming out of the east—a bad sign. When I got up the next morning two inches of snow had been blown in, turning the green world into a blank page.

Bill and I climbed into his old blue truck to go check his cattle—28 head of Hereford cows who were calving. Way out on a high meadow, we came upon a heifer who stood beside a still form in the slush. "Aw, Gaw," Bill whined, showing more emotion than he had for poor old Franklin, I thought. He jumped out of the cab, scooped the calf up and put it on my lap, then punched out of the field as he headed for the house.

"Elnor, Elnor," he screamed, "it's a calf!" and Eleanor came running with towels as Bill carried the baby into the bathroom. He swaddled it, rubbing it dry, until the calf began to shiver. "There," he said, " it'll be awright. Leave it stay here an' warm up."

After breakfast, the calf still lay on the cracked linoleum, making no effort to move. As I cleaned my teeth, I was disconcerted by its big baby blue eyes, circled white with terror, staring at me. It breathed hard, and mucous sprayed out its nose; it was as if its whole body was filled with liquid that shouldn't be there, and little squeaks, like birds caught in a chimney, came from its lungs. That calf reminded me of Franklin, the way it looked and never spoke and the way it couldn't breathe. I looked away from it into the mirror, where I caught the reflection of Bill, who was filling a big dripper with whiskey. "Get down here and rub its legs," he told me as he knelt and squirted the amber liquid into the calf's mouth.

I clenched my jaw, and we worked silently together. As I sat there on a peeling bathroom floor massaging a cow while it drank Ten High whiskey from a crazy man and it snowed outside in June, I figured I had no idea what to say about my life. I was coming to understand the ease of silence.

After the whiskey, the calf's breathing bubbled more. "Don't wanna git the little feller drunk," Bill said. "Come on." He headed back to his chair and again picked up Zane Grey. I looked at Franklin's empty chair and the air tank and grabbed his squeeze-it bottle to water the fireplace. The world was quiet but for the sigh of mist and the hiss of wet wood burning. It seemed so foolish of me, so foolish of Franklin, to try to keep up with the drying elements of the fire which had overcome any water in the logs and now crackled happily, the only happy noise in the house. The idea of happy sounds in that house evaporated as quickly and easily as the water I sprayed when I heard a clickety clack of hooves in the bathroom. Bill and I ran in, and the calf was still on its side, its legs galloping in a convulsion.

"It cain't breathe!" Bill shouted, and he loped out of the room, leaving me with the thrashing baby whose big wad of tongue, turning blue, was stuck to the floor. In a flash Bill was back, dragging Franklin's oxygen tank. He turned the lever, making the can hiss, and grabbed the mask, slipping it over the muzzle.

The opaque plastic cup, which used to cover all of Franklin's face, just fit over the big pink nose of the calf. Its thin lower lip jutted from underneath, and the pastel ridge of its ungulent gums gave a faint promise of teeth, just like a little human baby's. Pretty soon, the steady hiss had a regular rhythm, and the cow took its tongue back into its mouth. Bill removed the mask and gave it another shot of Ten High. "A coupla weeks of this, and the Nips'll want him," he said.

"What's that mean?"

"Kobi ."

"What's that mean?"

"Beef."

"What's that mean?" I followed him out of the bathroom, but he didn't answer. I stood not knowing what to do. Through the living room windows I could see that the weather was lifting, the sun filtering through the clouds, melting the slush, and the new grass outside was the color of cartoon green. I felt an intimation of hope. But just then there came a long, plaintive cry from the bathroom, so I turned back to see what the calf was up to. Its skin lay caved in around its soft ribs, the oxygen all gone from it, air and life expelled.

We loaded the corpse into the back of the pickup and drove it down and away from the cliff, far out and onto the ancient seabed. There we lowered it down like sailors would a body into the green ocean of land for the scavengers to eat. On the way back through the shimmering little grass, I thought about how that calf had died on bad whiskey and pure air. And that was all right. That was all I could think.

The rest of Bill's calf crop slipped with ease into summer, and then Eleanor's baby horses started coming, and the small ranch in the Crazy Mountains was like a miniature Genesis. It was all do and no talk for the most part, and it made me think of the Bible, how I never believed that in the beginning was the Word. I believed that in the beginning was the Deed, which wasn't invented; it was just done. The week the world started must have been a busy one, with light coming on and going off and water fountaining and grass and herbs and trees landscaping and fruit popping and man and animals self-generating. There wasn't any time to sit down and put words to it all. In fact, it wasn't until years later, when Adam and Even had to name the results of their deeds, and Abel and Cain theirs, and all those generations of begats theirs, that humans decided to write Genesis, and they lied, saying, "In the beginning was the Word." I felt myself becoming more and more like Eleanor and Bill, accepting that words were inaccurate and unnecessary. My longings for the poet lover became as dry and dead as the ocean which now grew fragile grass.

# Glen Chamberlain Barrett: *Off the Road*

The summertime came and went, flashing a dusty green and humming a busy song as it passed. And when it was gone, the place was quiet. There were few chores for me to do, so I began to take walks, and I would look at the high autumn clouds like dapples in the sky, grass that cured and spiraled into thin air, aspen leaves that sparkled like meteors as they fell in the sun, and pine that wove itself into the shade of mountainsides. The world that early fall was like a giant lens, smoke-hazed from range fires and casting a filtered but intense light on everything. I waited and waited silently, for what I didn't know—the horizon to the north to burst into flame, maybe, and the firefighters to scurry on it like the freezing flies were doing on the spotted and indifferent rumps of Eleanor's mares.

The first cold snap came then, and the quiet pools of the stream glassed over, entrapping a late hatch in the ice. The little black bugs looked like print emerging on its own out of the middle of some old parchment, indecipherable. I didn't care that I couldn't read it, though, for I had given up reading along with speech. Total silence came when the ravens left, their barks no longer rising on the thermal currents. I was passive with the weather and the landscape, just taking in the particulars of that Crazy world, beautiful and finely etched as foreign script.

Though they hadn't said anything, I sensed that Bill and Eleanor wanted me to leave. There was, after all, nothing for me to do anymore. But their silence continued, for I had come to let them treat me as they treated each other—not overtly unkind, but indifferent. Since they did not articulate their desire for me to leave, I did not need to articulate my reaction. What I would—wanted—to do remained unknown because it was unspoken.

Then one morning I woke with a start of fear. Maybe they would never ask me to go. Maybe I would stay on forever as the crazy hand who sprayed the moss rocks in the fireplace and played Chinese music in the dark. With a momentary energy fueled by panic, I came out of my dark basement dreams, out of the dark basement, up the stairs, out the door, and into the dark dawn. As the black ink slowly washed out of the sky I skirted around the cliff behind the house and up to the arena where Eleanor had ridden Sad, then down again and into the seabed field.

My breath was shaky because I'd been running and I was helter skelter scared, so scared all of a sudden, about becoming dumb. I felt unmoored, and I yawed around that land as the light changed from blue to yellow. There had been no blue to purple to red to orange to yellow, it seemed to me, and I sat down, winded, and wondered how the sky could go from one primary color to another. Given our invention of the color wheel, it seemed impossible. Then I remembered that I was living in a world which had not been overtaken by human invention. It just was. And that was what I thought I wanted.

I sat there frustrated and shivering, staring at the cured grass between my legs, and when I brought my head up, not twenty feet in front of me was a small blue rib bone. I stared at its blueness and its perfect curve which made a parallel arc with the horizon. Crawling toward the rib, I saw the blue fly away, and the bone turned white. It's a vision, I thought, but it wasn't. It was butterflies, tiny blue butterflies, and at least five hundred flitter-fluttered off the rib into the yellow air. I knelt on the ground like a dog staring at a bone, and then I saw the other ones scattered about. These belonged to the calf, the one that drank whiskey and used up the last of Franklin's air. I looked around for my bearing, to make sure it was the right spot. Right spot, hell; it was one of the centers of the universe, a hole in that September morning air where different spaces and times came together and for a crack were measurable with a curve of bone and landscape.

I remembered that once, before I'd given up on love and words, I'd read the Romantics. I learned from them that you can't have continuous epiphany. You can be surprised by joy, and the words that you use to capture that flashpoint of experience must be imitation. They are, after all, only words, and when they are put together by us, they seem like epitaphs to what was real. As I sat on my haunches in that fallen field of grass, I realized I had made a mistake. Those words—I love you—which had seemed so dryboned a half year earlier were not. They were the words of what it is to be human, to be trapped somewhere between the immediacy of life and the imagination it takes to live it, to be somewhere between bones and butterflies. I stared at the bleached rib a moment longer and turned away from the perfect curve. If I didn't, I knew I would go crazy. Or crazier.

As I walked back to the house I wondered if that was what had happened to Eleanor and Bill. Maybe that Crazy Mountain ranch had been a place where they thought they could just experience things, like Eleanor's horses did, without talking, without trying to figure out, for instance, what the word love meant, or how to use it in the dialects of body and soul. Since they wouldn't speak of joy, maybe the remembrance of its existence faded. If this was true, then even though words were epitaphs, they were promises, too. Without them, maybe Eleanor and Bill couldn't imagine love—or anything else, and so for them, delight never came to be. And they went crazy. Or crazier.

I went to the house and packed. They were eating breakfast when I came upstairs to tell them I was leaving and to explain why. My voice was hoarse from lack of use, and my sentences were faltering, but I did the best I could. I told them I loved them. They stopped chewing their cereal for a moment, looked at one other and at me, and then went back to chewing. They didn't say a word.

## WILL PETERSON
### POCATELLO, IDAHO

*Will Peterson owns and operates Walrus and Carpenter Books in downtown Pocatello, where visitors often can find him holding forth on all sorts of literary topics or launching into an impromptu poetry reading by himself or with guests. Peterson is the author of two books of poems,* Luctare Pro Passione *and* The Flows.

# Open Season

There's the story of the trail through the pass
shiny with horseshoes: and all of them
are supposed to be lucky.

But there aren't that many rocks
along West Fork of Mink Creek;
this is the only horseshoe I found.

Some want the whole story right off
and you were one.
By the time we got out of the car
it was like the walk you take
after a beating.

We never know the stories we'll have to tell
thank God and all his horses. It was cold
the creek thick with redbark and aspen
the steam rising from it like incense.

# RING OF FIRE

The deer could feel the cold coming, too
and were down low. Those beauties
that looked back at us would need luck
opening day if that was the pose they would use.

And then to find the ponds
transfigured by drought to stigmata of redwillow.
And to draw you close
under my wing
as night fell; and later that night
the first snow fell.

**Will Peterson:** *Poems*

# For Bill Hogan

He said the river's a lot like life:
there are stretches where the current
just takes you and you watch the trees
along the bank and sometimes deer that come down
in the morning to drink.

And it can be enchanting like at evening
when white birds rise and float
against the sky.

But the river will tell you
when the falls are coming; you'll hear them:
and the things you learn concerning
how water is changed by rocks
and what you learn beneath them
is harder to forget.

It's just that life won't let you know.

But the river will; and if you want
you can just get out and look.

## GENEEN MARIE HAUGEN
### KELLY, WYOMING

*Geneen Marie Haugen's work has appeared in* American Nature Writing 2000; Bugle, *and in other anthologies and journals. She has been the recipient of a Wyoming Arts Council literary award for nature writing. A version of this essay was included in the "Nature and Psyche" issue of the literary journal* Alligator Juniper.

# A Relationship of Substance

Earth: isn't this what you want,
an invisible re-arising within us?
—*Ranier Marie Rilke, The Duino Elegies*

Early Halloween morning, the last day of elk season, I woke in the dark to tree-snapping wind and volleys of hail against the skylights. I nudged David, who rolled deeper under the comforter, covering his head. "No way am I going out there," he mumbled, refusing to budge. Even the dogs only fluttered their ears before resettling on their beds. I stumbled into layers of fleece and GoreTex and walked into the dawn alone as I had so often that autumn, my first season as a hunter.

Friends had been betting one another whether or not I'd kill an elk. Every day someone called and said, "Well?" Stearnie Stearns, who had shot only a few animals in his long life, told me I'd regret it if I killed anything. He suggested I get a paint gun and mark elk with orange dye instead. "I shot a moose once," he said. "I felt so ashamed. It was like killing an old horse."

Other men were only interested in whether I'd fired my rifle—or, since I'd had the chance, why not? Women who were curious about my experience—not just their own opinion of it—wondered how I would feel if I did shoot. One of my sisters wouldn't speak to me about hunting.

I had not wanted the process of learning to hunt to be entirely about killing, but now it seemed that whether I killed or not had become the central point, the target, the bull's-eye. Could a person who had not killed be called a hunter? Was there any reason to stalk wild creatures besides killing? In *Meditations on Hunting*, the Spanish philosopher Jose Ortega y Gasset wrote, "Death is essential because without it there is no authentic hunting: the killing of the animal is the natural end of the hunt and the goal of hunting itself, not of the hunter.... "[O]ne does not hunt in order to kill; on the contrary, one kills in order to have hunted."

On Halloween, time took on an eerie, literal dead-line. After weeks of daily encounters, I hadn't seen elk or recent sign in two days. I was exhausted and wouldn't be sorry for the rest that the end of the season promised, but I didn't know how I'd feel if I ended elk season empty-handed.

Bare aspen arced at alarming angles in the press of wind. Hail pelted me like white BBs. Covered with crunchy ice and snow only days ago, the trail was now soggy and slick, though my steps were quieter. My waterproof jacket was not quiet, but my wardrobe options were minimal: get saturated or make noise. The hail and wind were so loud I figured a rustling jacket could hardly be heard, if at all. Even so, I tried not to move my arms. I held my binoculars still with one hand, and the shoulder strap of my rifle with the other. The sky barely lightened; mostly it turned a paler, tattered gray. Distant gunshots echoed off the mountains—rifles fired once, twice, five times in succession.

The sound accelerated my heart, turned my palms itchy with fear.

The only bullets I'd yet fired were carefully considered shots at a stationary, non-living target. I was not mentally prepared to shoot over and over to bring down an elk. No hunter I'd spoken with had mentioned such a thing except to say, almost as an aside, that I should eject the shell immediately, to be ready to fire a second time. No one had said be ready to shoot the whole magazine. Or more.

Were the hunters whose shots I heard firing at running herds? I tried to make a picture from the sound. Did the bullets miss or hit? A leg, a jaw or belly? How much suffering? Blood thundered beneath my skull like an inside-out drum, pounding out fear: what if I shot an elk and missed the lungs or heart and only wounded?

I knew that even the best hunters lost injured prey. It could certainly happen to me.

Beyond our gate, the land I hunted was a fragment of national forest too far from public access for most people on foot, and with enough fences to discourage horse travel. Surrounded by bigger hunt arenas with easier terrain for horses and ATVs, the pocket I chose seemed to be a small refuge. From the sign in the area, I guessed elk had been returning most of the autumn.

Hail veiled the shadows between aspen and spruce. Branches waved and shredded bark flew through the air like deformed wooden birds. I huddled, shivering, beneath thick trees, and traced a meadow's edge with binoculars. I unzipped my pack and unscrewed a thermos of tea. Because I could hear nothing but faraway gunshots and the storm, I assumed animals could not hear me and I allowed my movements to be casual. When I heard muted squirrel chatter amidst the staccato of hail, it occurred to me that the sonic world of animals is never muffled by walls, glass, steel or stereo headphones. The ears of wild critters must discern the textures of storms as well as the foreign, dangerous sounds layered within. Of course they heard the rustle of my jacket, the zip of my pack.

Of course, they knew I was there.

I thought of the Great Gray owl who had landed on a nearby lodgepole while I hunted a few days earlier. An owl unseen is unlikely to be heard: the leading edge of owl flight-feathers is sawtoothed and silent, and I was grateful to have witnessed the flight of this bird. The owl and I had tilted our heads, studying each other. The close-in squirrels and birds had stopped chittering and calling. The Gray stared at me with unblinking yellow eyes, lifted soundless wings and coasted to a branch directly over my head. The owl leaned down, angled over the limb to examine the odd, upright creature on the ground. I craned my head back to examine the bird's moon face, the twin suns of its eyes.

I knew something about owls; I had field guides to explain the calls, nesting habits, differences in range. I knew, for instance, that the Great Gray is the largest owl in North America, that outside the Yellowstone region, the Gray is rare. Without ever setting my own eyes on an owl I was privileged to information about them, but what encyclopedia of abstract knowledge do birds carry about humans? What knowledge did this owl have about me that was not won through its close attention, its own sensory experience? What knowledge did I imagine I possessed about this owl that was separate from the bird itself?

No field guide could inform me how the owl's feathers formed a hazy nebula around its body; no field guide prepared me for the intensity of the Gray's scrutiny, the fearless, unrelenting stare. No field guide primed me for the relationship, the reciprocal curiosity— but there we were, the owl and I, communicating in some immediate and physical way, arousing each other's senses. The fine hair on my own skin lifted.

The owl alternately peered at me and into the margin of the forest. Whatever drew its attention was not evident to me, not by sound or motion. After awhile, the owl shrugged and spread stealthy wings and drifted toward its prey like a gray ghost.

The silence of the great feathered hunter was its gift and message.

Unlike the owl, my own protective covering had not been designed for sneaking up on anyone.

In the Halloween tempest of hail, removing my noisy purple jacket would make me a candidate for hypothermia, a hunting season finale far more mortifying than not getting an elk. Still, even under petroleum-derived fleece and waterproof fabric, it was possible to move with greater care.

I crept into the pathless forest. Wild odors rose from the damp earth, a message for those who could decipher the language of scent. Stepping carefully over gopher mounds, flattened grass, bear scat and deadfall, moving so slow as to seem hardly moving at all— except when the unaccustomed slow motion caused me to lose balance and tip sideways— I followed faint animal trails. Listening. Turning my eyes toward any movement. Inhaling and sorting the textured odors. Bending to examine elk droppings for freshness. Noting the rise and fall of hair on my neck, tiny sensors that bypassed the analog brain, responding to currents I could not see or hear.

To extend attention beyond one's own body, to be conscious of the body's motion through space, aware of twigs, the moistness or dryness of plants, pine needles brushing a shoulder, musk on the wind, branches snapping in the distance, as if life depended on such attunement: surely this was how animals, both prey and predator, engaged the wild.

The demand on my ears, eyes, nostrils and antennal skin was so great, so exhilarating, so strenuous that I could hardly sustain it.

The storm burst and receded like breaking waves. Gunfire from Munger and Taylor Mountains accompanied the lulls between wind and hail. The atmospheric agitation blasted any sense of comfort or normalcy right out of me. Disoriented, rattled, alien even to myself, I plodded out of the pathless timber to a fenceline and discovered I was lost.

As if I had crossed into another country, I did not recognize any ridgetop or swale. A bulwark of steely clouds obscured the peaks. The terrain I mostly knew from hikes or ski tours was now colored and textured with decay: fallen brown grass, bare and vulnerable trees, blackened, rotting leaves. Gunfire blasted from all directions, unpredictable as drive-by shootings. Few were single shots. The rapidity of some resembled machine guns. I had an impulse to take cover, even though I knew the gunshots echoed from faraway. I walked one direction for a distance, then turned and walked the other, and slowly the terrain regained familiarity. But as if it were another country, the land I thought I knew had transformed into war zone.

Only one side was armed, and I did not find solace in being one of them. I felt like a spy in enemy territory.

Okay, I'll admit I went into my first elk season thinking most hunters were less-than-slime, a pack of power-starved guys who viewed animals as commodities, conquests or peripatetic targets. It was an impression reinforced by the dozens of poaching, antler-chopping, head-decapitating, wound-and-abandon-the animal tales I'd heard over the years, the general, blood-boiling theme of hunting stories tossed like bait to the general public.

I hadn't yet figured out what hunters shot in the middle of the day; my regular sightings had been at liminal light, when elk appeared and vanished with hardly a sound, like ghosts. So I was perplexed as always to hear shots throughout the afternoon all season.

But I was inexperienced, to say the least, with no intention or knowledge of shooting at enormous distance—three or four hundred yards—as some skillful hunters did. Maybe they were aiming at elk they'd tracked all morning. Maybe the lunchtime artillery was—as one cynic had suggested—frustrated hunters shooting at cans.

On Halloween, I had no way to gauge how many—if any—were besotted with both buck fever and last-day panic.

Although I suffered from deadline anxiety, not once during the season had I been tempted to take a wild shot. In my imagination, I was immune from buck fever, a self-protection that enabled me to walk about with a loaded gun. But in truth, does anyone know how they'll respond until a situation presents itself?

A few hours before Halloween sunset, I persuaded David to come out with me, to explore an area I hadn't hunted in a week.

I'd had better luck stalking elk by myself, but I was more than terrified to shoot one. I'd never seen anyone kill an animal. I didn't trust the words of other hunters or the ballistic charts: it seemed impossible that a bullet could take down an elk from any distance.

Which is why I'd kept creeping so close to the herds, so close that I couldn't raise my rifle or move without scattering them. I had felt electrified to be among the elk, hunching over like a four-legged creature, or standing still and erect as a tree, freezing when one looked at me, stepping only when they moved. But if I wanted to take an elk on homeground this year, I had only that afternoon. I could not afford to move into the herd as if I were one of them.

I don't know why I thought David's presence would help—it hadn't helped at all on previous occasions—but I was willing to try again. Surprisingly, so was he. I had a crazed notion that another eye, another voice to say, "Yes, that's a clear shot," might instill confidence.

And admittedly, on the season's last afternoon, David was the only choice I had for a companion.

I suppose I might never have begun hunting without him, even though he was not of a hunting mind and probably would not have considered it himself. He encouraged me in most wild schemes, as when I had hauled him—actually, he'd been a willing victim—to the Arctic to run a remote river that was so braided and shallow that our float trip had turned into an epic two-week raft drag. David had kindly never said a contrary word about my choice of outing.

When I wanted to learn to shoot, he'd offered his gun and gone with me to the firing range. When I wanted more familiarity with home terrain, he'd accompanied me on long, hot hikes. When I attended hunter safety class, he signed up. When I bought my elk license, he was there, buying his own.

But the first morning we hunted together, he had charged ahead, striding uphill as if we were racing to the top. I couldn't keep up, which made me fume. When he finally stopped, I signaled him to wait, and huffed alongside to ask, "Don't you think that hunting might involve some stopping to smell and listen?" He said, "I thought we needed to get higher, to sneak up on the elk." I couldn't imagine how two people practically running through dry, hip-high vegetation were going to sneak up on anything except stooges like themselves.

David had generously let me lead most of the time after that, but every time I sighted elk and knelt down, trying to slow my heart and get a steady aim, something happened. Such as David—who could read neither my jumpy mind nor clumsy body language—standing up and spooking the herd.

Clearly, I had needed to practice hunting alone.

But now, in the vanishing hours and fusillades of bullets, I had no enthusiasm for wandering about by myself.

※

A stream creased the draw and we crouched above it, in south-facing aspen, hoping the brush would soften our human silhouettes. I crushed sage, held it to my nose and rubbed its sharp resin on my clothes. I glassed the edge of the thick timber. The weak sun dropped behind the ridge and the temperature plummeted.

David unzipped his pack and pulled out another jacket, hat, his thermos. He stood and removed his orange vest, shrugged into the red jacket, pulled the vest back on. He layered his orange hat over a warmer hat with ear flaps. He sat down and uncapped his thermos, poured hot chocolate and slurped it. He looked at me.

"Do you suppose if there are elk waiting in the trees, they don't hear you or see you?" I whispered.

"Maybe," he said, gulping the hot chocolate as if we were now only on a casual sunset picnic, as if we—especially I—had not spent the better part of October tracking elk, intending, eventually, to shoot one.

I gave David the evil eye. My scowl didn't phase him at all, accustomed to it as he was. He accepted our different priorities in a most infuriating way. "You can do what you want, Geneen. I support you to do whatever you need to do," I often heard. Which burned me up when it meant he was welcoming me to go in a direction he was not leaning.

And clearly, on this last afternoon of elk season, David was unconcerned about hunting. I tried to hold on to my irritation. This was, after all, my last window of opportunity to shoot an elk close enough to home to pack it to our door without a vehicle. It was my last window from which to announce, "Yes, I did it," to friends waiting with expectation or horror.

A cloudburst of confusion gathered in me, amplified by the slosh of hot chocolate. How fortunate that David had come along: a person never knew when she'd need someone to blame.

I did not expect the tiny bubble of elation that began to form, loosening knots and snared thoughts accumulated over weeks of going into the woods with a gun: I was worn down from worry, rising early, and exercising an intense, expanded attention that was seldom required in my life.

Truth was, I wasn't sorry to come to the end of the first season's hunt. Not sorry for the commotion we made. If elk did not appear now, we—I—would not have to decide whether to shoot one. Wouldn't risk either buck fever or a wounded animal. I could truthfully say what more than a few hunters had been saying all season: Today, I didn't see any.

The bubble rose and burst inside me with the effect of champagne, making me slightly loopy with happiness.

I unzipped my own pack and pulled out a pair of hand-warmers, tore the cellophane, shook the warmers to activate them and stuffed them inside my thin gloves, knowing they would prevent me from operating the rifle. What did it matter? I'd had multiple chances to shoot an elk in my first season, and I'd never even flipped the rifle's safety off. The reasons I hadn't already taken a shot were layered and interwoven—wasn't that bull too old? how would we haul that cow out of the deadfall? would that high brush deflect the bullet? what if I miss?—but underneath there was only one explanation. It hadn't been appropriate. Yet.

I had gone about hunting in my usual I-can-do-that conquistador style. Not to conquer animals but to master the hunter's skill. I'd hunted alone because I didn't want to accompany a wild shooter, or someone who would take a shot on my license, or someone who would laugh if I made (as I knew I would) a ceremony of the elk's life and death. I'd gone hunting with only the barest guidance from elders, mostly because I'd begun the season acquainted with only few hunters, even fewer with whom I felt I could entrust with my first experience of killing, who unquestionably regarded animals as joint tenants of earth, worthy of respectful deaths. As the season went on, I became acquainted with more hunters whose ethics and values I trusted. I followed what spoor they left that I could decipher. But the trail that appeared for me was not anyone else's path.

I needed to walk out to the elk alone, to learn in the way I learned best, from my own kinesthetic experience. Naturally, in keeping with all previous attempts at instant mastery, the biggest revelation was how wide was my space of not-knowing.

I had never before followed the migration so closely, never known exactly what stand of trees the herd favored for cover. Never before had I found generations of antlers shed in undisturbed groves, never had an elk pass me a few dozen feet away, only the flicker of her ears registering any disturbance. I'd never before had a bull stare at me without fear while I raised and lowered, raised and lowered my rifle; never turned my ears and feet toward the eerie sound of bugling before dawn. I'd never before heard the rough warning barks of the guardian cows, the bleats of anxious calves. I'd never scented elk before I saw them, never heard fencewire sing as an elk band plucked it with leaping hooves.

In a small way, I'd begun an acquaintance with the elk of my homeground.

Did the Great Gray owl who had scrutinized me from an overhanging limb understand that I was also studying it? Was it outrageously anthropomorphic to imagine the elk and I had been engaged in such relationship, such reciprocity of attention? It seemed foolish to assume otherwise: elk senses are far keener than mine.

I imagined them waiting, now, for the cover of darkness. I imagined their relief, and mine, when the shooting was over, when the herds would survive the winter or die quietly—of old age, disease, perhaps starvation—not by bullets. I did not know if "natural" death was preferable to elk or even to me, but it certainly seemed less violent, a lesser holocaust. Though I had been among the armed humans stalking elk throughout October, something less clearly defined than a kill drew me into the dark timber.

As the light left the sky, the gunfire from Taylor and Munger came in less frequent bursts. Bowing after every shot, I blessed the lives and red deaths of elk.

The dark days around Halloween are said to be the time when the veil between the worlds is the thinnest, the time to remember all souls, all saints, all the dead. The ancient Babylonian goddess Inanna descends to the underworld, as does the Greek Persephone. Artemis the huntress becomes Hecate, the death crone. Animals den or migrate; visible vegetation dies, goes underground to await spring. The great wheel is turned to death, decay and disappearance.

The flesh of my body, the matter that binds me to earth, recognizes that autumn is the time for hunting. The flesh knows this, but the mind is thousands of civilized years removed from responsibility for the kill. To recover such lost territory of the psyche is not an act of will or acquisition, but a stripping away, like Inanna relinquishing her fine garments and head-dress as the price of passing through the gates to the lower world.

I had hunted elk throughout the twilight of October, but if killing was the point, I hadn't gotten it yet. Even so, I felt myself tracking toward a wilder center. It was not simply the deaths of animals I sought, but a sure-footed place in the phenomenal world, a relationship of substance, a relationship that matters.

I'd gone hunting because, in the words of Paul Shepard, I'd "ceased to listen to a million secret tongues in the wilderness." I didn't remember how to hear them.

I hunted for a species memory, a crack in the hypermodern layering, a break in the shell that has kept me disjointed from the organism that fuels our lives, that has kept me disconnected from the breathing and sentient companions in the great web.

On Halloween evening, the sky blazed with the first brilliance of the day. Scattered clouds flushed coral, lavender, gold. In the east, Orion huddled below the horizon, rising to fullness hours after the hunt was over, hours after David and I returned home.

Another autumn, I would follow elk into the dark timbered veins of these mountains. When given another chance to close the loop of predator and prey, perhaps—in the moment of balance—I would pull the trigger. Or perhaps I would stand watch, hands open and full of wild prayers.

Either way, I would not go hungry.

## LYN DALEBOUT
### MOOSE, WYOMING

*Lyn Dalebout has served as a poet in the schools, managed a bookstore in Jackson, and performed her poetry in collaboration with other artists for organizations such as the Grand Teton Music Festival, the Greater Yellowstone Coalition, Yellowstone National Park, the Snake River Institute, the Teton Science School, and others. Her first book of poems,* Out of the Flames, *appeared in 1996.*

# Ceremony
## *For Boiling River*

This dryland bone of death
I brought to break
was eaten clean.
The hawk hovered last spring.

I'll probably throw
it toward the Gardner River—
River of Cobalt Beam—
which will give it to the Yellowstone, I hope
for that is where I'd like these wishes to go.

But maybe
it will settle downstream
from the Boiling River—
the River That Breaks Bones—
and be cloaked in emerald satin
of teaming algae, and soon
resemble itself no longer.

# Lyn Dalebout: *Poems*

Soon a fish will nibble away
the bone's coat of green
and once again
it will be eaten clean,
this time by water.

Then kicked loose by crossing elk,
this time, floats toward the Yellowstone—
River of Viridescent Rose—
washed clean and free

for that is how
I'd like to be.

# Journey

If you stare out a window
you came to be quiet by,
what's on the other side
is not necessarily what you see.

My eyes drift past
the barrack buildings of Yellowstone,
past elk grazing
scared to cross the paved straight road
while cars rush too quickly by.

My eyes reach farther than the
northeast edge of Yellowstone,
dust through the vast expanse of mid-Wyoming
into the red heart
of the Black Hills
and there, come to rest.

I have journeyed thus.
You probably have too.

We do so much
we were not trained
to understand.
There is so much
we were trained not
to understand.

## TAMI HAALAND
### BILLINGS, MONTANA

*A faculty member in the English department at Montana State University—Billings, Tami Haaland has served on the Board of Directors for the Montana Wilderness Association. Her poems and essays have appeared in* Calyx, Petroglyph, Alkali Flats, The Florida Review, *and elsewhere.*

# Cleaning the Office

Essays and handouts go into files.
I toss memos into the recycling, old mail
into the trash, wipe down the desk top,
dust off the shelves, and the office
is clean except that poems
scatter around the computer,
chocolate smears the keyboard,
and this note written on birch bark, found
in the pages of a secondhand book,
leans against the calendar:
"Sweet Sara, tonight we sleep
under the full moon, maybe hear wolves
and breathe the scent of fir and pine.
You would like it here, Sara. Beargrass
lies along the mountain, paintbrush
and gentian stretch up from the creek,
sparks from the fire swirl
and dissolve under stars."

# In Celebration of Burdock

Stretching up through crags
along the Stillwater, among chokecherries
or in rows in my mother's garden
it grows showy as any dahlia or iris,
persistent as prickly pear.

On the stone covered sandbar
along Rock Creek one summer
I found its purple blossoms
just opening, then dreamed about it
in February, how its roots felt their way
through the rocks to the wet sand below
and the clay below that,
how its leaves extended from its center
toward the cottonwoods that reflected
and filtered the sun, toward
potentilla and plantain and
the smell of mossy water
slipping past.

## PATRICK DAWSON
### BILLINGS, MONTANA

*A native Montanan whose ancestors prospected for gold, homesteaded and established ranches, Patrick Dawson is the author of* Mr Rodeo: the Big Bronc Years of Leo Cremer, *and wrote the text for the photo book,* The Montana Cowboy. *Dawson's essays have appeared in the anthologies* Montana Spaces *and* Writing Montana: Literature Under the Big Sky. *He also reports for* Time *magazine.*

# Why We Kill The Yellowstone Buffalo

There was a long pause between each boom from the big-bore rifle. It was a sub-zero morning near Gardiner, Montana, early in 1986, and Yellowstone National Park was leaking buffalo. A few lucky licensed hunters had their names drawn to come out and shoot them, for wild buffalo were outlawed in Montana. Though my right cheek was becoming frostbitten from the movie camera's chilled metal casing, my first concern was to keep the film rolling.

They called it a special hunt, but it was not a hunt. There was no scouting, tracking or stalking. The images popping through the camera's viewfinder were like nothing I had ever seen. Mostly, the dark, shaggy ones just stood on the snowy ground and were fired upon again and again before toppling over, getting up, then falling again. Some shooters used telescopic sights at close range. Then the hunter and his helpers ambled over, slit the throat, sliced open the hide and turned a stream of hot blood onto the snow. A hunter in insulated canvas coveralls posed atop the carcass for pictures, bouncing with pride, waving his rifle for the cameras. Then a team of harnessed draft horses pulling only a flopping singletree hitch plodded into position and the carcass was roped and dragged off between the clumps of sagebrush, blood and entrails streaking the snow, the hunter riding atop his kill as if it were a prehistoric sleigh.

That was the first and last time I ever worked on a snuff film, but it was not to be the last time I would see Yellowstone's buffalo shot down in Montana. Western pioneers and travelers ate a lot of buffalo meat in the 1860s and 1870s, because that was often the most plentiful as well as the best meat obtainable. So the scene should not have come as a shock. Even though it had been a hundred years since any Montanan legally shot wild buffalo, there persisted this dormant tradition: We kill the buffalo because that's the way we've always done things here.

These buffalo were fifteen to twenty miles away from the nearest cattle, which were safely contained behind barbed wire fences. The cattle owners, the Department of Livestock, the governor and other wise leaders said that many of the Yellowstone buffalo carry a virus called Brucella aborta, or brucellosis, also known as Bangs Disease. Local press reports kept repeating that if the cattle should catch this virus, then the Angus and Hereford and other valuable cows would abort their first calves. But aborted calves were not the real issue. It's not fatal to cattle, but humans cannot risk catching undulant fever, which historically was contracted from dairy cattle with brucellosis. Maybe human health was not the issue, either. Ultimately, it was more a matter of commercial concern. After many years of testing and inoculating, Montana was finally rated brucellosis-free by the U.S. Department of Agriculture. When cattle interests in some other states heard that wild buffalo were wandering around outside Yellowstone, they used it as an excuse to stigmatize every cow in the entire state as possibly contaminated, even if some cattle were 600 miles away and buffalo had never been known to pass brucellosis to cattle. This makes for, as they say, marketing problems for Montana beef producers. The point was not that those cattle were in imminent biological danger, but that Yellowstone's buffalo were a mile inside Montana and fair game because of traditional livestock policy.

"It might prove impossible for various reasons to eliminate brucellosis from bison and elk in the Greater Yellowstone Area, so the best that could be achieved would be risk control," concluded a 1998 National Academy of Sciences study. "Bison might continue to require artificial control (such as shooting bison that leave the park), either at current or redrawn lines." But that rigid, fatal line was not expanded by the state to accommodate the wandering buffalo. Forced to rely more on speculation than on any scientific evidence, the NAS study conceded: "The risk of bison or elk transmitting brucellosis to cattle is small, but it is not zero."

Inside the park all summer, the buffalo run their ancient trails and swim the rivers in groups. They are always on the move, aerating the topsoil of their ranges by trampling, not loafing around water holes like cattle. The cinnamon-colored calves cavort among the wildflowers and the big bulls snort, bluff and fight each other. They live and behave much as they did a thousand years ago, and they don't need man to feed them, help them reproduce or protect them from predators. To them, invisible boundary lines mean nothing.

When the last of the herds were eradicated from the Southern Great Plains, out-of-work Texas buffalo hunters moved north to the Yellowstone and Missouri river valleys of Montana and Dakota territories. In 1889, William Temple Hornaday, chief taxidermist of the National Museum (later the Smithsonian Institution), conducted a bison census. In the entire country, which 10 years earlier still had millions of buffalo, he found 85 free-ranging animals, 200 inside Yellowstone, and a few more in zoos and private reserves. Two years before that, he had a hard time finding specimens for his museum's buffalo exhibit, but managed to take 25 from the remote badland plains between the Yellowstone and Missouri rivers of eastern Montana. The following year, 1887, an expedition from the Museum of Natural History in New York City came out looking for bison specimens to take back. They hunted the same area for three months and found not one buffalo.

## Patrick Dawson: *Why We Kill the Yellowstone Buffalo*

Millions of buffalo hides were shipped down river by steamboat from Montana until the early 1880s. Then the new railroad carried out the last of the hides and pickled tongues. By the turn of the century, buffalo were such an exotic commodity that poachers sneaked into Yellowstone to gun them down for some of the world's last hides and heads. In 1880, there were 600 native bison counted in Yellowstone. In February of 1894, Army scouts on snowshoes trailed Ed Howell of nearby Cooke City into a back country camp where they found his cache of several buffalo heads which he planned to sell to taxidermists for up to $300 each. Approaching Howell downwind, the scouts caught him stalking a small herd of buffalo with his rifle. When they arrested Howell, he was so upset with his dog for not warning him of the approaching scouts that he tried to shoot it. Howell's case resulted in almost instant passage by Congress of the Lacey Act to protect the park's wildlife. But by then poachers had nearly wiped out Yellowstone's buffalo. In 1901, the park herd was down to 25, though contemporary biologists speculate that there might have been forty to fifty remaining.

Some concerned conservationists back East realized the crisis and bought 21 head from private herds in Texas and northwestern Montana. The transplanted animals were coddled with hay and nightly confinement and protected by day herders at the Buffalo Ranch in Yellowstone's Lamar Valley. The animals in this growing foundation herd were the larger plains Bison bison. They thrived and were eventually turned loose to roam free with the survivors within the park, the smaller wood, or mountain buffalo, Bison bison athabascae, Yellowstone's original subspecies. A crossed hybrid emerged. Some of those transplanted plains buffalo came from the private herd of the prominent Texas cattleman, Charlie Goodnight. Nobody tested them then, but Goodnight's cattle may have passed brucellosis to his buffalo, and they may have brought it to Yellowstone.

But nobody really knows how buffalo contracted the brucellosis that was first tested for and found in 1917. Park biologists say they were never observed spontaneously aborting, nor had they shown any other signs of the disease, and so must be immune to the symptoms that affect cattle. In hindsight, biologists speculate that had the government only provided protection from poachers, those last 25 to 50 mountain bison could have recovered nicely and multiplied in no time without bringing in outside blood.

For years, very few bison ever wandered out of the protective boundaries of Yellowstone. Then came the big migration attempt during the winter of 1984-85. Under scrutiny by animal-rights groups, park rangers at first tried to haze them back in by firing rubber bullets, erecting cattle guards and using other schemes meant to turn them back or prevent them from leaving Yellowstone. But 88 crossed into Montana and were shot dead by state game wardens.

Montana hunters resented these few state employees monopolizing this frontier experience, and they demanded some of the action. So the 1985 Montana Legislature passed a law making the buffalo a big-game animal, subject to a special hunting season. The law was intended to solve the buffalo's perceived brucellosis threat to cattle.

During that first civilian buffalo season of 1985-86, selected hunters killed 57. The next year they shot only a half dozen that wandered from Yellowstone, and the next year 39. But during the winter of 1988-89, they shot 569, and the carnage proved to be a public relations embarrassment for the state.

In early 1989, more buffalo than ever came out to forage for grasses after the Yellowstone fires and drought of the previous summer. Again, the special-hunt lottery brought to the north entrance armed Montana citizens who had paid $200 for the honor of bagging a buffalo. I returned to the scene without a movie camera.

On a frigid morning, they shuffled into the Gardiner forest ranger station to listen to a state game warden captain explain how to do the job. Montana had never had a big-game hunting season for buffalo, so this was new to most of them. Warden Captain Bud Hubbard pointed to a photograph of a cow buffalo and told them to aim for two spots: "The best place is to get a side view and a head shot," he explained. "You want to go from the base of the horn and about that far back. If you're going to get that big vertebrae, right there on the end of the spine, or you're gonna get a brain shot, then just drop 'em right there, you've got a real good hit. It won't wreck the skull or the part you're gonna put on the wall."

The second-best place to aim for, he said, is the heart. "If the animal is walking, or you're just too far away to feel good about a head shot, go to the heart. That's fine, and that'll do it quick. But stay behind the front leg, and stay way low. What people tend to do is think like they're shootin' an elk or deer and get up there in the ribs, and believe me, we've had these things shot clear through, in the ribs, hole that big around, and they just keep on walkin'. We've had a lung-shot buffalo keep up with a bunch two miles away. They've got so much lung, they can go a long way. It'll kill them eventually, but not as quick as we need it for our purposes here. Between the eyes is good, just above the eye. That's fine with a younger bull or cow, you'll dump 'em right there. It's not really that big a target, and really, unless you're pretty sure of yourself, I wouldn't advise it."

He warned them not to be choosy, not to hold out for a big head, because this was a "damage hunt," not a trophy hunt. Off they went, into their pickups and Jeeps, down Highway 89 to the gathering point near where the Yellowstone River emerges from the narrow gorge of Yankee Jim Canyon. It was below zero that morning, with an inch of fresh snow on the ground, and low clouds left over from the storm bumped into the mountainsides. All along the road were small groups of bighorn sheep, elk and buffalo. But only the buffalo were targeted, because they were suspected of carrying brucellosis. The elk, Montana's premier big-game animal, but also known carriers of the disease, were exempt from the "damage hunt" because they were thought less likely to mingle with cattle.

I saw some mighty buffalo bulls along the road, looking timeless and lordly, blowing steam vapor into the cold morning air, but these were not to be shot that day. The hunters were directed to a group of forty, mostly cows and calves, that were by now acting wild, for they had been shot at repeatedly and chased since leaving the park behind.

Montana game wardens took more than an hour to haze the animals down from high ground, through private land and out to an open space for the hunters. Genetically, these must have been mostly Bison bison athabascae, descendants of Yellowstone's original, wily mountain buffalo. They were evasive and unpredictable, but they stuck together. Across a steep, rocky hillside, they moved with a speed and agility you would not expect from such big animals. Domestic cattle could not move like that.

The buffalo clan halted on a low hillside near a ranch road, and the first two hunters were loosed on them, with the wardens directing. The hunter who had drawn number one fired again and again. The buffalo's knees were shot. It stumbled, fell, rose again to hobble up the hill, exhibiting classic bison stamina. There were more shots, and it fell one last time. Number two hunter was luckier, knocking down his with one shot. The surviving buffaloes took off over the hill.

Wardens and hunters gave chase, but then came back, as the buffalo had circled around and were now on the other side of the road, on level ground obstructed only by short juniper trees and big boulders, good position for the hunters. A 34-year-old woman and a teenaged boy were the next two in the lineup. She, a nurse about five feet tall, knocked down a buffalo cow with one shot from her .358 Winchester. The boy's one shot from his 7mm rifle sent his young cow off the ground, flipping it completely over backwards. The rest of the herd, stirred up, danced around the fallen buffaloes, but then settled down.

Another woman rested her rifle on a boulder, took her time, squeezed off one shot and scored. After the shot, she told me she had been nervous. Another teenaged boy fired into a young bull three, four times. Each shot hit, but didn't knock the bull down. The boy's father was behind him, recording the event with his video camera. The rest of the herd rumbled off, disappeared over a rise down toward the river. The wounded one emerged alone a few minutes later, standing tall, head raised proudly but bleeding from his nostrils. A warden drove the boy closer so he could lean his rifle on the pickup box for the kill.

It turned out that the sure-shooting nurse hadn't killed her buffalo after all. It took about twenty excruciating minutes of several coup de grace shots before it was over. Audubon's journal of a buffalo hunt records that one bull took 24 shots before falling to the ground. The buffalo is an amazing animal, evolved to adapt and survive or outrun most any earthly adversity, be it drought, blizzards, wildfires or natural predators. From the Ice Age until 1885, the buffalo proved it could endure saber-toothed tigers and stone-tipped spears. But not the unrelenting bullets of Manifest Destiny.

Further up the canyon, the hunters drawing later, higher numbers brought down their quarry in a sagebrush clearing at the edge of the forest. An 81-year-old man drew a bead on a fine looking bull, and fired several times. But the bull did not die until a warden finished it off. They cut its throat and melted the snow with rivulets of warm blood. Then they rolled the bull onto its back, its polished, ebony like hooves turned to the bright sky, and the old hunter proudly hacked open the brisket with a long-handled cleaver.

A hundred yards away lay the last buffalo of the day, shot by the third woman hunter who had little trouble knocking down the young cow. The young woman with a pleasant smile said she had been anxious and sleepless since learning a day earlier that she had been picked in the drawing. Now that it was over, she said she felt better. She passed her hand gently around the cockle burrs in the dead bison's coarse fur, admiring the tones of color ranging over the cow's hide, from coal black to golden, and asked, "Isn't she pretty?"

The afternoon winter light on the scene of hunters and their buffalo carcasses illuminated a strange modern version of an ancient North American ritual. Bright red blood colored the new snow as bison were laid open and hunters and their helpers wearing surgical gloves pulled out stomachs, lungs and other heavy entrails. The gloves were a precaution against humans catching undulant fever if the buffalo was carrying a virulent strain of brucellosis.

I drove back down the road and encountered Yellowstone research biologist Mary Meagher, who had driven up from the park and was listening to warden chatter on the police radio as she scanned the landscape with binoculars. She said that killed-bison blood samples so far that season tested at around fifty percent exposure to brucellosis, which was no surprise. It was a good sampling, since 250 had been killed so far.

Yellowstone's bison have been her project for a good part of her life. She started as a naturalist there in 1959. She flew over the park often to observe them from the air. On the ground, she examined their range, their muddy wallows, their calving grounds, their use of thermal areas for wintering, their forage, their winterkilled corpses—before the wolves were brought back. She knew these animals intimately. On that day in 1989, dressed in her dark green winter ranger coat, she said they were migrating because of the drought damage to the range, and because the population of the herds was higher than ever. It was only natural that they move out, she said. They are gregarious animals and if left alone would recolonize the upper Yellowstone River valley.

I asked her what she felt as she watched her bison being killed by Montana hunters. She looked away quickly, up the river. Ever the reserved, objective scientist, she would not comment on any aspect other than biological. But she added that she hoped the political solution would be compatible with the biology of the park herd, and had no reason at that point to fear otherwise.

The political solution, of course, was to kill bison, theoretically to prevent them from spreading brucellosis to Montana cattle. There were few, if any, cattle then on that part of the upper Yellowstone River and the bison were not dropping calves.

In 1973, the U.S. Department of Agriculture proposed that as many bison as possible in Yellowstone National Park be rounded up, corralled, and tested for brucellosis. USDA suggested that all those testing positive be destroyed and those left roaming free on the range would be hunted down and killed, just to make sure. USDA wanted to wipe out all of Yellowstone's buffalo based on a shaky scientific premise. The National Park Service said no deal, and then admitted it had acted wrongly earlier when it intentionally reduced the park's herds by wholesale slaughter. Over the three winters between 1954-57, the herds were cut from 1,500 to 500. Between 1961 and 1966, at USDA's insistence, they fell from 900 to 300, below the park's preferred management numbers. The park's 1974 master plan changed all that, decreeing, "Yellowstone should be a place where all the resources in a wild land environment are subject to minimal management." Park rangers killed three buffalo bulls in 1974 and one bull in 1978. No more bison were killed by man inside the park.

To Mary Meagher, the Yellowstone bison always made a remarkable comeback over the years, and that's why she said she wasn't worried about that latest "damage hunt" threatening the 2,700 remaining buffalo left at that time in 1989.

By the side of the road at the mouth of the canyon that afternoon, a party of modern buffalo hunter helpers had a massive hide staked out on the ground, drying in the warming air. On the bed of their truck was a buffalo carcass, splayed open, neon red in the sun, naked to the world. It certainly looked like the day's migration had been stopped there.

But no. A few miles further down the road there appeared a startling sight out on the valley floor. About a dozen buffalo trotted closely together, like an oldtime football team rushing downfield. They were pointed north and looked determined, as if guided by some collective instinct. They had eluded the wardens and the hunters and seemed to be off to find some new ground where they could graze in peace and drop calves in April. They were headed toward their species' ancestral country, in spite of government resistance, barbed wire fences, highways and plowed ground. It was obvious to me that these buffalo were trying to come back to Montana.

Why couldn't they just find their way onto some of the 26,773,255 acres of federal land in Montana and multiply? The state would then have the distinction of hosting the only free-ranging buffalo outside of Yellowstone. The tourist-attraction potential would be sensational. How many came to Montana to look at cattle standing behind fences? The state could also sell a few expensive permits to hunt America's original big-game animal. But no, the ancient habitat of the buffalo had been turned into real estate. Cattle, fences, cropland and rural subdivisions prevailed over such atavistic nonsense. Those lonely visionaries who actually suggested such a plan during the drought-ridden 1980s were shouted down for heresy at public forums in small prairie towns by hostile farmers and ranchers who still managed, proudly, and with help from their lenders, to eke out a living on the land. Those locals intrigued by the idea kept quiet at the meetings.

In the late fall of 1876, some Diamond R freight-team oxen got loose near Fort Keogh at the confluence of the Tongue and Yellowstone Rivers and were feared lost and starved in the deep snows of winter. But they turned up alive in the spring, and in fine condition. The quality of the dried native grasses that had sustained them surprised the post commander, General Nelson Miles, who predicted, "When we get rid of the Indians and buffalo, the cattle and sheep will fill this country."

After Montana's millions of buffalo had been shot for their tongues and hides and their bones and skulls picked from the prairies and hauled out by freight trains for fertilizer and sugar refining, cowboys pushed in wave upon wave of Texas longhorns to eat the free native grass on the great, lawless expanse of public domain. Had there been any buffalo left out there, they would have cruised through the brutal winter of 1886-87. Instead, the snow, wind and cold wiped out most of the big speculator herds from the overstocked ranges. Nature's lesson was lost on optimistic Americans. What was left of the reorganized open-range cattle business hung on until the railroads shamelessly enticed thousands of settlers for the land boom stimulated by the Enlarged Homestead Act of 1909 that allowed for homesteading of 320 acres of arid prairie land.

Between 1910 and 1922, homesteaders filed claims on 93 million acres of Montana's public domain, even though more than eighty percent of it was unfit for crop agriculture. During the World War One grain-growing delirium, they plunged into debt buying seed, gang plows, gasoline tractors and threshing machines. And it rained. Then it was over. No more war. No more subsidized grain market. No more rain. Just widespread destitution and farm foreclosures. Half the state's banks closed years before the Wall Street crash of 1929. After the war came drought, locusts, wind and dust. The old buffalo range that had evolved along with the animal so perfectly since the Pleistocene was patriotically transformed into cropland, flourished briefly, and then baked by sun and scoured by wind into stretches of wasteland, not just in the eastern two-thirds of Montana, but throughout

Oklahoma and the Texas Panhandle on up into Saskatchewan and Alberta. These were eerily similar conditions to how the desertification of northwest Africa began.

Homesteaders abandoned their dreams and their blown-out lands. A few flush specu-lators among the fittest who survived bought their ex-neighbors' farms at county tax sales for fifty cents or a dollar an acre and put together big spreads. Ultimately, on the Northern Great Plains, the Homestead Act resulted not in the Jeffersonian vision of many happy yeoman citizens, but in de facto privatization of the public domain. It was a swift, monu-mental transfer of real estate into the hands of bankers or to a minority of the settlers who had come only twenty or thirty years earlier.

Despite its social and ecological disasters, the Homestead Act was permanently exalted in our national mythology. Politicians of the late 1800s claimed credit for civilizing with homesteaders what early maps once marked as the Great American Desert. "Consequently," wrote Paul Wallace Gates in a 1936 American Historical Review article, "there was built up around the law a halo of political and economic significance which has greatly magnified the importance to be attributed to it and which has misled practically every historian and economist who has dealt with land policies." Those very politicians, Gates noted, had during the same time quietly conveyed vast tracts of western public domain to large commercial interests. "Such imperial generosity was at the expense of future homesteaders who must purchase the land," he wrote.

In less than forty years, America's old northern buffalo range was transformed. Under the Bankhead-Jones Act of 1937, the federal government resettled many failed farmers elsewhere and bought up 1.8 million acres of eroded Montana homestead land. It was but a swatch of what had been ruined by the plow. If all that failed land had been re-nation-alized, that is, returned to the public domain, it could have been planted back to native grasses and some buffalo brought out and turned loose to renew the balanced cycles of nomadic grazing.

But instead of reviving the year-round standing forage of nutritious buffalo grass, blue grama and fescues known for their resiliency through drought and fire, there were instead widespread blocks of eroded federal and private land assiduously planted with imported Asiatic grasses such as crested wheat grass and Russian wild rye. These plants were touted as hardy erosion fighters, but they were inferior to buffalo grasses because crested wheat grass declines in forage value and palatability by late summer. Just mechanically cultivat-ing soil to plant these Asiatic grasses, in the words of Alberta range scientist and historian Alex Johnston, "releases nitrogen and organic matter, and breaks down the prairie complex that's taken thousands of years to develop. I, personally, believe that native grass is the cover of choice, and I feel very strongly that plowing marginal lands is not a good idea."

If crop farming was so marginal and cattle ranching so unprofitable most years, then why did the Government-Smarter-Than-Nature let this go on? Under Bankhead-Jones, the government altogether bought up ten million acres of failed homesteads in the Great Plains for an average of four dollars an acre. In Montana, if it had bought up most of the delinquent-tax homestead properties and reclaimed them to native grass, it would not later have had to pay out millions every year for crop subsidies, defaulted farm loans, and cash incentives to not grow surplus crops on erodible land. Fly over that country in the daytime and you can easily imagine what happened.

One might wonder why the Government-Smarter-Than-Nature did not just take a fraction of the money it paid to help farmers fail over the years and buy back all the old homestead land and restore it to native range. Or why Congress, which has always had the power to do so, did not take back the rest of the twenty million acres (in Montana alone) of old Northern Pacific Railway Land Grant sections that by law were intended to be sold to settlers for no more than $2.50 an acre, in parcels of no more than 160 acres, instead of sold in lots of thousands of acres to foreign ranching interests, lumber and mining companies, or held as corporate real estate assets. And then why, one might wonder, didn't the government pay experienced farmers using the no-till method to reseed the old range back to native buffalo grasses and end the erosion? Wouldn't there be room for cattle in the many river valleys as well as room for buffalo on the prairies and badlands?

Then, perhaps, the bison from Yellowstone would have a chance to resuscitate the hammered prairie and maybe restore some of the vast, natural, reliable reservoir of protein. It could again be a prairie rich in low-maintenance meat, but without erosion, farm bankruptcies, or surplus grain harvests. After all, the federal farm bill that provided for all those subsidies was entitled the Food Security Act. Why not unequivocally secure the food supply with a great, self-sustaining source of quality protein on the plains? Because that's not how we've always done things around here.

In the early 1990s, the bison problem was taken away from the citizen hunters and run for awhile by the game wardens. Then, after some states threatened to require testing of exported Montana cattle, the problem was turned over to the Montana Department of Livestock. This time, there were fewer blazing buffalo guns. Instead, the state workers hazed the animals migrating from Yellowstone into capture pens, prodded them onto trucks and shipped them off to slaughter houses where they were killed, skinned, beheaded, quartered and the meat, hides and heads sold at public auction. Sometimes, reservation Indians were invited down to the edge of Yellowstone to take away dead bison, a program which ignited rancorous ethical debates between some tribal members.

During the memorable winter of 1996-97, the buffalo just kept coming out of the park and the rangers and state wardens and brand inspectors shot a few and trapped the rest and trucked them off to slaughter houses. That winter, 1,084 Yellowstone buffalo were killed in Montana. Some had come as close as twenty or thirty miles of supposedly vulnerable cattle. The carnage did not go unnoticed. Park headquarters was blitzed with more than six thousand letters from people upset with the killing that year. Over in the Dakotas that winter, severe cold and snow wiped out thousands of cattle, while in all the private and tribal herds, only two buffalo died.

In early February 1997, I went to a Montana Department of Livestock auction of Yellowstone buffalo parts held at a country slaughter house. There were stacks of heavy, dark buffalo hides and small piles of buffalo heads, some with eyeballs bulging and frozen tongues sticking out. The auctioneer first sold off hind quarters and sides of fresh meat to the highest bidder. Men staggered along the iced-over county road to their cars and pickups carrying heavy, raw quarters of flesh and bone. Most of the meat was taken away in a big refrigerated truck by a South Dakota purveyor of buffalo meat. It was a profitable trip for the company, because lots of premium buffalo meat went cheap.

President Ronald Reagan appointed a Secretary of Interior, James Watt, who wanted to privatize federal lands and ordered the buffalo on the department's logo changed to face right instead of left. Reagan appointed to the federal bench in Helena a judge, Charles Lovell, who that winter rejected scientific arguments presented in court that bison were unlikely to pass brucellosis to Montana cattle, and he refused to stop the state from further slaughtering. Reagan had earlier turned down a plan by the U.S. Forest Service to buy Malcolm Forbes' ranch near Gardiner for buffalo and elk winter range. Later, many buffalo were killed there.

Montana's two senators cheered the killing of the buffalo. While one senator had inherited an interest in a large cattle and sheep ranch, the other senator once worked as a livestock auctioneer and field man for the Hereford Association, so they knew how dangerous wandering buffalo might be—politically, at least. The issue seemed to bring out the best in us: One senator called Yellowstone's superintendent "that jughead." A woman protester was arrested for throwing a bucket of old buffalo guts at the governor and senators.

Western ranchers who raise bison told me that you can't cowboy them. No roping or branding or sorting bunches in traditional wooden corrals. But they also will say that they do not miss the winter feedings and midnight calf-pulling. They like it that buffalo cows produce calves for much longer than do domestic cows and require half as much feed. They like not having to maintain separate bull pastures. They like it that buffalo just turn their shaggy heads into the blizzard and use their heads to clear snow down to forage. They like the lower veterinarian bills. They like being able to sell whenever they want, not just when the cattle buyer representing the few monopoly packing houses says so. They say the range evolved with the animals into a perfect solar collector for producing protein. Most of all, buffalo ranchers enjoyed being paid double or better the prices they ever got during the highest beef markets.

Grain farmers and cattle ranchers must plant and harvest a crop every year, no matter what the market or the weather. In our semi-arid climate, such economic stress only adds more stress to the land. It seems a culture of desperation that seldom abates. Economic theorists would argue that the free market so revered by most ranchers mandates raising grass and buffalo instead of wheat and cattle. But that's not the way we've always done things around here.

In February 1999, a group of Lakota Sioux and members of twenty U.S. and Canadian tribes walked and rode horseback from the Black Hills of South Dakota to the north entrance of Yellowstone. They called it "Tatanka Oyate Mani," or The Way of the Buffalo Walk, and the 507-mile trip was meant to be more of a prayer than a protest march. Their path through the ancient buffalo country was largely dictated by highways and barbed wire. On the Crow Reservation, they passed dusty fields that had been plowed during the tax-shelter sodbusting mania of the early 1980s. Just outside Big Timber at dusk, I saw a half-dozen Indian men on horseback riding into the teeth of an approaching westerly snowstorm. At the town gymnasium, walkers, riders and supporters who prepared food all formed a circle and made a communal prayer. Most of the people were poor and could hardly afford to be so far from their reservations. But it was important to them, they said, to make other people understand that in the grander scheme of things, killing the buffalo from Yellowstone was not good medicine.

## Patrick Dawson: *Why We Kill the Yellowstone Buffalo*

Carolyn New Holy, an organizer from South Dakota's Pine Ridge Reservation, was there comforting her small children with head colds. She said the slaughter during the winter of 1996-97 and subsequent failure by the government to reach an acceptable alternative is what prompted the long walk. "It's gone on too long, and this is our way of saying we aren't going to tolerate it anymore. It's affecting our nations in different ways, whether people realize it or not. Other tribes feel this is affecting us, and it has to stop, because it's affecting nature. The buffalo did a lot for us, and this is the least we can do for all the sacrifices they made for us."

The northern herds were once vital to the well-being of native peoples in much of the inland northwest, not just to the Plains tribes. During the horse culture, several tribes from west of the Rockies made seasonal trips east to the buffalo ranges of the upper Yellowstone and Missouri rivers. Pierre-Jean DeSmet, the pioneer Jesuit missionary, reported that those mountain tribes which could not obtain buffalo meat suffered famine. It was not always easy. The Blackfeet patrolled the Rocky Mountain Front and attacked returning caravans for their meat and ponies. Under a treaty signed at the mouth of the Judith River in 1855, the Blackfeet agreed to allow their old enemies access to the buffalo country. In exchange, the national government promised to pay them off with regular provisions. Thirty years later, no buffalo could be found by any of those tribes. During the winter of 1883-84, the Blackfeet Tribe counted 555 deaths by famine caused by the meat shortage.

A couple of weeks after the Indians marched, federal livestock-health scientists in Denver told the State of Montana that Yellowstone's wandering bison did not pose a risk to the state cattle industry's brucellosis-free status, after all. Bulls, calves, yearlings and cows not birthing did not have to be killed, they said. It appeared that the longstanding economic stigma against bison might finally be lifted from the shoulders of Montana cattlemen. But no, the governor reacted by ignoring the federal low-risk policy determination and went ahead with trapping and killing bison, because that's the way we've always done it.

Federal scientists told the state that buffalo bulls and young females could not transmit brucellosis, and that probably the only way cattle could contract it would be from eating fresh afterbirth passed by an infected bison cow. While many blood samples had indicated exposure, very few bison tissue cultures showed live brucellosis, they said. Bison rarely calve later than mid-May, and most federal-land grazing permits are cattle-free until June 15. The chances for bison coming into contact with summering Montana cattle was considered slim, but not slim enough for the Montana Department of Livestock, which continued to trap wanderers outside of West Yellowstone and to arrest young protesters interfering with the operation.

Some would suggest that since it was federal policy which greatly degraded the natural balance of the interior West, then only federal policy can redeem it, or at least mitigate some of the damage done over about 120 years. The Indians on the Buffalo Walk claimed that continuing the slaughter bodes badly for everyone and upsets the balance even more. Perhaps accidentally, the Yellowstone buffalo issue represented for the state politicians and cattlemen a continuing struggle of wild-versus-tame that intruded uncomfortably beyond frontier mythology.

We Montanans have a history of being gamblers, and hindsight always reveals much foolishness. But we keep it up, betting against Mother Nature, going for broke. You would think in 120 years of playing for high stakes we should have learned what most casino players find out sooner or later—that you can't beat the house. The bison skull on our state license plate says something about our past. I wonder what it says about our future?

By the end of the twentieth century, here's how things looked in Montana: Cattlemen felt besieged for several reasons. Since the early 1980s, the state had killed two thousand Yellowstone bison to protect cattle from brucellosis, and the cattlemen caught the blame. Prices for wheat and live beef were the lowest in years, but not retail food prices. Meanwhile, privately raised buffalo cows and calves were selling at auction for six to ten times the price cattle were bringing. Nationwide, private bison ranchers could not keep up with the demand for buffalo meat, low in fat and cholesterol, high in protein. Several tribal herds were thriving, helping to make up the more than 200,000 head in private herds in the United States: an astounding recovery from the near-extinction of 1901. President Bill Clinton announced hopeful news for the Yellowstone buffalo in the summer of 1999: the feds would finally buy the old Forbes ranch bordering the park's north entrance and dedicate it to wildlife habitat.

For whatever reason, the weather was acting funny and great clouds of loose topsoil were in the wind more than usual. If ever that day comes when the drought has dragged on and the crops fail again and again and the soil blows and the Asian grasses of the pasture shrivel and the cattle run out of water, we will stare into the dark sky of dust and wonder how this could happen to our great agrarian experiment. And maybe then, whenever a buffalo from Yellowstone National Park shows its face in Montana, we will shoot it, this time not to protect our cattle, but to feed our children.

Should there be no drought or pestilence and all is going well, we will probably shoot it anyway, because that's the way we've always done things around here.

## LYNNE BAMA
### CODY, WYOMING

*A Pennsylvania native, Lynn Bama graduated from New York University and the Germaine School of Photography before moving to northwestern Wyoming in 1968. Both a poet and prose writer, Bama's essays and articles have appeared in* Sierra, Orion, High Country News, *and several anthologies.*

# Sandwort

is too lumpish a name
for this neat green mound.
And the Latin, Arenaria,
is no better. Nothing airy
about this plant. It hugs
the ground like a tuffet
of unfriendly velvet,
each tiny leaf a prickle.

It lives a long time.
One that sprouted in my garden
two decades ago is not half
the size of this clump
on the bare hillside,
unwatered and unloved.

# RING OF FIRE

When the bulldozer slammed its way
through here to make a road, it left
this living pincushion dangling
upside down from its long taproot,
like some sad pomander hung
in a closet. In a few months it will fall.

But on this June morning
it is covered with so many
starry white flowers
I can hardly turn my eyes away
from that exultant, hopeless flare of bloom,
shimmering like a revelation
out of the mortal dirt.

Lynne Bama: *Poems*

# Casualty

The summer river is an eye looking back at the sun;
the winter river is an open mouth steaming,
sucking light out of the air.

Last week it froze from the bottom up
into green caverns full of lumpy teeth.
This week it's rising again, towards a spot
on the ice where all the coyote tracks converge—
a crumpled fawn.

Snow sticks to the cold fur, the small hoofs lie in slush.
Near the chest, blood has seeped into the rotted ice
and spread away into ocherous stains.
The flank gapes open.

By next day, the black tongues of water
have licked the spot clean.
The sun is blazing in the winter grasses.
A mob of finches rollicks by
in a shining cloud.

If not for the raven that flaps downriver—
one darkness looking into another—
you could forget what happened here.
You could be blinded by the light.

**DAVID QUAMMEN**
**BOZEMAN, MONTANA**

*David Quammen has been awarded a Lannan Literary Award for Nonfiction and an Academy Award in Literature from the American Academy of Arts and Letters. He is a two-time winner of National Magazine Awards for works that have appeared in* Outside *magazine. His books include* Natural Acts, The Flight of the Iguana, The Song of the Dodo, *and* Wild Thoughts from Wild Places.

# Synecdoche and the Trout

It's a simple question with a seemingly simple answer: "Why do you live in Montana?"

Repeatedly over a span of some years you have heard this, asked most often by people who know you just well enough to be aware of the city where you grew up, the tony universities you attended, and a few other bits of biographical detail on the basis of which they harbor a notion that you should have taken your place in New York café society or, at least, an ivy-adorned department of English. They suspect you, these friends do, of hiding out. Maybe in a way they are right. But they have no clear sense of what you are hiding from, or why, let alone where. Hence their question.

"The trout," you answer, and they gape back blankly.

"The trout," they say after a moment. "That's a fish."

"Correct."

"Like lox."

"In some ways similar."

"You like to go fishing. That's why you live out there? That's why you spend your life in a place without decent restaurants or bookstores or symphony orchestras, a place halfway between Death Valley and the North Pole? A place where there's no espresso, and the *Times* comes in three days late by pontoon plane? Do I have this straight, now? It's because you like to go fishing?"

"No," you say. "Only partly. At the beginning, that was it, yes. But I've stayed all these years. No plans to leave."

"You went for the fishing, but you stayed for something else. Aha."

"Yes. The trout," you say.

"This is confusing."

# David Quammen: *Synecdoche and the Trout*

"A person can get too much trout fishing. Then it cloys, becomes taken for granted. Meaningless."

"Again like lox."

"I don't seem to fish nearly as much as I used to."

"But you keep talking about the trout. You went, you stayed, the trout is your reason."

"The trout is a synecdoche," you say, because these friends are tough and verbal and they can take it.

A biologist would use the term indicator species. Because I have the biases of a literary journalist, working that great gray zone between newspaper reporting and fiction, engaged every day in trying to make facts not just talk but yodel, I speak instead of synecdoche. We both mean that a trout represents more than itself—but that, importantly, it does also represent itself.

"A poem should not mean/But be," wrote Archibald MacLeish, knowing undeniably in his heart that a good poem quite often does both. Likewise a trout.

The presence of trout in a body of water is a discrete ecological fact that nevertheless signifies certain things.

It signifies a particular complex of biotic and chemical and physical factors, a standard of richness and purity, without which that troutly presence is impossible. It signifies aquatic nutrients like calcium, potassium, nitrate, phosphate; signifies enough carbon dioxide to nourish meadows of algae and to keep calcium in solution as calcium bicarbonate; signifies a prolific invertebrate fauna (Plecoptera, Trichoptera, Diptera, Ephemeroptera), and a temperature regime confined within certain daily and annual extremes. It also signifies clear pools emptying down staircases of rounded boulders and dappled with patterns of late-afternoon shade cast by chrome yellow cottonwood leaves in September. It signifies solitude so sweet and pure as to bring an ache to the sinuses, a buzz to the ears. Loneliness and anomie of the most wholesome sort. It signifies dissolved oxygen to at least four or five parts per million. It signifies a good possibility of osprey, dippers, and kingfishers, otters and water shrews, heron; and it signifies Oncorhynchus clarki, Oncorhynchus mykiss, Salmo trutta. Like a well-chosen phrase in any poem, MacLeish's included, the very presence of trout signifies at more than one level. Magically, these creatures are literal and real. They live in imagination, memory, and cold water.

For instance: I can remember the first trout I ever caught as an adult (which was also the first I ever caught on a fly), and precisely what the poor little fish represented to me at that moment. It represented (a) dinner and (b) a new beginning, with a new sense of self, in a new place. The matter of dinner was important, since I was a genuinely hungry young man living out of my road-weary Volkswagen bus with a meager supply of groceries. But the matter of selfhood and place, the matter of reinventing identity, was paramount. My hands trembled wildly as I took that fish off the hook. A rainbow, all of seven or eight inches long. Caught on a Black Gnat pattern, size 12, tied cheaply of poor materials somewhere in the Orient and picked up by me at Herter's when I had passed through South Dakota. I killed the little trout before it could slip through my fingers and, heartbreakingly, disappear. This episode was for me equivalent to the one in Faulkner's "Delta Autumn," where blood from a fresh-killed buck is smeared on the face of the boy. I slew you, the boy thinks. My bearing must not shame your quitting life, he understands. My conduct for ever onward must become your death. In my own case, of course, there was no ancient Indian named Sam Fathers serving as mentor and baptist. I was alone and an autodidact. The blood of the little trout did not steam away its heat of life into the cold air, and I smeared none on my face. Nevertheless.

The fish came out of a creek in the Bighorn Mountains of north-central Wyoming, and I was on my way to Montana, though at that moment I didn't yet know it.

Montana was the one place on Earth, as I thought of it, farthest in miles and spirit from Oxford University, yet where you could still get by with the English language, and the sun didn't disappear below the horizon for days in a row during midwinter, and the prevailing notion of a fish dinner was not lutefisk. I had literally never set foot within the boundaries of the state. I had no friends there, no friends of friends, no contacts of any sort, which was fine. I looked at a map and saw jagged blue lines, denoting mountain rivers. All I knew was that, in Montana, there would be more trout.

Trout were the indicator species for a place and a life I was seeking.

I went. Six years later, rather to my surprise, I was a professional fishing guide under license from the Montana Department of Fish, Wildlife, and Parks. My job was to smear blood on other young faces. I slew you. My bearing must not shame your quitting life. Sometimes it was actually like that, though quite often it was not.

*Item.* You are at the oars of a fourteen-foot Avon raft, pushing across a slow pool on the Big Hole River in western Montana. An August afternoon. Seated in front of you is an orthopedic surgeon from San Francisco, a pleasant man who can talk intelligently about the career of Gifford Pinchot or the novels of Evelyn Waugh, who is said to play a formidable game of squash, and who spends one week each year fishing for trout. In his right hand is a Payne bamboo fly rod that is worth more than the car you drive, and attached to the rod is a Hardy Perfect reel. At the end of the doctor's line is a kinked and truncated leader, and at the end of the leader is a dry fly that can no longer by even the most technical definition be considered "dry," having been slapped back and forth upon and dragged through several miles of river. With this match of equipment to finesse, the good doctor might as well be hauling manure in the backseat of a Mercedes. Seated behind you is the doctor's wife, who picked up a fly rod for the first time in her life two hours earlier. Her line culminates in a fly that is more dangerous to you than to any fish in Montana. As you have rowed quietly across the glassy pool, she has attacked the water's surface like a French chef dicing celery. Now your raft has approached the brink of a riffle. On the Big Hole River during this late month of the season, virtually all of the catchable trout cluster (by daylight, at least) where they can find cover and oxygen—in those two wedges of deep still water flanking the fast current at the bottom of each riffle. You have told the doctor and his wife about the wedges. There, those, you have said. Cast just across the eddy line, you have said. Throw a little slack. We've got to hit the spots to catch any fish, you have said in the tactfully editorial first-person plural.

As your raft slides into this riffle, the doctor and his wife become tense with anticipation. The wife snags her fly in the rail rope along the rowing frame, and asks sweetly if you would free it, which you do, grabbing the oars again quickly to avoid hitting a boulder.

# David Quammen: *Synecdoche and the Trout*

You begin working to slalom the boat through the riffle. The wife whips her fly twice through the air before sinking it into the back of your straw cowboy hat. She apologizes fervently. Meanwhile, she lets her line loop around your right oar. You take a stroke with the left oar to swing clear of a drowned log, then you point your finger over the doctor's shoulder: "Remember, now. The wedges." He nods eagerly. The raft is about to broadside another boulder, so you pull hard on both oars and with that motion your hat is jerked into the river. The doctor makes five false casts, intent on the wedges, and then fires his line forward into the tip of his own rod like a handful of spaghetti hitting a kitchen wall. He moans. The raft drops neatly out of the riffle, between the wedges, and back into dead water.

*Item.* You are two days along on a wilderness float through the Smith River canyon, fifty miles and another three river-days from the nearest hospital, with cliffs of shale towering hundreds of feet on each side of the river to seal you in. The tents are grouped on a cottonwood flat. It's dinner hour, and you have just finished a frigid bath in the shallows. As you open your first beer, a soft-spoken Denver architect walks back into camp with a size 14 Royal Wulff stuck past the barb into his lower eyelid. He has stepped behind another fisherman at precisely the wrong moment. Everyone looks queasily at everyone else, but the outfitter—who is your boss, who is holding his second martini, and whose own nerves are already frazzled from serving as chief babysitter to eight tourist fishermen—looks pleadingly at you. With tools from your fishing vest (a small pair of scissors, a forceps, a loop of leader) you extract the fly. Then you douse the architect's wound with what little remains of the outfitter's gin.

*Item.* Three days down the Smith on a different trip, under a cloudless July sky, you are drifting, basking comfortably in the heat, resting your oars. In your left hand is a cold Pabst Blue Ribbon. In place of your usual T-shirt, you are wearing a new yellow number that announces with some justice, "Happiness Is a Cold Pabst." On your head, in place of the cowboy straw, is a floppy cloth porkpie in a print of Pabst labels. In the bow seat of your raft, casting contentedly to a few rising trout, is a man named Augie Pabst, scion of the family. Augie, contrary to all your expectations, is a sensitive and polite man, a likable fellow. Stowed in your cargo box and your cooler are fourteen cases of Pabst Blue Ribbon, courtesy. You take a deep gulp of beer, you touch an oar. Ah yes, you think. Life in the wilderness.

*Item.* You are floating a petroleum engineer and his teenage son through the final twelve miles of the Smith canyon, which is drowsy, meandering water not hospitable to rainbow trout but good for an occasional large brown. The temperature is ninety-five, the midday glare is fierce, you have spent six days with these people, and you are eager to be rid of them. Three more hours to the take-out, you tell yourself. A bit later you think, Two more hours. The petroleum engineer has been treated routinely with ridicule by his son, and evidently has troubles also with his wife. The wife is along on this trip but she doesn't fish; she doesn't seem to talk much to her husband; she has ridden a supply boat with the outfitter and spent much of her time humming quietly. You wonder if the petroleum engineer has heard of Hemingway's Francis Macomber. You are sure that the outfitter hasn't and you suspect that the wife has. The engineer says that he and his son would like to catch one large brown trout before the trip ends, so you tell them to tie on Marabou Muddlers and drag those billowy monstrosities through certain troughs. Fifteen minutes later, the boy catches a large brown. This fish is eighteen inches long and broad of shoulder—a noble and beautiful animal that the Smith River has taken five years to grow. The father tells you to kill it—"Yeah, I guess kill it"—they will want to eat it, just this one, at the hotel. Suddenly you despise your job. You despise this man, but he is paying your wage and so he has certain prerogatives. You kill the fish, pushing your thumb into its mouth and breaking back the neck. Its old sharp teeth cut your hand.

The boy is a bad winner, a snot, taunting his father now as the three of you float on down the river. Half an hour later, the father catches a large brown, this one also around eighteen inches. You are pleased for him, and glad for the fish, since you assume that it will go free. But the father has things to prove to the wife as well as to the son, and for the former your eyewitness testimony of a great battle, a great victory, and a great act of mercy will not suffice. "Better keep this one too," he says, "and we'll have a pair." You detest this particular euphemistic use of the word keep. You argue tactfully but he pretends not to hear. Your feelings for these trout are what originally brought you out onto the Smith River and are what compel you to bear the company of folk like the man and his son. My conduct for ever onward must become your death. The five-year-old brown trout is lambent, spotted with orange, lithe as an ocelot, swirling gorgeously under water in your gentle grip. You kill it.

I don't guide anymore. I haven't renewed my license in years. My early and ingenuous ideas about the role of a fishing guide turned out to be totally wrong: I had imagined it as a life rich with independence, and with a rustic sort of dignity, wherein a fellow would stand closer to these animals he admired inordinately. I hadn't foreseen that it would demand the humility of a chauffeur and the complaisance of a pimp.

And I don't seem to fish nearly as much as I used to. I have a dilemma these days: I dislike killing trout but I believe that, in order to fish responsibly, to fish conscionably, the fisherman should at least occasionally kill. Otherwise he can too easily delude himself that fly fishing is merely a game, a dance of love, played in mutual volition and mutual empathy by the fisherman and the trout. Small flies with the barbs flattened are an excellent means for allowing the fisherman's own sensibilities to be released unharmed—but the fish themselves aren't always so lucky. They get eye-hooked, they bleed, they suffer trauma and dislocated maxillae and infection. Unavoidably, some die. For them, it is not a game, and certainly not a dance. On some days I feel it's hypocritical to profess love for these creatures while endangering and abusing them so wantonly; better to enjoy the thrill of the sport honestly, kill what I catch, and stop fishing when I've had a surfeit of killing. On other days I do dearly enjoy holding them in the water, gentling them as they regain breath and balance and command of their muscles, then watching them swim away. The dilemma remains unresolved.

"Yet each man kills the thing he loves," wrote Oscar Wilde, and I keep wondering how a person of Wilde's urban and cerebral predilections knew so goddamn much about trout fishing.

"Why do you live in Montana?" people ask. For the trout, I answer. "Oh, you're one of those fanatical fisherman types?" No, not so much anymore, I say. It's just a matter of knowing that they're here.

## DOUGLAS AIRMET
### POCATELLO, IDAHO

*Douglas Airmet's poems and translations have appeared in* The Temple, The Formalist, Light: A Quarterly of Light Verse, Idaho's Poetry: A Centennial Anthology, *and* Mountain Standard Time. *His book,* Anything But Poetry, *appeared in 1996 and was followed by a chapbook in 1998 called* Bards of the Numinous. *He holds a Ph.D. in English from the University of Iowa and is the editor and publisher of The Acid Press. He enjoys hiking and camping and has been known to visit pool halls throughout the Yellowstone region.*

# Palisades

And we came down together
naming flowers
latin delphinium
lavender
larkspur
monkshood
hound's tongue
and the simple oregon grape
two kinds of pea
bee balsam
white rockcress all around
by the trail that winds
as the creek winds
after the stolen hours
on a high knoll
in the May sunshine
with the snow on the peaks
all around us gleaming.

# RING OF FIRE

And we came down together
naming kisses
in the shadow of the ridge
and pine scent in the air
in the tangle of growing things
one from the heart
and one from the mind
and the old one
from the body of desire
and the fourth the kiss
of feeling and fragrance
of air in the mouth
on the tongue and lips
in the chambers of light
where the names
of the flowers are.

# Picturesque Moment in the White Clouds

We stopped there and laughing made love
because it was picture-perfect
for "natural love in the mountains"
five hundred feet above Slickenside Creek
and Castle Peak rising thousands
of granite and limestone feet behind us
as we lay on the grassy ledge
too high for mosquitoes
in the sun and mountain air
and not an ant touched us.
One fly only entered and left the stage
as if directed and all we lacked
to complete the moment
was a cigarette to dangle
between my fingers
as I stood afterward looking through volumes
of air across the creek
and you said you wished you had
a picture of my white bum
but we don't take pictures
and neither of us smoke
and when I turned around
to say I love you
you were lovely and naked
except for your socks and the ribbon
holding your hair.

## RANDALL GLOEGE
### BILLINGS, MONTANA

*Randall Gloege is a faculty member in the department of English and Philosophy at Montana State University—Billings, where he teaches composition, creative writing and other courses, and serves as the editor of* Alkali Flats, *an annual journal of creative writing.*

# Pryor Mountain Camp

Tempered by the setting sun,
the bentonite hills cool
to blue-black;
the pellucid dark
rises
with faintly pulsing lights:
time for the rattler
to slide to sleep and for the delicate
scorpion
to crawl to our fire ring,
luminous stinger
daintily held aloft
as it seeks the singeing stone.

# Spring Meeting, Wyoming Badlands
## *(for my father, 1904-1996)*

I didn't ask you to come along.
One moment, all by myself
with the weather-wrinkled
land forms,
the next, here you are.
We falter as we sink
into the soft skin of early spring.
It hurts to move,
feels like no flesh
between foot bones
and cracked earth.
Hey you, father,
dead is dead,
no magical, mystical
comings and goings,
none of that bunkum.
Snow-melt seeps into gullies,
a black beetle scurries overland,
up slope, fractured concretions hold
the dune faces,
a dry wind buoys
a golden eagle,
a silhouette hunting in circles.
Is this your legacy,
this surreal, sun-puckered, whispering
piece of planet?
We know life through traces,
mirrored half-moons
of antelope tracks,
and puddled hoof prints
along the barbed wire fence.
The sand bleeds dark and cool.

# WILLIAM HJORTSBERG
## MCLEOD, MONTANA

*William Hjortsberg has lived in Montana for half his life. He has published seven works of fiction, including* Alp, Gray Matters *and, most recently,* Nevermore. *His novel,* Falling Angel, *has been translated into twelve languages and was filmed by Alan Parker as "Angel Heart." Screenwriting credits include "Thunder and Lightning" and "Legend." He is currently working on a biography of Richard Brautigan.*

# The Sidekick

Fast? Recollect a sidewinder's lightning tongue and you'll know the move. Right or left, he was good with both hands, same as dealing cards. Blink and you'd miss the play. He never blinked a-tall. His eyes stayed cold and steady as that aforementioned snake. And he always had an edge. Them boys all do or else go out of business feet first. What he done was pour a little barber's talc inside his holsters. Sweetest draw in the west.

He wore matched .45 calibre Smith & Wesson Schofields, butts of walrus ivory with abalone inlay. Mexican silver conchos prettified the belt. It was some rig. Caught your eye right off, even before you saw him smile. When local ordinance compelled him to check his iron at the door, heads turned all down the bar. His every move looked dangerous. Even the smile.

He never feared hanging up his outfit. A sidewinder'll strike with his head cut off. Under his midnight blue frock coat and brocade vest, secure in pockets known only to his tailor, a brace of tiny Remington over-and-unders awaited his need. Most saw only the smile.

Gambling was his true profession, although he worked off and on as a cowtown lawman and once appeared in a New York City variety hall. Seven-up and stud poker were his games, table-stakes his creed. He kept his fingers busy practicing fancy shuffles, flourishes, one-handed cuts and the like. I never saw him cheat, but it wasn't because he lacked the know-how.

He always called me Monk on account of the way my ears stick out and my mug in general. I first run into him in Helena, Montana, the year after the big strike. He was hanging around the Gulch and running a Faro layout over at Chicago Josie's log hurdy-gurdy in the evenings. A traveling show had come to town and set up in the mud out back of the livery stable. The audience perched like crows along the top rail of the corral fence. He stood by the gate, munching roasted goobers.

# William Hjortsberg: *The Sidekick*

I knew him by sight, though he was a stranger to town. He'd picked up a reputation during the war and had killed two men down in Bannack the previous spring. He was in high spirits, laughing when the dancing bear fell asleep between fiddle tunes. It wasn't much of a show being as the bear was the main attraction. The mangy critter finally dropped face-first off his wooden ball into the mud and folks started drifting away. There'd been no time to pass the hat. The dago running things was looking down in the mouth. This made the stranger laugh like hell, stopping the show with all them pretty teeth.

"Hey, Luigi," he called. "Your bear's a bust, better get some other breed. Try that monkey sitting yonder." Then he pointed straight at me and my ears got so hot you could of lit a cigar on them.

All he done was plant the seed, I suppose, but he didn't lift a finger when a bunch of miners and roughnecks grabbed me off the rail and hauled me over to the wooden ball. "Give us a dance," they hooted and the whole damn corral echoed with laughter. Even the Eye-talian was having a good time.

Sometimes it's best to get into the spirit of things, so I did a quick buck and wing, skipping like a lumberjack as the circus ball spun beneath my feet. I wasn't much improvement on the bear and soon joined him in the mud. Everybody was laughing and having a good time. You'd of thought it was the Fourth of July.

When I wiped myself off, I saw him standing there like a well-fed priest after the funeral. Smiling down, he tossed me a goober and said: "Come on, Monk, I'll buy you a beer."

And that's how we met, contrary to what it says in the dime novels. If everything happened like it does between the pages of *Beadle's Half Dime Library* life would be a pretty picture indeed. We repaired to the Muleshoe, a tent-bar sporting a white-washed wood front, where he bought bucket after bucket of beer, laughing all the time and flipping goobers at me through the cigar smoke hanging like ground fog under the flapping, canvas roof.

I caught them in my mouth. I seen straight off it was what he wanted. "Here you go, Monk," he'd laugh, and the whole place'd laugh with him. Got to be just about his favorite joke. Said it brought him luck. He'd tote around a pocketful of goobers and toss one to me whenever he took the notion. To this day, I can't stand the sight, smell or taste of the damn things.

And it wasn't all gunsmoke and player piano melodies neither. Sitting in nickelodeons don't do folks a world of good when it comes to dealing with the facts of life. Sometimes months would go by with the iron cool except for practice. He'd spend an hour every morning in whatever dump was handy, shooting rats on the move or having me throw tins and bottlenecks high above the cottonwoods.

Once in a while, he'd miss. At the fairgrounds in Denver, in a public display of fancy marksmanship, he shot the tip off a senator's nose instead of nipping the ash from his cigar. There was a lot of nose left over so no real harm done.

Another time, we were traveling by buggy between Tombstone and Bisbee in the Arizona Territory when he spotted a reservation Apache asleep under the mesquite, naked save for his blanket and a battered stovepipe hat. We was moving along at a good clip. He pulls his hogleg and cuts loose. It was better'n fifty yards but the redskin tumbled off the rock just as easy as you please. We reined in and had a look. The ball went right between the Apache's startled eyes. "Nice shooting," says I, knowing how he loved a compliment.

"Terrible," says he. "I was aiming for the hat."

Most of the men he killed deserved killing same as rattlesnakes and skunks. Thinning the competition was what he called it, always with that smile. Course, even the best make mistakes. Old "Duck-bill" Hickok gunned down one of his own policemen in the streets of Abilene. Wes Hardin once shot a fellow for snoring, and that other Texican, King Fisher, plugged a bald man just to see if lead would richochet off his gleaming pate. It didn't, but it made for an interesting experiment.

What I got to say next ain't very pretty, but it's the truth. His biggest mistake was believing he had a soft spot for children. Far as I could see, he was flint clean through, but he always toted them goobers and penny candy like I told you and when he wasn't making me play the chimp, he scattered handfuls among the tattered immigrant urchins that seemed to gather in the mud of them first towns like flies on a festering wound.

He could of been the Pied Piper the way kids followed him around, squatting on the board sidewalks outside saloons for hours just to catch a glimpse of his swagger. They come in handy when he wanted someone to fetch a cigar or the weekly newspaper. The snap of his fingers sent them tots scampering like "Dog" Kelley's greyhounds.

The usual reward for such devotion is much beloved by journalists and no doubt you've read of it a dozen times in the *Police Gazette.* He'd give the lucky kid a brass bar token or barbershop token or suchlike to toss in the air and drilled it with a single offhand shot. Said it was his true signature, pen and ink being forger's tools. Them dented tokens became his trademark throughout the territories and are much sought after by collectors today.

One time in Ellsworth, Kansas, a fight broke out between a pair of ragamuffins, each claiming ownership of a newly-fallen, bullet-punctured prize. They gouged and bit and kicked over that token until he waded in and hauled them apart. "Look here," he smiled, "gentlemen don't settle disputes in the dirt like animals." Still smiling, he slipped his sidearms from their holsters and handed each kid a revolver.

Their tiny shoe-button eyes grew big and round as double eagles. They had to cling to them sacred pistols with both hands, that's how small they were, little bitty kids no more'n seven or eight years of age. I tried to talk some sense but he wouldn't hear none of it, saying he was just having fun.

He made a pretty speech about the Code Duello and paced off the distance in the alley. The two urchins hung on his every word like it was Scripture and he was some golden-throated angel direct from heaven. When he told them where to stand and directed them to fire on his count of three, I tried to call him on it but he stared me down. "Little snot-noses couldn't hit the barn wall from the inside," he whispered. "Be a laugh to see them fall on their asses."

With that, he counted one, two, three, and the children blew themselves to kingdom come at his command. It's an education to see what a slug from a .45 will do to something that small. "Those brats had real talent," was his only comment. I told the law the kids had swiped the guns while he was napping on the bench out front.

It didn't amount to much. One little tyke was a homeless orphan who lived in the barn behind the express company. His pal had a mother, an Irish widow who took in washing back of the tracks. The town held a benefit turkey shoot to pay for the funeral. He sent the grieving mother a letter of condolence, together with a two-dollar lapel watch and one of them autographed bar tokens.

# William Hjortsberg: *The Sidekick*

Women. That's what most folks ask about after I've satisfied their curiosity regarding the Squaw Creek massacre. What was he like with women? Was he ever in love? Did he send flowers? Well, there weren't no lonely schoolmarms nor any wild-eyed rancher's daughters far as I could tell. Mostly, he hung around with whores.

Don't look so shocked. If he'd been a preacher he'd of sung with the choir, as the saying goes. The chippies and dancehall girls all took to him straight off. He had an easy way with a compliment and was always ready to buy a lady a drink. He could of had his pick of the flock wherever we traveled but his mind was on other things.

What he would do now and again was treat me to the best in the house. "There's a blooded filly," he'd say, "like to take her for a ride?" I never let on how hot I was to trot, which tickled him all the more. He'd give the nod and off we'd go, him flirting and whispering all the way up them carpeted steps.

Course, the lady the whole time was thinking she'd have something to tell her grandchildren. Not every tart got to diddle the most famous cock in the country next to President Garfield's. Imagine her surprise when she saw it was me hauling off my trousers. Sometimes, the more refined Jezabels would grow indignant and that's when he got that tone in his voice, so his word cut like a scalping knife. "Strip," he'd tell them, his eyes gone hard as nailheads. He only had to say it once.

Oh, they were some fine-looking women, skin whiter'n flapjack flour and soft enough to drown in. I'll never forget them perfumed nights, gaslights all ablaze, shadows dancing across the papered walls. Something else I'll never forget: the sound of his mirthless laughter echoing in them tiny rooms like a coyote pack yipping on a windless night.

What he liked to do was pull a big comfortable chair up to the foot of the bed and observe the proceedings like he had a front-row music hall seat. He'd smoke a cigar and roar with laughter at my frantic coupling. It sure tickled his funny bone. "Go to her, Monk," he'd shout, clapping his hands with pleasure. It got so after a while I didn't listen anymore, but that sort of thing can play havoc with a man's concentration.

Guess by now you can see what a sense of fun he had, always turning everything into a joke. "Treat life as a comedy and you'll go to the grave smiling," was what he told me. Even at the horror that was Squaw Creek it was him had the idea to prop all the corpses up on logs around the campfire. The boys laughed about it all the way back to Munson's Ferry. He sure was a joker.

Over the years I guess he played about every kind of trick you might imagine. On my birthday one year in Denver he presented me with a fancy gilt-engraved hat box from Rheinlander's. Expecting to replace my trail-worn sombrero with a brand-new Stetson, I yanked off the lid and found myself facing the fighting end of an angry she-skunk. I had to burn my clothes and must've taken two dozen baths before I rid the polecat perfume from my hide.

He enjoyed them animal surprises. I never knew what might turn up in my bedroll, but gopher snakes and quilly-pigs were recurring favorites. One time, I found my boots full of horned toads. On another occasion, he bribed the cook at the Inter-Ocean Hotel in Cheyenne to fry up crow for my dinner instead of chicken. Like a fool, I ate it.

I always promised myself someday the joke'd be on him. Not just a cockie burr under his saddle blanket or some dumb kitchen-match hot foot. I wanted a stunt worthy of a master prankster. It was on that last famous rainy April Sunday in Fort Worth that I finally got my chance. We had our usual set of rooms at Fanny Porter's bordello and was just setting down to a fine big dinner when the colored girl brought word that a gentleman downstairs wished a word with him. She handed over a calling-card.

"Please tell Mr. Crawford I am having my supper and will await his pleasure on the street outside when I've done." Them was his very words and he spoke so easy you'd never know "Cimmeron Jack" Crawford'd been dogging our trail for months. My pal gutshot Crawford's younger brother Danny over a disputed coin-toss at the Wichita racetrack and it had only been a matter of time before the rent come due.

He rushed his meal not a jot, but went at his boiled beef and dumplings with a steady hand, serving up second helpings all around. The girls at the table never caught on to the nature of the business attending him outside. From the easy way he lingered over brandy and coffee, puffing a cigar without a care in the world, they surely assumed it was a matter of little consequence.

At last, he rose and brushed the crumbs from his vest. He asked me to lay out his shaving kit and as I repaired to the adjoining room, he ushered the lovely ladies to the door. When we was alone, he checked the loads in his revolvers, opening the breakfront action and turning the cylinder as carefully as a jeweler peering at the innards of a pocket watch. Next, he picked up the talc canister, giving me a sly wink, and powdered the insides of his holsters. "Time to carve another notch," he said, heading down the stairs and out into the rain.

I followed right behind, not too close because he never liked me to crowd his play. I cut across the cobbled street to where I could watch from a safe distance. The two gunmen stood fifty paces apart, bareheaded in the drizzle, and he just grinned as "Cimmeron Jack" called him every low name in the book.

When the bluster was done he was still smiling, just like always. "You spoke your peace, Jack," he said, "now make your play." What happened next is still being talked about around campfires and pool tables from the Rio Grande to the Rosebud. Crawford reached under his slicker where he had a sawed-off shotgun hanging by a cord over his shoulder. He give Crawford plenty of time to get the weapon into view so's the witnesses'd know it was self-defense; then he dug for the big Schofield on his right-hand hip. He grabbed that ivory grip and tugged hard but the piece never come clear of the holster. At that last moment before "Cimmeron Jack" Crawford tore his head clean off with a charge of double-ought buckshot, I caught his eye and returned the wink. I think he got my meaning.

It was a good joke, one he'd of laughed at himself. Maybe he's laughing in Hell this very minute. I took my cue from an old trick of his. He was all the time slipping gunpowder into my pipe tobacco or pulverized alum into the bicarbonate I brush my teeth with, so when he sent me for his shaving kit, I filled the talcum canister with plaster of Paris. Out there in the rain it seized-up right quick, them Smith & Wessons froze hard and fast in his hand-tooled holsters. When the time come, he died laughing.

The coroner's jury ruled it justifiable homicide and no charges were ever brought. There was an all-night wake at Fanny Porter's with the girls weeping like widows. He had a grand funeral. They say five thousand people followed the glass-walled hearse to the graveyard. A fence had to be erected around the tombstone to keep souvenir-hunters from chipping it away to a pebble. I turned down a handsome offer to travel with a medicine show and took to hanging out with "Cimmeron Jack" Crawford. But then, that's another story.

## CAROL L. DEERING
### RIVERTON, WYOMING

*A native New Englander, Carol Deering also lived in Arizona, Michigan, Germany, and Washington before coming to Wyoming. Her poems have appeared in The* Owen Wister Review *and the anthology* Wyoming: Prairies, Peaks and Skies. *A 1999 recipient of a Wyoming Arts Council Literary Fellowship in Creative Writing, Deering is the Director of Library Services at Central Wyoming College in Riverton.*

# Twilight, Angus

They've chewed up this edge of the pasture,
Ripping out the stitches from the land.
Shadows, shaking their white breath,
Lumber through the irrigated grasses,
Feeding on twilight's energy.

Time steers the horn-tipped moon
In paths worn through the sky,
And now and then a sonorous remark
Travels to odd corners of the night
Where darkness flowers.
Legs on the offbeat, shifting
With awkward ghostly grace,
Dark cattle move among white clover
Stars.

# Homespun

Snow stirs, like a shiver of birds
Past the uprooted moon, then settles
Back within the sage. A whisk of skirts,
And a woman turns inward. Her breath
Leaves the pane a blister of stars.
She moves in lantern shadows, silent,
Scraping the quills of ice from the chinks.
The baby sleeps in his packing crate.
Over the girls lies a braided rug,
Wild blankets blossoming with frost.

What madness drove their dreams to wander
To a land where the wind was born?
The biting chill preys on her senses,
Her fingers swollen raw. A spider's
Web was draped awry, flaunting moths
Like trinkets to the glass, spangles
Fading in the storm. Such arrogance
From a frozen artisan—a weaver
Like herself, poised in the tracery of awe.

# Absaroka Blues

Blue breath of the Absarokas
broods upon the dawn. Shadows
drag my thoughts like horses
loath to climb.
              This river,
glacial, swift and self-
abiding, flows past rocks
with hearts of fire.

We passed this way. Your eyes
deep azure-brown like rivers
charmed me, fishing the dark
for glow.
              This river,
eyes closed, haunting,
counts the bones and finery
which buck beneath the ice.

I cross the river, trusting
stone, shy of the icy
yoke, the skin around the rock
curdling into stars.

# PAUL SCHULLERY
## YELLOWSTONE NATIONAL PARK

*Paul Schullery has been involved with Yellowstone National Park since 1972, when he first worked there as a ranger-naturalist. Ten of his 28 books are about Yellowstone, including* Mountain Time, Searching for Yellowstone, *and* The Bears of Yellowstone. *He is the recipient of an honorary doctorate of letters from Montana State University and the Wallace Stegner Award from the University of Colorado Center of the American West. Schullery lives at Mammoth.*

# The Bear Doesn't Know

There is no trail to the pond. It lies, unnamed as far as I know, in a flat alpine saddle between Gray and Little Quadrant peaks, a perfect mountain meadow. There are a few whitebark pine trees, and the whole little plain, a few acres, is quite level. The pond is toward the north end; it may be a spring, or it may get its water during spring melt from the surrounding mountain walls. The elevation is near 9,000 feet. I doubt that the place is as warmly hospitable most of the year as we found it that day in early September.

We'd been told that we could leave the Fawn Pass Trail, to the south, and ride over the saddle by following animal trails and meadows. It's not possible to get lost, with the surrounding mountains serving as such unmistakable landmarks, but I was still a little edgy about such an extended bushwhack. Horses need a lot more space than hikers, and this was steep country.

The pond has a tiny overflow on its east end. The trickle goes a few yards and turns northward, dropping into a forested ravine. The ravine was our recommended avenue north, but it was mostly trailless. We soon were hopping back and forth over the stream, seeking the easiest course for the horses. Too often to suit us, we could only travel in the little streambed itself; steep banks and deadfall kept us pinned there, and the horses slipped and lurched along the wet rocky streambed.

We didn't notice tributaries, but they were there. Within a mile of the pond the rivulet was a genuine creek, tumbling and twisting over logs and rocks and making passage even more difficult for the horses.

Once, seeking safer trails for the horses, we climbed the east slope of the ravine for some distance above the stream, so far that its noise was inaudible. While moving through fairly open timber on a gentler slope, we heard a large animal crashing through the brush and deadfall ahead of us. My companion, riding ahead of me, got a glimpse of the animal. "I think we scared up a bear."

I was skeptical. We'd been jumping elk for two days, and one large animal can sound pretty much like another when it's running frightened.

Traditional wisdom has it that a surprised bear will often flee until it locates a good spot from which to check out what frightened it. About 150 yards farther along my companion pointed up the slope to our right. "There's the bear."

She stopped her horse, and as I caught up I saw an adequately large grizzly, about fifty yards off, standing on his hind legs. He was watching us from the edge of a tight stand of lodgepole pines.

My companion asked, "Should we take his picture?" just as the bear seemed to decide something; he came down on all fours and took a step down the hill toward us.

"No, the horses haven't seen him yet and I think we'd better just keep going."

We rode quickly out of his sight, but within a few minutes we were rimrocked by a sharp side ravine off the main creek, and we had to retrace our steps back to the bear. He was gone, and we moved on down to the stream and continued north.

The horses amazed us that way. On this trip they plodded past any number of elk and coyotes, and one moose we encountered at about thirty feet, without any sign of noticing. We heard but did not see bighorn sheep; their tenor baaing at least got Midget to perk up his ears. On several occasions, bull elk, getting in voice for later recreations, bugled hoarsely from the slopes above us. The horses plodded on.

But of all that trip—the echoes of elk bugles ringing across the stone walls, the stark lawnlike alpine meadows, the midnight mountains half lost in starshadow, a golden eagle soaring off the point of Gray Peak, and all the rest—that moment near the bear lingers most persistently in my memory. I've relived that encounter hundreds of times, chasing it around in my mind, picking at it for detail or depth and often finding them; running those frames through the projector, editing, enhancing, and embellishing them without wanting or needing to. The bear came down on all fours. He (we both made him male in our minds) watched us until he knew we saw him. He decided something. He came down on all fours and took a step forward. He decided something, he came down on all fours and took a step forward down the hill and into my soul.

That, I had often been told, is the way to see your grizzly—a chance meeting on his doorstep. Whether in a moment's glance or through a morning of distant observations, you must see him at home. The time it takes to see a grizzly, the waiting involved, makes it an event long before it happens. Anticipation and romance crowd into your consciousness so that you may worry, while you're "getting ready," that the bear will somehow disappoint (which isn't possible), or that you will somehow be inadequate and will fail to enjoy, or comprehend, or be adequately enriched by the encounter. That is probably not possible either, if only because once you have realized just how special the event is your subconscious will take care of making the experience memorable. Like your first kiss or shaking hands with the President, it is memorable even if it went wrong.

And, appropriately, the bear doesn't know; it all means so much to you, but the bear forgets it almost right away.

Since the 1890s, until recently, you could see your grizzly a lot more easily, and a lot less approximately, at a garbage dump. In the 1960s those few people who knew somebody who could get them into the Trout Creek dump (not near public roads, and off limits except to researchers and park officials) were likely to see anywhere from twenty to a hundred grizzlies at once, a visual overload I have trouble imagining, and am just as glad I can't share, because these dozens of bears were all up to their appetites in garbage.

Feeding Yellowstone's grizzlies at dumps was just as much an institution as feeding the black bears along the roads, and feeding the black bears was the most desired of all visitor experiences for millions of people. I remember the black bears myself. In the early 1960s my parents brought me to Yellowstone and a small black bear tried to eat my sister's camera (or my sister; we never were sure). What I've seen in Yellowstone has convinced me that feeding wild bears, in dumps or along roads, is a stupid, ugly, typically human thing to do. What bothers me most is not so much the people who get hurt but what it does to the bears. Hundreds of people were clawed or scratched in those days (the black bears did some mean work on a few, but most were just scratched and scared; six people have been killed by bears in Yellowstone since 1872, out of more than 115 million visitors), but look what they were doing: ignoring all sorts of warnings; smearing jelly on a child's face so they could photograph the bear licking the child; placing children on the bear's back for a picture; feeding bears film wrappers, cigarette butts, ice cubes, cherry bombs, and even food; running over an occasional cub...in short, doing everything to test the forebearance of an incredibly patient providence. Providence frequently took the form of a mama black bear who finally had had too much and took a swat at the hundredth citizen of Poughkeepsie to make a grab at her cubs that day. Then the rangers would be called to destroy the "dangerous bear." The rangers, who were in on the problem and yet preferred the company of bears most of the time, ended up destroying dozens of bears. Life is not simple, even for idyllic types like rangers and bears.

The rangers knew the bears shouldn't be fed. It had been illegal since 1902. The people did, too; a survey conducted in 1953, when the great Yellowstone "bear-jams" were beginning to reach their mile-long boiling radiator peak, revealed that 95 percent of the people knew they were breaking the law when they fed bears. Only the bears didn't know. Being bears, extraordinarily adaptive omnivores, they were simply cashing in on an obvious good thing. The Rocky Mountain Free Lunch. Dill pickles, twinkies, ham on rye...the wilderness was never like this.

The only difference at the dumps was that servers and served were more select groups. Park employees, researchers, and a chosen few dignitary-gawkers were privy audience to lunchtime for one of North America's most spectacular evolutionary achievements, the grizzly bear. But, I am happy to say, this culinary camelot was doomed.

In the early 1970s Yellowstone officials cut off the gravy train. They stopped roadside feeding and they closed the open-pit garbage dumps. The dumps had been frequented by grizzlies for more than eighty years, and their closing (with the bears thus deprived of trash food) caused a monstrous national controversy, with political influence, scientific careers, outrageous egos, and, perhaps, the bears' welfare all at stake. By 1977 only one garbage dump remained open, a small scar near the north entrance, used by the town of Gardiner. Through a long-standing agreement between the park service and the town, this dump was a part of the community's way of life. For all the usual political and practical reasons, it was more difficult to close this dump, which serviced a private community, than it was to close the others, which serviced only park facilities. In every case, something else had to be done with the garbage, and it was harder to convince a small border town to spend the extra money than it was to organize better garbage disposal in the park.

Everyone knew the dump would have to be closed eventually. Not only was it unnaturally influencing the movements of the neighborhood bears, not only was it a flagrant violation of E.P.A. standards, it was a fabulously disgusting sight, even as dumps go.

Someone in the park decided that it would be useful, both scientifically and politically, to know more about the bears who used this dump. It was common knowledge that on most nights there were a few grizzlies at the dump, only a mile or so from town. Kids shot at them with .22's. Grown-ups (ha!) drove around the locked gate at the main road and went down the old service road to the dump so they could sit in their cars and watch the bears. But nobody could say how many bears there were, or how many of them were grizzlies, or if any had radio collars or ear tags from the Interagency Grizzly Bear Study Team. Bears move pretty far sometimes, and knowing how many use what areas is important information when figuring out population levels and such.

A few rangers began taking turns monitoring the dump. Some time after 10:00 p.m., they'd unlock the gate, drive in, lock it behind them and drive the dirt road to where it passed behind a rise and ended at the dump. They'd sit there an hour or so, trying to identify individuals by their size, colors, markings, and other features (bears are as individual as people in appearance, but very few people get to see them enough to get to know what to look for; I never got any good at it).

I'd only been to the dump once before, in daylight, so I didn't have a very good fix on the setting. The Gallatin Mountains, specifically Sepulchre and Electric, slope quickly into the Yellowstone River valley on the park boundary. Between the river and the mountains is a narrow shelf, actually a rolling flat, mostly bare of trees, about half a mile wide. In a hollow, between a low ridge and the base of the mountains, sat the dump. Well, it didn't really sit; it sort of festered. It was perfectly accessible to the grizzlies who roamed the extremely rough country in the north Gallatins.

That evening, as we rounded the rise and bounced along into the dump, Les played the spotlight across the footslopes of the mountain to our left, locking onto four or five brown bear bottoms as they galloped over the ridge into a gulch.

"The engine scares them away. They come back in twenty minutes or so."

We parked at the very end of the road, engine and lights off, with garbage dump on three sides and a small hill immediately to our right. The car sat on a little earth ramp that pointed out over the portion of the dump then in use, but off to our left and behind us stretched several acres of American Fantasia: washing machines and couches, cellophane and freezer wrapper, detergent boxes and tin cans—the broken, the rusty, and the disposable.

"They usually come in through that draw." Les pointed straight ahead to the far side of the clutter, where the hillside split into two humps with a gap between them. "Sometimes they come right over that hill," he continued, pointing to my right, "and right past your side of the car." I voted for the draw.

Fifteen minutes later, our eyes now fully accustomed to the weak moonlight and our ears searching the night for sounds (a rat scrambling over a pile of tin cans sounds a lot like a bear when you're expecting a bear), Les pointed at the draw. "There's one."

Later, I had time to realize that my brief daytime visit to the dump had left me with a poor notion of its size. In the flat moonlight my eyes had misplaced the draw about twice as far away as it really was. So, laboring under this significant misimpression, I saw a bear twice as large as a bear should be. "God, lookit how big!" Eloquence under pressure is natural to the experienced woodsman.

Les didn't answer. I assumed he was as agog as I was, but when I looked over he wasn't even watching. He was calmly taking notes—his clipboard resting on the steering wheel—about the bear's arrival. I squirmed and gaped. The bear lumbered silently down the draw toward the dump (and us), casting a moonshadow like the Astrodome. This bear wasn't large; this bear was *vast*.

Before long, he placed himself in a helpful context. He wandered past an old ice box and didn't dwarf it quite as much as I would have expected. I then realized that I'd been seeing wrong, and that he was a reasonable grizzly bear after all, maybe 300 or 350 pounds. A boar, a little lean, a little ratty; he looked as if he'd slept in his clothes.

Most of the others we saw, on that and subsequent nights, were sleek and fat. Strictly speaking, it isn't true that a partial diet of garbage makes bears sick, but it may increase the risk of natural sickness as essentially solitary animals get together in big groups where diseases that might normally be restricted to one can be transmitted to many.

Before long the boar was joined by a few others, a family group of sow with two young of the year. A coyote skirted the place nervously, almost seeming to need the company more than the food.

I'm sure that the scientists who spent years studying the dump bears in the 1960s got to the point where every moment of watching wasn't a thrill, but I didn't spend years at it, and the excitement didn't wear off. Even after an hour or so of watching them, there was always a gut-tightening surge of adrenalin when a new one wandered close, or when a giant head suddenly loomed up directly in front of the car (one ranger who made his first trip with me later couldn't get over the size of the heads; whenever I'd pick up the clipboard he'd tell me to "make sure you say that they have really large heads").

And watching them, just sitting there watching them feed, was enchanting. Sorting through the junk (one imagines the bear casually pitching a refrigerator over his shoulder, but most of the sorting was of a more delicate type), poking a claw through some wet paper (did I miss any lettuce here last night?), or strolling along swaying that big head back and forth, the bear is just like any other open-minded shopper. Is this detergent good in cold water? Are the tomatoes fresh? Do the coupons apply to the day-old bread? No, you can't have that, I saw it first. There is so much curiosity, so much of the small boy picking up pretty rocks, that you quickly begin to see personhood in the bear. Or you begin to see bearhood in yourself. It's all the same.

They can get used to the same things, too: cans with sharp edges, rubbery vegetables, a table too close to the kitchen, fire…. Fire? Yes, fire, the great Bad Guy of all children's animal stories (along with Nasty Hunters and Wolves, of course). It seemed that some of the stuff the dump received every day was burnable, and desultory efforts to light it usually left a couple of hot spots at night. The bears pawed all around the flames, their noses so close they'd reflect orange. I understand that this happens at other bear dumps, and occasionally a bear gets too close and gets burned or singed. Adaptive omnivores indeed.

Though I learned a lot at the dump, watching those grizzlies feed, search, nap, and occasionally square off for a few therapeutic loud noises, my basic convictions about the bear were only strengthened. Most basic of all is my belief that even though grizzly bears are capable of explosive devastation, they can be lived with in places like Yellowstone. Look at the facts. Here is an animal that can bite through your skillet, or dismantle your recreational vehicle (removing the side nearest the refrigerator), or kill an elk with a good swat (ask yourself how many times you'd have to hit an elk with your hand to kill it), or reduce a dead tree to sawdust to get some ants, and it hardly ever *kills* anybody. Grizzlies can kill people, and we give them plenty of chances, the way we crowd into their country; in recent years grizzlies have been killing more people, a sign that we've reached some limit of their tolerance and the capacity of their country. But they continue to show a restraint that amazes me, and that we hardly deserve.

I don't underestimate them, and I've had my share of memorable dreams involving me, a grizzly bear or two, and small crowded places; being mauled by a grizzly bear has always struck me as one of those wilderness experiences where the novelty wears off almost right away. But look at what the bears put up with: all the thousands of sweet- or sour-smelling, careless, bacon-frying hikers who intrude on them for every one "incident" (an unfortunate euphemism that probably can't be avoided) that results in tragedy. Like a nuclear reactor, or a heart, we take the grizzly bear for granted until it does something we weren't expecting. I think, in the bear's case at least, that the problem is in our expectations, not in the bear's behavior.

We certainly make too much of the viciousness of the bear. Any species that survives by eating its neighbors is bound to make the community jumpy, but keep in mind that most of the time bears do no more than eat their neighbor's lawn, or dig up his flower bed.

Partly because in modern America being killed and eaten by a wild animal is incredibly rare, and partly because such an event is great press, we have a distorted view of the ferocity of grizzly bears. Every precaution must be taken—I always carry some honest fear into grizzly country—but let's be realistic about what the grizzly bear is and isn't.

The grizzly *isn't* a man-eater in the traditional sense. Unlike the famous lions and leopards of Africa or the tigers of India, the grizzly doesn't make its living eating people (a population of brown bears once got reasonably good at it in an isolated part of Russia, but even then relatively few people were killed). Some of the big cats have killed over a hundred people *each*. Fifty years ago, when Jim Corbett was hunting down man-eaters in the Kumaon Hills of India, he wasn't just some rich white hunter off on a sporting jaunt. He was a national hero. Those people were being dragged from large settled villages, nightly, by tigers that lived in good part on human flesh.

Rare is the grizzly bear that has killed more than one person. Many became famous as stock killers, back before 1900, but even then some profitable exaggeration occurred to the advantage of aggrieved stockmen and glory-seeking hunters. Unlike the cats, the grizzly is primarily a vegetarian. Both grizzlies and black bears can and do kill people, and once in a while eat them, and even less once in a while kill them *to* eat them, but not as a matter of habit.

A friend of mine once outbluffed a young grizzly. She was hiking alone when the bear rushed toward her, apparently interested in dinner. She waved her arms, growled all manner of foul insults, and informed the bear in her biggest voice that he must understand that she was larger and meaner than he, and was in no way to be considered dinner. Each of his charges was met and stopped by a louder and more blustery one by her. Each time the bear backed off, just unsure enough of himself to chicken out. She doesn't remember how many charges there were, but knowing her normal calm I wish I could have been there. She's gifted with language, and I would have loved to hear her when *really* inspired. The bear finally went away.

Friends have seen bison, or elk, or their own horses, grazing in the same meadow with a bear. There are times of truce, apparently, as there seem to be times that the predator only preys when the prey "acts like dinner," that is, runs or panics. A ranger I know once saw a grizzly charge an unsuspecting elk. The elk continued grazing, even after the grizzly was clearly in view. The bear stopped, probably puzzled at this imperturbable ungulate. After studying the elk from a short distance for a moment, the bear wandered away (perhaps thinking, "Gee, I could have sworn that was dinner").

Now I don't recommend charging or bluffing grizzly bears, or even ignoring them. I find the whole thing delightfully confusing. Grizzly bear authorities tell us that if we are confronted by a grizzly bear and cannot escape by climbing a tree, we should play dead. It seems that the most damaging grizzly-hiker encounters (statistically speaking; there are exceptions) are unexpected, when a hiker surprises a bear on a kill or with a mate or young. In those circumstances the bear's response may be instinctive and quick defense, and a grizzly's defense puts most good offenses to shame. The idea behind playing dead is that an inert reclining being is not threatening. Though not a sure thing, playing dead has proven itself, statistically again, the best choice. Sometimes the bear will come over and roll the "body" around a little, or munch thoughtfully on an elbow (imagine lying quietly during this), but unless the hiker panics and struggles (acts like dinner?), the odds are good that the bear will go away.

What puzzles me is that grizzlies eat lots of dead bodies, feeding heavily on winter-killed elk in those springs when carrion is available. How is it that *this* dead body, a frightened hiker, doesn't get the same treatment? I suppose part of the answer is that at the moment of the encounter the bear wasn't looking for carrion, though I'd hate even more to be in that hiker's shoes in early spring, when elk carcasses are most available.

Like almost everything else about grizzlies (or many other things worth knowing about), we can't be sure we understand. We have to admit that their food habits surprise us. A few years ago scientists observed a Yellowstone grizzly passing up easily available dead meat to hunt and kill elk of its own. Even the carcass feeders are still teaching us. The prevailing attitude about bear food makes them "foul feeders." Any old-time hunter will tell you that "them bears don't get really worked up about a carcass until it's good and ripe." Actually, no one has proved that bears have a taste preference for rotten meat over fresh meat, but it has to be a lot easier for them to sniff out a rank carcass than a new one. For that reason they may feed more on the rank ones. They may also prefer a rank carcass because it will contain more maggots, a bear delicacy. What bears need and what people find disgusting tell us more about people than it does about bears. As the beggar and dump bears most dishearteningly demonstrated, willingness to try new foods is the bear's special blessing; even were the animal able to do so, it could not afford to worry that its diet causes people to suspect a character deficiency. Maggots, escargot; rancid elk meat, buttermilk; who's really deficient here? No one, I think, but I figure we're more suspect than the bears; at least bears never make judgments about people.

# Paul Schullery: *The Bear Doesn't Know*

A 600-pound grizzly bear, a nearly black boar, was being held for helicopter relocation at the Fire Cache. His culvert trap, a circular metal tube about twelve feet long and four feet across (made from corrugated metal culvert tubing) mounted on a pair of wheels for towing, was parked in one of the long garage stalls. It was a cool dark tunnel, away from the prying eyes of tourists and most employees, a quiet and rather dank spot that I imagined might even be to the bear's liking were he not caged up in the trap.

I shuffled self-consciously the length of the passageway to the culvert at the far end—not sure whom I was afraid of disturbing—and took a seat on an upended bucket about a yard from the metal grill at the front end of the trap, the end the bear faced.

There was enough light from small high windows to see him well. He was resting on his belly, his paws drawn up near his chin, his nose a few inches behind the grill. He didn't move as I seated myself, or during the fifteen or so minutes that we sat staring at each other in that damp corner.

Bears don't have big eyes, so they are lost in that infinity of fur and fat and ripplingly smooth motion, two small dark sparks evolved to deal primarily in the nearby because what else need a 600-pound grizzly bear worry about? Like the Union officer who threw the auxiliary sails overboard shortly after his huge ironclad battleship was launched because nobody was going to make *him* hurry, this bear needed better eyes nowhere near so much as his neighbors did. If I'm too far away for him to see me, it's my responsibility to keep it that way. I try to look him over, but I keep coming back to the eyes. I have big hands, and his claws seem as big as my fingers; I am darkly amused that he could probably hook his claws into the grate that separates us and rip it from its welded frame. In this case, what the bear doesn't know won't hurt me. But from the claws I am drawn back to the eyes, steady, unblinking, either dull beyond my comprehension or perceptive beyond my imagination, staring with evident but unlikely calm back at me. His ears are reduced by the bulk of their surroundings—a massive round skull over heavily muscled jaws—to unimportance, like some anatomical afterthought stapled indecisively to the finished animal after it left the factory. Bears hear well, but, as with their eyesight, from my bucket in front of this one I figure that they don't really need to. I wouldn't insult this one if he was stone deaf.

When I'm not held accountable to human reason or scholarly accuracy, which is to say when I'm alone, I lapse into a rather personal approach to what interests me; I talk to things, trying to calm a squirming fish as I struggle to free a hook and release it, reasoning vainly with a horse that is more interested in trailside clover than in getting to the corral by dark (then cussing him as I rein him in), or greeting the elk, bedded in the snow by my door, with a mixture of joy, respect, and fear. So I want to talk to this bear. I sit there wanting to understand, wanting to see something in those eyes besides my reflection (and not being seduced by the rhetorical opportunities of seeing oneself reflected in grizzly eyes), something in his passive stillness besides brute patience. But I don't know how to start. What to say? I know that the trout doesn't understand my reassurances, I know the horse recognizes impatience in my voice and figures he can get one more mouthful of clover before the reins pull him away, and I never have figured out what those elk think of my silly greetings, but the talking is useful, at least for me. It's a kind of reaching out. But the bear is too much. I would ask questions if I thought the bear had answers, or if I thought that by asking them, out loud, I might sense an answer of my own. I most feel a need to express regret or apology for the circumstances of our meeting, to apologize for the idiot who baited the bear into a settled area where he had to be trapped before someone was hurt; again the bear would have no answer. I would express admiration for his size and power, or for his wildness...admiration, at last, for his utter independence of my admiration, or of anything else I think or want.

That is probably why he is so important to me; it's a one-way street of fascination, I caring most for his detachment and nearly alien disregard for me, caring that he can exist without caring about me. This bear is at my mercy, vulnerable to the moronic growth of commerce, the mindless pressures of human population, and the mechanical finality of a good rifle, and he doesn't even know it. He'll die some day, and all like him, never having grasped where he stood in relation to humans, never having sat on a bucket and studied one.

This is good, I decide, and it's also a little spooky. The bear in the trap suddenly seems a lot farther away, not just a yard but uncrossable distances, and I am chilled and uncomfortable on my bucket in the presence of so untouchable a spirit. I must stir uneasily, for suddenly the audience is over. From somewhere deep in the cavernous innards of the bear, like a train still far away in a mountain tunnel, a rumbling hum begins. Impatience. The menace in the sound is palpable, though the actual animal, eyes unblinking, claws at rest on the culvert floor, has not moved at all. I still can't talk to the bear, not even an "Okay, okay, I'm going," as I right the bucket, return it to its place by the wall, and with one last wishful look at those incredible eyes, hurry from the building and into the bright morning sun.

# Contents by State

## Acknowledgements

Douglas Airmet's poems, "Saying My Name" and "Palisades," are from his collection, *Anything But Poetry*, copyright © 1996, by Douglas Airmet. "Palisades" also appeared in the anthology, *Mountain Standard Time*, published by Walrus and Carpenter Books, Pocatello, ID. Reprinted by permission of the author.

Glen Barrett's essay, "Off the Road, or The Perfect Curve Unfound," copyright © 1999, by Glen Barrett, first appeared in *Northern Lights*. Reprinted by permission of the author.

Tim Cahill's article, "Trusty and Grace," copyright © 1999, by Tim Cahill, first appeared in the magazine, *Outside*. Reprinted by permission of the author.

Lyn Dalebout's poems, "Journey" and "Ceremony," are from her collection *Out of the Flames*, published by Blue Bison Press, Moose, WY, copyright © 1996, by Lyn Dalebout. Reprinted by permission of the author.

Carol L. Deering's poem, "Twilight, Angus," first appeared in the journal *Westering*. "Absaroka Blues" was first published in the anthology, *If You Would Love Wyoming*, and "Homespun" appeared in the collection, *Wyoming Promises*, published by High Plains Press, Glendo, WY. All poems copyright © 1999, by Carol L. Deering. Reprinted by permission of the author.

Gary Ferguson's selection here is from his book, *The Yellowstone Wolves: The First Year*, published by Falcon Press, Helena, MT, copyright © 1996, by Gary Ferguson. Reprinted by permission of the author.

Randall Gloege's poem, "Pryor Mountain Camp," first appeared in the literary journal, *Alkali Flats*. Both poems, copyright © 1999, by Randall Gloege. Reprinted by permission of the author.

Jamie Harrison's selection is from her book, *Going Local*, published by Hyperion Press, copyright © 1996, by Jamie Harrison Potenberg, and St. Martin's Paperbacks, New York, NY, copyright © 1998, by Jamie Harrison Potenberg. Reprinted by permission of the author.

Geneen Marie Haugen's essay, "A Relationship of Substance," copyright © 1999, by Geneen Marie Haugen, first appeared in the journal, *Alligator Juniper*. Reprinted by permission of the author.

William Hjortsberg's short story, "The Sidekick," copyright © 1999, by William Hjortsberg, first appeared in *Rocky Mountain Magazine*. Reprinted by permission of the author.

Julia Hoskin's short story, "Personal Effects, " copyright © 1998, by Julia Hoskin Hoagland, first appeared in *The Owen Wister Review*. Reprinted by permission of the author.

Greg Keeler's poems, "Llamas in the Landscape," "On a Bend of the Jefferson Near Three Forks, Montana," "Rock Chuck Hears a Logging Truck," and "Salmon Fly Hatch on the Henry's Fork" are from his collection, *Epiphany at Goofy's Gas*, published by Clark City Press, Livingston, MT, copyright © 1991, by Greg Keeler. His poem "Stuck in the Surface Film," is from the chapbook, *A Mirror to the Safe*, published by Limberlost Press, copyright © 1997, by Greg Keeler. All poems reprinted by permission of the author.

## Acknowledgements

Douglas Airmet's poems, "Saying My Name" and "Palisades," are from his collection, *Anything But Poetry*, copyright © 1996, by Douglas Airmet. "Palisades" also appeared in the anthology, *Mountain Standard Time*, published by Walrus and Carpenter Books, Pocatello, ID. Reprinted by permission of the author.

Glen Barrett's essay, "Off the Road, or The Perfect Curve Unfound," copyright © 1999, by Glen Barrett, first appeared in *Northern Lights*. Reprinted by permission of the author.

Tim Cahill's article, "Trusty and Grace," copyright © 1999, by Tim Cahill, first appeared in the magazine, *Outside*. Reprinted by permission of the author.

Lyn Dalebout's poems, "Journey" and "Ceremony," are from her collection *Out of the Flames*, published by Blue Bison Press, Moose, WY, copyright © 1996, by Lyn Dalebout. Reprinted by permission of the author.

Carol L. Deering's poem, "Twilight, Angus," first appeared in the journal *Westering*. "Absaroka Blues" was first published in the anthology, *If You Would Love Wyoming*, and "Homespun" appeared in the collection, *Wyoming Promises*, published by High Plains Press, Glendo, WY. All poems copyright © 1999, by Carol L. Deering. Reprinted by permission of the author.

Gary Ferguson's selection here is from his book, *The Yellowstone Wolves: The First Year*, published by Falcon Press, Helena, MT, copyright © 1996, by Gary Ferguson. Reprinted by permission of the author.

Randall Gloege's poem, "Pryor Mountain Camp," first appeared in the literary journal, *Alkali Flats*. Both poems, copyright © 1999, by Randall Gloege. Reprinted by permission of the author.

Jamie Harrison's selection is from her book, *Going Local*, published by Hyperion Press, copyright © 1996, by Jamie Harrison Potenberg, and St. Martin's Paperbacks, New York, NY, copyright © 1998, by Jamie Harrison Potenberg. Reprinted by permission of the author.

Geneen Marie Haugen's essay, "A Relationship of Substance," copyright © 1999, by Geneen Marie Haugen, first appeared in the journal, *Alligator Juniper*. Reprinted by permission of the author.

William Hjortsberg's short story, "The Sidekick," copyright © 1999, by William Hjortsberg, first appeared in *Rocky Mountain Magazine*. Reprinted by permission of the author.

Julia Hoskin's short story, "Personal Effects, " copyright © 1998, by Julia Hoskin Hoagland, first appeared in *The Owen Wister Review*. Reprinted by permission of the author.

Greg Keeler's poems, "Llamas in the Landscape," "On a Bend of the Jefferson Near Three Forks, Montana," "Rock Chuck Hears a Logging Truck," and "Salmon Fly Hatch on the Henry's Fork" are from his collection, *Epiphany at Goofy's Gas*, published by Clark City Press, Livingston, MT, copyright © 1991, by Greg Keeler. His poem "Stuck in the Surface Film," is from the chapbook, *A Mirror to the Safe*, published by Limberlost Press, copyright © 1997, by Greg Keeler. All poems reprinted by permission of the author.